FINANCIAL TIMES GUIDES

Alternative Investments

JACKIE WULLSCHLÄGER

Financial Times Business Information

Published by
Financial Times Business Information
7th Floor, 50–64 Broadway
London SW1H 0DB
Tel: 01-799 2002
Registered number 980896

Typeset by Florencetype Ltd., Kewstoke, Avon
Printed in Great Britain by Camelot Press, Shirley Road,
Southampton SO9 1WF
ISBN 1 85334 013 8

First edition 1989

CONTENTS

PREFACE

Over the past 20 years, so-called 'alternative' investments, and especially buying and selling works of art, have shown better returns than many conventional investments, including equities and UK property. Inevitably, buoyant markets have attracted many new investors, and as these sectors have grown in size, they have also developed in sophistication and become more vulnerable to the effects of wider economic events.

This book analyses the forces at work in some key sectors of the art market, in associated areas like wine and veteran and vintage cars, and in two independent markets – backing theatrical productions and buying woodlands.

The choice of viable alternatives for the serious investor is greater than ever, and the spectrum ranges, as it does for conventional investments, from the blue chip to the highly speculative, and from the traditional to the barely tried-and-tested. Some demand a capital outlay which would not deter a child with a few months' savings in the piggy bank; others are more or less the exclusive territory of the millionaire; most fall in between. I have tried to cover a broad range, but all the sectors discussed include opportunities for investors with £5,000 or more, and in many an initial outlay of £1,000 or less is possible. As a bonus, all share one extra dividend – enjoyment over and above the thrill of the marketplace.

In researching this book, it has been a great pleasure to become well acquainted with two invaluable publications dedicated to a lively charting of the fortunes of the art market, Sotheby's *Art Market Bulletin* and the magazine of the Antique Collectors Club, *Antique Collecting*. It was an even greater pleasure to meet their creators, Jeremy Eckstein and John Steele, and I have benefited enormously from their expertise and ideas, both written and spoken, and from their kind permission to use certain statistics and figures, acknowledged in the text. In addition, I am grateful to Jeremy Eckstein for reading the manuscript and making many useful and wise suggestions. The remaining infelicities are the result of ignoring his advice.

Another joy of writing this book was wandering through the cavernous interiors of Christie's, Sotheby's and Phillips to talk to the experts over a newly consigned Old Master or a batch of Meissen china. Many thanks to Paul Bowker, Anton Gabszewicz, Paul Greenhalgh, Jonathan Horwich, William Lorimer and Lord Poltimore at Christie's, Olivia Bristol, Edward Dolman, Nicholas Lambourn and Trixie Millar at Christie's South Kensington, Jon Baddeley, Bunny Campione, Roy Davids and Mark Newstead at Sotheby's, and Fiona Baker, Anne-Marie Benson, Peter Card, Robert Dawkins and Anna Marrett at Phillips. Special thanks too to the Press Offices of all the auction houses, and especially Marianne Wheeler-Carmichael at Christie's, for their help and patience.

Many other people turned out to be founts of knowledge and enthusiasm on subjects arcane and complex, in particular Nick Allet at Cameron Macintosh, Martin Beck at Armitage, David Brass at E Joseph, Grigor Fyskin at Coys, Barry Gamble at Fountain Forestry, David Gittings at Tilhill Forestry, Henry and Jonathan Green, Nigel Greenwood, Titus Kendall and Edmund Laird Clowes at Spink, Susie Paolis at John Armit Wines, Anthony Rota at Bertram Rota, David Taylor at John Clegg, Olympia Theodolou at Colnaghi's, and Harriet Wynter.

Finally and importantly, I would like to thank Robert Ansted, who to someone who couldn't tell the front of a computer from the back of a bus seemed like a magician, for initiating me into the wayward activities of the *Investors Chronicle* statistics department, and producing many of the charts for this book.

FINANCIAL TIMES GUIDES

Alternative Investments

THE ECONOMICS OF THE ART MARKET

What's aught but as 'tis valued?
Shakespeare, *Troilus
and Cressida*

Cecil Graham: What is a cynic?
Lord Darlington: A man who knows the price of
everything and the value of nothing.
Oscar Wilde, *Lady Windermere's Fan*

Like the British Rail platform indicator on a bad day, the illuminated currency exchange board in the corner of the massive trading floor is struggling to keep up with the lightening quick changes imposed on it. As it battles to accommodate ever larger sums, the dealers at the front of the room are gesturing wildly at each new figure they hear; those at the back, late arrivals who hadn't bargained for a day out at the casino, are flushed with excitement as they try to get noticed. Someone pays $20,000 for a piece of paper that cost $7,000 six months before; someone else offers $6,500 for one he could have had for $4,500 a few hours earlier.

This is not Wall Street or the City, but Saturday afternoon in Manhattan, and the pieces of paper changing hands are modern prints – $20,000 for *Sweet Dreams, Baby!* by pop artist Roy Lichtenstein and an easy $6,500 for a Robert Longo lithograph which the buyer could have had for a couple of thousand dollars less at dealer Brooke Alexander that morning.

Open on a Saturday to entice those whose weekdays are taken up with the frenzied earning of money to come and spend it with the same passion, Sotheby's in New York is doing brisk business; indeed, the frenetic activity of auctioneer and dealers would make a fine Lichtenstein-style comic strip. Yet, close your eyes for a moment, try to break the obsession with mental arithmetic that buzzes around the huge expanse of the main auction room, and another cartoon comes involuntarily to mind. This one is in black and white, and it shows matchstick men from the 1920s in pinstripe suits and bowler hats speed-walking into Colnaghi's print shop in London, breezing round the corner to leave their newly acquired etchings at Christie's, and pocketing a fat profit a few weeks later. That collapsed along with Wall Street in 1929, and prints which had cost 100 guineas in the 1920s fetched just two or three guineas in the 1930s.

In the American print market, the cartoon is in colour, and the sums are larger, but the route to easy profit is the same: Diebenkorn's print *Green*, which rolled off the presses in 1986 at $15,000, sold for $42,000 in 1987. But there is no sign of a collapse.

THE ART MARKET AND THE WORLD ECONOMY

Modern prints are just one of many buoyant sectors which have kept art investments fizzing away for a couple of decades now. The case for investment is simple, and rests on capital gains alone. Works of art don't pay dividends, but they are assets which rise in value so much faster than inflation that the sacrifice is worthwhile for anyone who doesn't need a steady trickle of income. Established sectors like English furniture and Chinese ceramics have traditionally been safe bets, although there may be short term weaknesses in the market; over the last 20 years areas like these have also turned out to be among the most lucrative investments around.

Sotheby's Art Index, which has monitored prices in key sectors – paintings, furniture, porcelain and silver – since 1975, shows that an antique which cost £1,000 in 1975 would now be worth £8,380. That represents an average annual return of 18 per cent, which in a period of generally low inflation indicates a very strong market. An equivalent hamper of items from the Retail Price Index has crawled along at a snail's pace in comparison (see Figure 1.1) and the art market has even outshone the inflationary housing market (see Figure 1.2), the most comparable of conventional investments because it also depends solely on capital appreciation.

Fig. 1.1: Sotheby's Art Index/RPI

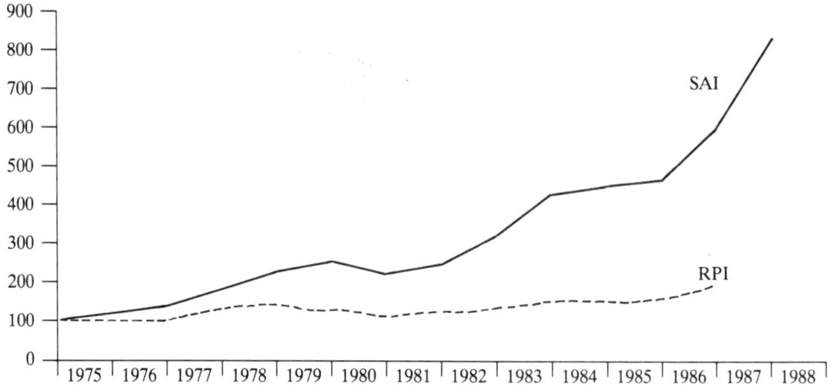

Art prices and the stock market

But the crunch is the relationship with the equity market, and this is a complex affair. A pattern of association between wider economic factors and art investment can no longer be denied by anyone who watched the art market cruise along in the generous wash of the mid 1980s equities boom. While times were good, investors creamed the froth from their stocks and shares profits and directed some of the surplus cash towards works of art. But when equities peaked in October 1987, art prices continued to rise, little affected by the Crash. Very rapid growth in some sectors slowed down a little, and buyers became more discriminating, but this was compensated for, as, by highlighting the volatility of the stock market, the Crash actually encouraged more activity in some other sectors.

Fig. 1.2: Sotheby's Art Index/National House Prices (inc. London)

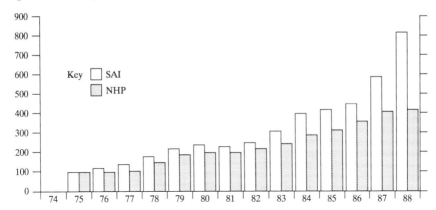

Figure 1.3 shows the art market and the stock market riding in tandem along the same route, give or take a bump or two on either track, until the road forks sharply in 1987, and art prices continue their upward trend. That £1,000 invested in antiques in 1975 is now worth almost £2,000 more than the same amount deposited in shares. And the only time since 1975 when art prices have lagged behind equities was in the frenzied two years which culminated in Black Monday.

Figure 1.3 suggests that while the highs on the Art Index seldom touch the peaks of a stock exchange boom, the art market does better than equities in more humdrum times and positively sparkles in comparison when the City's luck runs out.

Fig. 1.3: Sotheby's Art Index/FTA All-Share Index

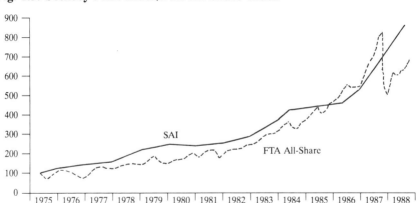

The inherent stability of the art market

This implies a stability which results from something much stronger than a simple flight into assets when the going gets rough. 'Fear' money has always been a feature of the art market, both in inflationary times – the British Rail Pension Fund diversified into art in the late 1970s as a hedge against inflation – and as an alternative to mediocre performance on the stock market. But men who have lost their fortunes are not usually in need of somewhere to put them. The present strength of the art market comes from something else.

The opposite of 'fear' money, one would suppose, is 'desire' money – buying because you want to rather than because you fear you may lose if you don't – and it is this that the art market was busy fostering in the happy economic clime of the mid 1980s. More private individuals bought art for the first time between 1985 and 1987 than at any period in the last 20 years. Although Black Monday curbed the activities of some of them, many turned into the genuine collector who may be aware of the prospect of financial gain, but who buys primarily for the love of it, and who will go on buying until he simply can no longer afford to – whether his limit is £1,000, or £10,000 or £1m.

That sort of *purity of demand*, which has been so well boosted this decade, is unique to the art market, and the more 'pure' buyers there are, the more effortlessly the market can ride out slumps in the world economy. 'Fear' money, money diverted to art because of a lack of confidence elsewhere, on the other hand, is unlikely to stay for long – witness the BR Pensions Fund, which began to divest itself of its art purchases in 1987.

The art market gains an inherent stability, much to be welcomed by the investor, from the solid band of collectors who form its backbone. Like any other group of people with a disposable income, their economic optimism conditions their willingness to spend, and it looks as if this is derived less from Stock Exchange indicators than from inflation.

In the last couple of years, record art price rises of 31 per cent in 1987 and 39 per cent in 1988 have been achieved with inflation running at below 5 per cent. That goes some way towards debunking the myth that art does best in inflationary times. A comparison between the annual percentage changes of Sotheby's Art Index and the UK Retail Price Index (Figure 1.4) shows not an uncanny likeness but an uncanny *unlikeness* – the two form an almost precise mirror image of one another. When inflation rose to over 20 per cent in 1980, the Art Index registered its only decline since 1975; when inflation tapered off to under 5 per cent in 1983, the art market boomed.

Much, but not all, of this tallied with the good and bad times on the Stock Exchange, but the correlation here is a lot clearer. It suggests that for many collectors, art is not a hedge but an indulgence: raging inflation means belt-tightening all round; people are aware that their money is losing in value daily, and they feel poorer, so they don't buy. Conversely, low inflation inspires economic optimism, and the willingness to spend.

THE ECONOMICS OF TASTE

While men fall in love with aesthetic objects, the art market retains an inherent stability. While men fall in love with works of art, the art market will always be volatile. A paradox called the economics of taste is the axis on which it spins.

Fig. 1.4: Annual % change Sotheby's Art Index/RPI

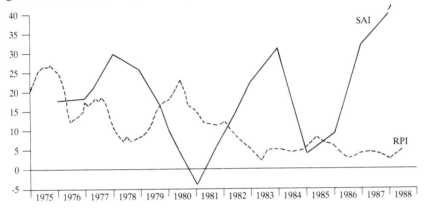

Lord Darlington's cynic would never have been happy here. Unlike any other tradeable commodities, works of art are two-faced coins: they have a quotable value, the price at which they are estimated or sold, and an unquotable one, their worth to an owner or potential owner. And because every work of art is unique, what is useless to someone who doesn't appreciate it becomes literally priceless – invaluable and irreplaceable – to someone who does.

For all the talk of tangible assets, a painting has no more intrinsic worth than a share certificate; indeed, it can be argued that a share certificate buys some future flow of income and is always likely to command some value as long as there is some income, although it is always possible, of course, that it may one day stop paying dividends, and end up worth no more than the paper it is printed on.

Sectors of the art market, too, can go down as well as up, and it is also possible that an Old Master painting may at one time or another be quite unsaleable. But it cannot go bankrupt, and although tastes change, an asset that has held its value for centuries is likely to survive a short term period of weakness. Nonetheless, at the end of the day value depends on fashion and sentiment alone, and this inevitably brings a volatility to the market from the very source – the love of fine objects by rich men – of its strength.

For a work of art, it all depends on who is looking at it, on what cultural prejudices they bring to it, on whether, for example, it has just been downgraded to a copy and if so, on who *knows* that it has been downgraded. This is the catch of every graph and index which tries to analyse price trends and growth prospects. Historically they are fine – and they are all we have – but no amount of sophisticated economic analysis, or measuring of 'constant quality' price changes, can ever determine something which operates outside the economic framework – changing tastes.

'It is charming to totter into vogue', wrote Horace Walpole. He also complained about the diminishing supply of masterpieces coming on to the art market, which suggests that over the centuries changing tastes have been not only inevitable but essential for self-preservation. There is always a top rung to be filled, and if the supply of what was once regarded as the very best dries up, the market more or less adjusts by promoting something else. That is at least one reason why Impressionist paintings, in abundant supply, have become so much more expensive than Old Masters, where the most desirable – the Leonardos and the Botticellis and the Vermeers – have long been stacked away in museums. Another major reason is the lesser chance of modern works proving to be fakes, as they are better catalogued and researched.

So dazzlingly quick and splendid has been the rise of the Impressionists that the time when they were *not* the powerhouse behind the entire market seems to belong to another era. Yet as recently as 1980, Sotheby's Old Master Index showed a faster rate of growth than the Impressionist Index (see Chapter 4); by 1988, the position had reversed and the Old Master Index finished at 516, the Impressionist at 1399.

The annals of art market history read like one extended lesson in the virtue of the long view. During their lifetimes the Impressionist painters could barely sell a canvas, and it was not until the famous Cognacq sale in 1952, when a Cézanne made £100,000, that they began to get expensive. In 1899 Monet tried to help the impoverished Cézanne by paying someone to bid against him for *Neige Fondante*; he managed to push the price to £270.

A year earlier, Burne-Jones' *Love and the Pilgrim*, a massive 16 foot affair in which winged angels disport themselves across the English countryside, had made £5,775; in 1942 it was bought in at £21, the most wretched victim of a violent swing in the first half of this century against Victorian values. But by the late 1960s, Victorian art was creeping back into favour: John William Waterhouse's *Ophelia*, 20 guineas in 1950, was 420 guineas in 1968, 3,000 guineas in 1971 and £75,000 in 1982. And the much-despised Burne-Jones? Another painting, *The Prince Entering the Briar Wood*, was bought in in 1987, this time at £520,000 – which says something about the development of greed, as well as the development of taste.

THE CHANGING FACE OF THE ART MARKET

In 1963 Gerard Reitlinger published the first volume of his account of three centuries of art market history, *The Economics of Taste*, and concluded that 'the identification of art with money' had first taken root in the 1960s.

In the 1961-1962 season, Christie's and Sotheby's joint turnover was £11m and collectors were still reeling from the shock of 1961, when on the other (reckless) side of the Atlantic someone paid $2.2m for Rembrandt's *Aristotle Contemplating the Bust of Homer*. Since then, the £1m mark has long ceased to be a psychological barrier, and no price represented quite the same quantum leap in the public imagination until 1987, when *Sunflowers* fetched £24.75m. Though Van Gogh's *Irises* beat it at $53.9m (£30.2m) a few months later, and holds the record for the most expensive work of art ever sold at auction, mythological status has stayed with *Sunflowers*.

In 1988, the record for the world's most expensive painting was 25 times higher than it was in 1962; Christie's and Sotheby's combined annual turnover, however, had gone up over 100 times, from £11m to £1.5 billion. Ever eager to fuel their own success, the salerooms are by now practised self-publicists and have made much of this – news about prices not only reaches the headlines but also worms its way into sober financial affairs: in 1988 the BBC *Money Programme* featured a Christie's sale of modern British pictures. It comes as something of a shock, then, to remember that the art market is still tiny when compared to the equity markets – the salerooms' 1987-88 turnover of £1.5 billion looked decidedly puny when announced along with the £2bn trade deficit for July 1988 alone.

Figure 1.5 shows the combined annual turnover of Christie's and Sotheby's since 1975, and the significance is of course the growth as well as the size. For you cannot widen your appeal without changing first your image and then your very nature. The art market today offers investors a very different package from 20 or even 10 years ago.

Fig. 1.5: Combined worldwide net sales of Sotheby's and Christie's (£m)

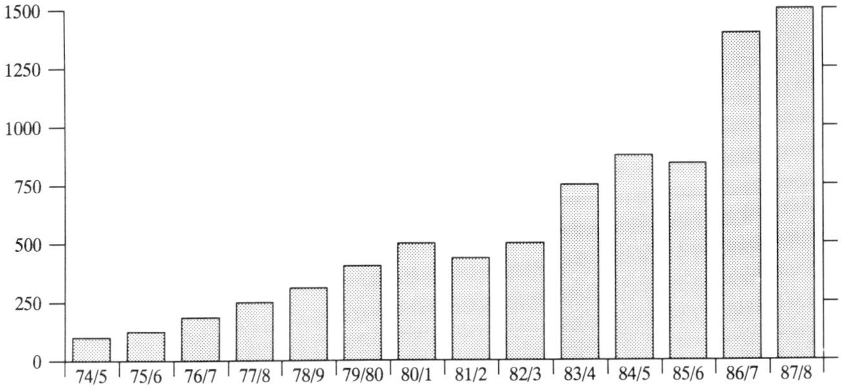

Source: Sotheby's Art Market Bulletin

The salerooms have always existed to make money, but a half-genteel, half-frosty facade used to make a good cover for such vulgar concerns. Now they are both more approachable and more worldly, a trend confirmed by the recent chairmanships of Lord Gowrie at Sotheby's and Lord Carrington at Christie's, both men of the business world rather than of the arts (although Lord Gowrie has also spent time as a dealer).

Sotheby's, moreover, also seems to have taken the prevailing spirit of deregulation to heart. Not only has it pioneered a development which enables works of art to be used as collateral for Lloyds, it has also aspired to some of the roles of a finance house, and among other services on offer is a credit scheme allowing payment in instalments for works bought at auction. That, it is rumoured, is how it got *Irises* away for over $50m.

If art prices continue to rise by over 30 per cent a year, even raging interest rates look derisory in comparison. But if you remember a time when a mortgage meant a loan of one and a half times or perhaps twice an annual salary, close your eyes for a minute and let your mind wander on the long-term possibilities of art-related credit. The art market is already more buoyant than the housing market, but it does not go in for repossession and there is a general Micawberish sentiment of living within your means. If the top end should ever destabilise, the foundations would be unlikely to survive intact.

Art as an international currency

Along with deeper financial waters comes a bigger pool. In the last 20 years, the salerooms have found themselves the centre of a growing international base of collectors, and have developed an international sales mechanism – telephone bidding, worldwide touring exhibitions of pieces such as *Irises*, deemed to be of international importance – to meet it. Both Christie's and Sotheby's look forward to opening in France when the present restrictions on foreign auctioneers are withdrawn (currently they content themselves with some very glitzy sales in Monaco), and Sotheby's brave experiment of selling Russian avant-garde and Soviet contemporary art in Moscow in July 1988 paid off handsomely, making a total of £2.1m and only 2 per cent unsold.

The salerooms' international profile has been helped by a growing breed of migratory purchasers happy to sale-hop from New York to London to Hong Kong to Geneva, or to bid down the telephone if they can't make it in person, and by a number of entrepreneurial dealers who have also realised that a bit of international publicity never did anyone any harm. Auction-fever at Sotheby's heady sale of modern prints was in part the result of the activities of Japanese dealer Ikkan Sanada, who arranged an exhibition of Robert Longo's prints at a Tokyo gallery a few months earlier. It was Japanese buyers, mostly represented by Sanada, who pushed up records for Longo, and they accounted for a full 40 per cent of the purchases at the sale.

The Japanese used to be regarded as the obsessive buyers of Impressionist art and in particular the natural recipients of second-rate Impressionists. They certainly fuelled the Impressionist boom, and indeed when they stayed away from some key sales at the end of 1987, a couple of pretty Renoirs turned out to be unsaleable, though the effects were not as disastrous as when they stayed away from sales immediately after the 1974 oil crisis. But recently Japanese taste has diversified, moving into modern and contemporary paintings, especially pop art, and even into Old Masters: a Japanese buyer established a record price of £638,000 for a Murillo, *Virgin and Child*, in 1987.

For the moment, Japanese demand in general is filling the void left by American caution and a falling dollar, while in 1988 English interest was reported to be stronger than ever at London's prestigious antique fairs, once the antiques equivalent of an abundant Garden of Eden laid out to tempt easy American cash. That makes the point that, whichever way the wind blows, the best works of art can boast of a cosmopolitan appeal which nationally quoted equities can never match. Works of art are a powerful international currency which is cushioned against local downturns and invulnerable to exchange rate fluctuations. Yet prices benefit from the historical accident that has left the UK and the US, countries with weak currencies, as the saleroom powerbase and magnet which attracts buyers from countries with strong currencies, notably the Japanese, the Germans and the Swiss.

In any market there is safety in numbers, and the collapse in the price of Imperial Ming when the activities of two of its six major collectors were disrupted by the Portuguese Revolution of 1974 highlights the danger of a market dependent on local or narrow demand. On the other hand, nothing ties the fate of the art market more closely to the world's financial markets: so far, the going has been good, but once again the stakes are upped. Against this backcloth, the odd steadying influences like museum budgets, which operate independently of world markets – the Getty's pocket money is $2m a week – are a drop in the ocean.

The new breed of buyer

Also potentially destabilising are the buying habits of the new rich who have kept the market so buoyant. Twenty years ago most investors started their art-collecting lives in a dealer's shop, training their eye and accumulating facts. Now the salerooms, once little more than a source of wholesale supply for dealers, have coaxed in private buyers, who simply buy on whim. Joining forces with them in the early 1980s, and continuing to be a significant factor, is the interior decorator buying simply on 'look'. Together they have created a market where instant appeal is as important as authenticity, originality or superior technique. In the art market, the 1980s will be remembered as the *decade of the decorative*. First impressions are what count.

Never has the paradox on which the art market is hinged, the economics of taste, shown itself more dramatically at work. Old-fashioned collectors who would save up to buy a well-considered antique, a walnut bureau, say, which has always held its value, have watched their sectors unceremoniously swept aside as new impulse-buying has pushed ahead the flashy and the flamboyant.

Any sector which has seen a large influx of private buyers at auction is bound to be more volatile; sectors still dominated by dealers, who like stability and never let a rush of blood to the head determine what they buy, remain steadier, though even here values are changing. Furniture is one area where the dealers have held on, but still a daintily pretty style called Regency which no one had heard of in the 1970s is leaving traditional areas like eighteenth century walnut high and dry.

THE MODERN ART MARKET AND THE IMPRESSIONISTS

In the fine arts, all the world loves a pretty girl or an easy, unchallenging landscape, and few want a difficult abstract or historical work, let alone something which smacks of religion. And Impressionists, true to their name, have the sort of immediate impact which makes Old Masters look very low key.

The mood of the modern art market follows the fortunes of the Impressionists like a faithful shadow. But in a sense, the history of the Impressionists *is* the history of the art market since 1980. The massive leaps

Quantum leaps in prices for Impressionist and modern art: Van Gogh's Sunflowers *became the most expensive work of art sold at auction when it made £24.75m at Christie's in March 1987; Van Gogh's* Irises *exceeded it, at £30.2m, in November 1987 . . .*

and Picasso's Acrobate et jeune Arlequin, *which Christie's sold for £20.9m in November 1988, a record for a twentieth century work of art sold at auction.*

in price, the influx of private buyers to the saleroom, attractive subjects determining saleability, the development of an international currency traded by the rich and status-hungry: all the key factors have reached their apotheosis here. As a result, the Impressionists have come to be seen as something of a barometer for the health of the art market as a whole. Along with modern art, sales account for around a third of saleroom turnover, and there is a feeling that if all is well here, the rest of the market will look after itself – a kind of inversion of the idea of the pennies controlling the pounds.

In particular, the Impressionists were the first to show on a large scale symptoms of a phenomenon which has long been a feature of the art market on a smaller scale, and is co-existing in an uneasy truce with the love of the decorative: an ever-widening two-tier market, with a flight into quality developing faster after the stock market crash in October 1987.

Not everyone loses money when the economy begins to slide, but everyone suffers from the psychological fall-out, and so caution prevails even among men whose fortunes have remained intact. The resulting flight into quality in the long run promises stability for the market anyway. In the short term, it means prices go higher than ever at the top while a huge slice of the second rate, the stale and the difficult sits unsold in dealers' shops or is bought in at auction.

Some sales held in November and December 1987 did well in spite of high reserves, but others suffered acutely because hefty reserves fixed months before the crash left some estimates looking impossibly pie-in-the-sky. Sales of lesser Impressionists especially, which dealers had hoped to pass on to undiscriminating wealthy individuals at a quick and effortless profit, were around 35 per cent unsold, and for many dealers sitting on stock acquired before the Crash, 1988 was a disappointing year. Meanwhile, at the top end of the market there were more records than ever, including the one for *Irises*. Historically, the best works of art have always held their value, and a two-tier market should shield the investor who has bought well from any economic slump.

Meanwhile, in a buoyant market the top tier is keeping the confidence spiral twirling. When Sotheby's sold Rembrandt's *Head of a Girl* for £7.26m in December 1986, a cluster of bidders remained interested at the £3m mark. A few months later, Christie's discovered a handful of buyers who stuck it out to around £10m for Van Gogh's *Sunflowers*, which fetched £24.75m. And whatever else has become apparent since October 1987, it is clear that there are still an awful lot of people around with an awful lot of money. Records for works of art seem to tumble daily, and the 1987-1988 season went out with a bang as it celebrated a number of multi-million pound sales in its last three months: $10.12m (£5.32m) for a Degas sculpture, *Petite Danseuse de Quatorze Ans* (it was £380,000 in 1971), $9.24m (£4.86m) for a Cézanne, *La Côte du Galet à Pointoise*, $4.84m (£2.58m) for a Jackson Pollock, *Search*, HK$17.05m (£1.16m) for a Chinese copper-red decorated vase, £1.54m for an English Book of Hours, and £14.3m for an exceptional Monet, *Dans la Prairie*. And in the 1988–89 season, with new records established for a twentieth century work of art (£20.9m for Picasso's *Acrobate et jeune Arlequin*) and for a work by a living artist (£9.4m for Jasper Johns' *False Start*), as well as a host of other records – £3.74m for Giacometti's *L'homme qui Marche I*, which makes it the most expensive twentieth century sculpture, £1.65m for a Paul Klee, £297,000 for a Munch print – in its first spate of autumn sales, the boom shows every sign of continuing.

While death, divorce and bankruptcy ensure a flow of good antiques on to the market at any time, strong prices are currently bringing out the best quality pieces – *Dans la Prairie*, for instance, was considered to be the best Monet seen in the salerooms for a couple of decades – which in turn fetch higher prices than ever and inspire yet more bullish sentiment.

2 THE MECHANICS OF INVESTING IN ART

There are few ways in which a man can
be more innocently employed than in
getting money.

Samuel Johnson

What concerns investors poised on the brink of any market is the risk-reward equation. History can and does (selectively, of course) prove the art market to be as safe as houses, and in many cases safer, but investing in art still seems like a gamble.

Part of this is psychological. The thrill comes from putting your taste on the line to be judged by that harshest of arbiters, market forces. What is at stake is both more and less than financial gain: your decision is made in terms that are not quite financial, yet evaluated in terms that are. It comes down to not wanting to look a fool.

Another part is mythical. From the outside, the art market inspires a certain wish-fulfilment, whipped up from all those rumoured possibilities and lamented near misses every time an obscure painting turns out to be worth half a million pounds, or a once-cheap sector is suddenly all the rage. A bowl which cost £6 in 1960 sells at Christie's in 1985 for £7,000, and the spotlight falls instantly on contemporary ceramics. A teddy bear makes £360 at Sotheby's in 1983, and by 1987 there are more grizzlies in the salerooms than at a charity bazaar. The step from wish-fulfilment to self-fulfilment is very clear in dreams about the art market.

Of course any market is at least as much about what people think could happen as about what is happening, and self-interest probably creeps into aesthetic appreciation subtly enough to make people like what they think will become expensive. But if you get it right, it always looks like effortless profit, which suggests again that the *frisson* of speculation is much more exciting than a familiar dividend or a share that has had to work hard for its money.

SECURITY

Security for works of art comes first from the confidence that they have been traded, mostly, though not always, at a profit, for centuries; that they are uniquely valuable. This puts a premium on authenticity, and gives an enormous boost to the traditional collecting sectors – the fine arts, furniture, porcelain and silver – while the younger markets, generally, have a greater chance of being devalued. If you pay £8,800 for a teddy bear today, you are less likely to find someone to buy it for £8,800 tomorrow than if you had bought an Old Master painting.

The more sophisticated the art market becomes, the more watertight are the guarantees about authenticity. Almost all the fine and decorative arts are under-researched, and in almost all of them there are historians, scholars and market-makers anxious to make up for lost time, and so the market is becoming increasingly underwritten by authority. A research paper or a *catalogue raisonnée* always raises prices; so does an exhibition, because it usually increases the popularity of its subject.

'Buy-back' guarantees

Authenticity is sufficient inspiration for dealers to offer what must be every investor's dream: a buy-back guarantee, including an agreed minimum rate of growth, which the buyer can cash in on a 'redemption date' of his choosing, but to which he is not tied: he can sell at a higher profit to someone else if he can get it.

That is one answer to those who compare the stability of art investments unfavourably with so-called fixed interest securities. But if speculation begins where guarantees end, there is no such thing as a non-speculative investment on either market.

In return for low profits, on the conventional markets you can get bonds, convertible stocks or gilts which offer quantifiable returns and a known cash-in value on an agreed date. But as long as they operate in an economy where interest rates, exchange rates and inflation fluctuate, their security is meaningless.

Of course, a dealer's guarantee is equally shaky in a market where growth rates are unpredictable. And like gilts, you also have to pay for your 'security' – buying through a dealer is more expensive than buying in the saleroom: profits, like risks, are lower.

Statistical information

On the open market, no amount of 'art portfolio' management will ever be able to satisfy the investor who pines for a given return on a given day, and this is the insecurity that the art market shares with the stock market. In a sense, it is worse, because the statistical information is so ephemeral. All you can infer from an auction result is that two buyers were prepared to bid to a certain level on a certain day; it tells you nothing about chance factors like the weather, which might have kept a wealthy buyer at home, or about the accident of two similar pieces turning up at the same sale, leaving one to be picked up cheaply after intense competition for the first. And the very individual features – details of style, condition, history – which make a piece unique and determine its price, are lost in a list that sets a figure against a name and date.

Knowing what you are doing

But if risk is about information – is, in fact, the *inverse* of information, since the more you know the less risk you take – it is the art market which wins the security race. For a start, you know where your money is – you are looking at it, or sitting on it, or pouring coffee from it – which puts you one step ahead of the ordinary investor in the stock market.

The small investor inevitably relies on limited information about the workings of the financial markets, as the victims of Barlow Clowes found out to their cost. Led to believe that they were investing in British government bonds sold by a company that had passed the DTI's scrutiny, the investment looked reassuringly risk-free. In 1988 it emerged that most of the money was nowhere near a gilt fund, and that even the fund managers were unaware of this fact.

There are crooks in the art market too, but the small investor's shield is information and knowledge – harder to get than ever in today's conventional markets, but quite impossible to do without when buying art. And 'insider dealing' is a nonsense in a market which depends on the knowledge and interest of as many participants as possible. Even the notorious 'ring' can be beaten by a collector who knows the worth of what he is selling and insists on a fair reserve (minimum price).

That sort of control gives the investor the best security of all, and it is backed up by the guarantee of authenticity: the salerooms agree to compensate buyers if a piece turns out to be a forgery within five years of a sale, and reputable dealers give written guarantees including a description, date and, where relevant, attribution of the piece.

LIQUIDITY

Security is also about liquidity. In the short term, works of art can be converted – though sometimes at a cost – into cash within hours if you have a buy-back arrangement with a dealer who is – unlike his counterparts in the City on Black Monday – not prone to disconnecting his phone at the precise time at which you need to sell.

It is obviously better to shop around, and this does take longer, while reaching the widest market of all – through the salerooms – *involves a time lag of at least three months* and often more. In terms of activity, the art market is cyclical, and most of the important sales take place in a couple of clusters in November and December and then in March, May and June, tailing off in July for the salerooms to close for the summer. For some minor sectors, there are only one or two significant sales a year.

There is also the problem of disposing of a collection, or rather of part-disposing of it. A collection is a better investment than a group of unrelated items, and should be refined rather than randomly sold off. Moreover, while you can sell half a batch of shares, you cannot sell half a work of art, and if you have a painting worth £25,000 and you need £10,000, you will be forced to liquidise more of your asset than you need. This becomes particularly acute if your money is invested in just one, very expensive, object, like a veteran car. For financial and strategic considerations, it is vital that investors are aware of the *typical unit costs of different categories of works of art*, and choose what to buy accordingly. And even within a sector this is important: two paintings valued at £10,000 each make a far less liquid investment than 10 paintings valued at £2,000 each.

In the long term, the hazard is timing. To be forced to sell at the wrong time is unfortunate in any market, but it is complicated here by the art collector's obsession with 'freshness', which puts a premium on anything that has not been seen on the market for a long time. Dealers especially are reluctant to buy a piece which has been traded recently, and it is normally advisable to keep a work of art for seven to ten years before you consider selling; the longer the better. For the investor, the perils of a quick resale is an important point to bear in mind, though there are exceptions, and plenty of examples of pieces which have been sold on at a comfortable profit after only two or four years. But dealing expenses, whether you buy and sell at auction or through a dealer, can be as high as 25 per cent, which means that the first couple of years' capital appreciation may have to be discounted.

PLAYING THE MARKET

However the market performs, certain features, such as the two-tier market, hold true for almost all sectors, and thus certain rules for building up a collection almost always hold true. These rules are amplified in the discussion of individual sectors, but are the key to how the whole market works. The most important of them are listed below.

1. *Buy what you like* If you do not derive aesthetic pleasure from works of art, you should turn at once to Chapter 14 and continue reading from there. If you do, you should indulge your own taste. This is at once a strategy and a hedge. The chances are that if one collector falls in love with a piece, there is something exceptional about it that will ensure that someone else does too (hopefully at a higher price). There is no substitute for developing your own eye and taste, and refining your knowledge to recognise the very best. Private collections formed with love and care do consistently better than works of art bought for investment alone. And if by chance you do fail to sell on at a profit, at least you have had the dividend of enjoyment and you are left with something you like.

Few 'pure' collectors can be unaware, as works of art become bigger business and unit costs go up, of the potential gains to be made, and conversely, 'pure' investors, if they exist in this market in any numbers at all, will be quite unable to spot a bargain, predict a trend, or indeed, make any shrewd business judgements unless they develop an intrinsic interest in their markets. This is a market which attracts players for varying reasons (see Chapter 1), and it is hard to draw a clear line between the investor and the collector. Nevertheless, an investment is not necessarily to be equated with collecting something which appreciates in value – a collector may never intend to sell – and by the same token, buying something cheaply as a collector does not necessarily make the purchase a good investment.

2. *Buy the best you can afford* Most collectors will want to do this anyway, but there is ample evidence that it pays off. Top quality works have consistently been shown to appreciate faster than the rest of the market, presumably because they are rarer and supply is diminishing faster than the rest of the market, setting an ever higher premium on what remains. By the same token, top quality works are most likely to hold their value should there be a general falling off: the best in any sector is the closest the art market comes to blue-chip investments.

It has been shown again and again that those sectors which used to be dominated by indiscriminate investment buying were precisely those which suffered most during periods of weakness – lesser Impressionists, for example, did very badly after the stock market crash.

There is the potential for a *two-tier market* in all sectors, and it is developing rapidly in most of them. Buying the best means discriminating rather than spending a fortune, seeking out good fresh examples and avoiding 'hype'.

3. *Beware of hype*   It is particularly important to beware of artificially hyped markets where prices are engineered rather than allowed to develop naturally – they seldom last. Always look at the reasons for a sudden surge – is it long-unrecognised quality at last coming into its own, or something else? One feature of the modern art market is 'nostalgia money' – the burst of interest in areas once popular with children or adolescents which peak when former fans reach the height of their spending powers. The rise in prices for pop and rock 'n' roll memorabilia – a guitar that belonged to a Beatle, an Elvis stage costume – are good examples, but less obvious ones may be more of a trap: the rise of certain children's books, for instance. Items that appeal to only one fairly short-lived generation may well not hold up in price.

The other warning here is not to be seduced by famous names. Look at the piece *before* you look at the name – most artists have off-days and exceptional days. An extraordinary price always raises sellers' expectations, but will not necessarily lead to a boom, so to buy on the basis of a couple of high prices is risky. Within two days in November 1986, for example, Christie's sold two portraits of young women by William Orpen. In the late 1970s an Orpen portrait cost around £500; at Christie's in South Kensington *Young Ireland* was £37,500, but at King Street *The Blue Hat*, depicting Orpen's favourite sitter, was £137,500.

In all sectors, *a good piece by a lesser known artist is a better buy than a mediocre example by someone well known.*

4. *Specialise*   A collection formed with love and care is always worth more than a miscellany of objects. A specialist collecting area gives you the chance to develop the knowledge to buy well and interestingly, and to keep informed about events that may influence prices – exhibitions, publications, the sale of a major collection.

5. *Buy works with a good provenance*   Provenance – the history and previous ownership of a piece – has a dramatic effect on prices because it substantiates authenticity, as well as adding interest.

Works of art have always been a luxury and a lot of them were commissioned for specific private collections. Most sought after of all are pieces which have stayed in the same family since they were made, but pieces from any private collection usually command a premium over those that have been traded between dealers. This is why freshness to the market place is so important.

Sales of large private collections always fetch the highest sums and often move prices to a new plateau by whetting the market's appetite with a display of the very best available.

When individual works from private collections are sold at auction, the catalogues mark them as 'property of a gentleman', 'property of a nobleman', 'property of a Swiss collector' etc. This is helpful, but not watertight, since the 'property of a gentleman' may well mean someone who is to all intents and purposes a dealer but happens not to trade from a shop.

6. *Don't compromise on condition*   Unless you can be sure that damage is slight or easy to restore, you will land yourself with more trouble than pleasure if you buy something that is falling to bits. Once you have bought

something, maintaining its physical condition is absolutely essential if a piece is to hold its value. This is where an art investment is more of a risk than a conventional stock market investment – the value of a share certificate is not decreased if it is damaged or torn.

More specific ground rules of conservation – don't hang watercolours where they will be regularly exposed to full sunlight, for example – are mentioned in the relevant chapters.

7. *Don't be afraid to exceed saleroom estimates*   These are notoriously conservative, usually fixed low as a ploy to please the seller for whom the salerooms are agents (though occasionally pitched too *high* to satisfy the ego of the seller). The most common regret among long-standing collectors is not that they paid over the odds for something but for 'the ones that got away' because they were reluctant to pay that extra 10 or 20 per cent. Something that seems expensive at the time can look like a very good buy a few years on.

8. *Get your timing right*   This is the essence of playing the market. The ideal, of course, is to buy before a boom and sell at its peak – to buy, in fact, when everyone is selling and vice versa. The catch, as in all markets, is to recognise the trough and the ceiling when they have been reached. But even if you do, it takes confidence to buy in a recession – this, however, is when there are bargains around: some of the best collections were started in the 1930s on a few pounds.

In a buoyant market, lesser examples will sell more easily; there will also be, at a price, more of the very best around, so this is the time to prune a collection and trade up.

JUDGING THE MARKET – WHICH SECTOR?

Figure 2.1 shows the breakdown by value of total worldwide sales in the art market in 1987-88, and gives some idea of the strength of various sectors. 'Fine arts' include all the graphic arts (see Chapters 4-7), 'decorative arts' comprise furniture, silver, porcelain (see Chapters 8-10) and works of art. The third slice takes in books (Chapter 11) and jewellery, both major collecting areas, and 'collectors' items', from the traditional

Fig. 2.1: Sales breakdown 1987/88

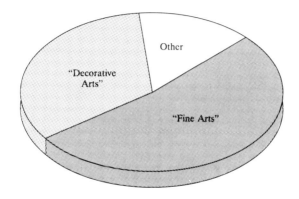

Source: Sotheby's Art Market Bulletin

(coins, stamps) to the newer fields. Two of these, at the serious and the frivolous ends of the spectrum, are discussed in Chapters 12 and 13.

In choosing which sector, the questions to ask are those that every prospective investor in any field must ask. First, can I afford it?; second, has it performed well and what is the evidence that it will continue (or for that matter, begin) to perform well in the future?; and third, how safe is it, or at least, am I prepared to accept the risk-reward balance the sector offers?

In this context, the investor should consider carefully the following points which apply to all sectors, as well as those particular variations on them which are highlighted in the discussions of the individual markets later in this book.

1. *Can I afford it?*   Over half the works of art sold at auction fetch under £1,000, and most sectors encompass a wide price range. The beauty is in trading up lesser pieces for better ones, refining your collections as you go. In the end it can become almost self-financing, while gaining in value all the time.

2. *Has it performed well?*   If you are buying in a traditional area, you can judge its health and stability from price records over the years. Figures 2.2 and 2.3 show Sotheby's Art Index as a yearly aggregate and broken down by sector at the end of the 1987-88 season.

In all sectors the estimates in saleroom catalogues, though on the conservative side, are invaluable as a guide to what you might have to pay, to relative prices within a sector and to what your own pieces are worth. When looking at the price lists, the most significant figure is the 'bought in' rate, or the percentage of the sale that was unsold. Erratic prices for single lots can be flukes, but if a high number of works fail to sell the whole field is likely to be in trouble. Up to 10 per cent is good, up to 20 per cent is acceptable; over 30 per cent starts to be very worrying.

3. *How safe is it?*   Sector by sector, the art market spans a 'safety' spectrum which parallels the risk rating from gilts to futures. If you want stability, look for a traditional collecting area – Old Masters, silver,

Fig. 2.2: Sotheby's Art Index — yearly aggregate

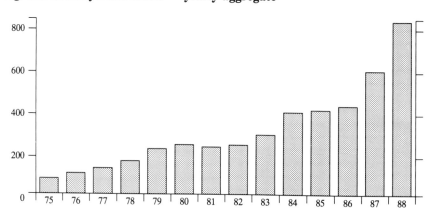

Source: Sotheby's Art Market Bulletin

Fig. 2.3: Sotheby's Art Index — % seasonal changes by sector

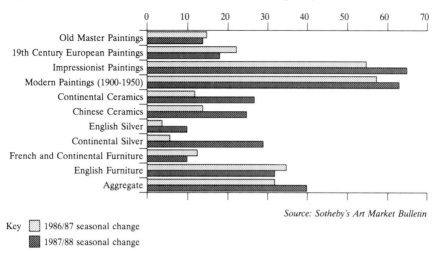

Source: *Sotheby's Art Market Bulletin*

Key 1986/87 seasonal change
     1987/88 seasonal change

porcelain, rare books – where you will almost certainly find a strong body of dealers with a keen interest in keeping price rises decorous rather than overwhelming. The presence of dealers usually means stability in a sector unless, as happens occasionally, high interest rates affect the cost of carrying stock, which in turn pushes up prices and weakens demand. This occurred in the early 1980s with Dutch and Flemish Old Masters, generally a very safe bet (see Chapter 4), which form the basic stock of many dealers.

Move to an area where private buyers hold the reins – modern British pictures, for example – and expect surging prices but always the possibility of a shakeout if things go too far. In a younger market, like twentieth century ceramics, indiscriminate buying early on can mean see-sawing prices until real quality comes into its own, along with huge rewards for those who got it right in the first place. But for those who don't, the upward swing of a trendy new market is lethal: the orientalist market boomed in the early 1980s and pictures by its brightest star, Augustus Lamplough, rose from a few hundred pounds to peak at £4-5,000 in 1984; by 1987 sellers were glad to be rid of them at £1,000, and many are now back in three figures again.

The orientalist market initially relied on one local group of buyers – Arabs who were attracted by nineteenth century views of their homeland. When the oil price fell, demand collapsed along with it. One further way of limiting risk without stunting growth is to *keep to collecting fields which enjoy wide international support*, or which at the very least are not dependent on vulnerable economies. Take the case of Thomas Baines, an Englishman working in South Africa in the nineteenth century. Very similar examples of his semi-surreal animal paintings fluctuated madly from £14,000 in 1982 to £90,000 in 1984, to unsaleability in 1985 and to £39,000 in 1987. The pattern of the Rand, and of South African political stability, looked rather similar.

4. *Maintenance* The physical problems of investing in different categories are also crucial for the investor to consider. Porcelain is clearly the most fragile, and that alone is enough to put some investors off for life. On

the other hand, so long as it doesn't get broken, it is easy to maintain – much of it lasted for centuries underground in the tombs of early Chinese owners. Furniture, on the other hand, which can well take a chip or two and is almost expected to show signs of use, is susceptible to heat and damp, and is also bulky to move. Silver is both easy to move and difficult to break, but demands frequent careful polishing, which also puts off some investors. It's horses for courses, but, as stated above, it is essential that investors are prepared to maintain a piece carefully, or its value will decline inestimably.

TAX CONSIDERATIONS

They were probably far from the Chancellor's mind, but the 1988 budget was not kind to works of art. The rationalisation of Capital Gains Tax and income tax lost art investment its status as a refuge against income tax; many collectors were left liable to CGT at 40 rather than 30 per cent, and to boot the CGT annual exemption was reduced to £5,000. The only cheering factor was the relaxing of the CGT base date to 1982, which reduces tax on sales and may thus stimulate the market by bringing out works whose owners were previously too frightened to sell.

With careful planning it remains possible to keep CGT liabilities to a minimum. Works of art qualify for the Inland Revenue's 'chattels exemption', which means that any object sold at less than £3,000 is totally exempt from CGT. The limit is doubled for a piece owned jointly by a married couple; moreover, if an item sells for only slightly more than £3,000, the CGT gain is assessed generously at 5/3rds of the excess.

Thus collectors in still-cheap areas can buy and sell to their heart's content – or almost: if you are shown to trade too many pieces, the Inland Revenue might decide you are in business and slap on income tax.

In other sectors, it is worth considering splitting up a collection into separate parts – a book of prints, say, which might sell for £20,000 could be broken up into separate prints selling at under £3,000 each. But as a collection itself sells at a premium, it is by no means always worth splitting it even to allow for the tax benefit. And where pieces are clearly made as a set – a set of chairs, for example they cannot be assessed independently; nor can a set of objects sold 'separately' to the same buyer.

Where works of art are subject to Inheritance Tax, the Inland Revenue is not known to press for the most up-to-date valuations, and works of art tend to be let off more lightly than assets in the conventional markets.

Early tax planning, taking into account potential long-term liabilities, is important for anyone building up a 'portfolio' of works of art, and essential for owners of very high quality (and expensive) works, where special exemptions apply. Works of exceptional quality may be designated 'museum objects' and owners receive favourable tax treatment if they are sold to a public institution by a private treaty sale (rather than auctioned). For such works, ongoing maintenance costs may also be set against income tax by establishing a special maintenance fund.

INSURANCE

Unlike any other asset, works of art expect to be kept rather than earn their keep. The chief costs are maintenance and insurance, which in London is around 1 per cent for collections excluding high risk objects like jewellery, which can be as much as 3-4 per cent, and as little as 0.375 per cent for a picture collection. Insurance also partly depends on size – large items are harder to steal!

Insurance is small compensation for the loss or damage to works of art, whose value and attraction lies in the very fact that they are unique and irreplaceable. Nonetheless, most collectors will sleep more peacefully if they feel they are at least covered if the worst happens.

A typical householder's insurance policy is likely to cover only a limited number of potential dangers such as theft and fire, and probably not accidental breakage, so a separate all risks policy may be necessary.

The following checklist is a reminder of how to make sure that your insurance policy really is as foolproof as you think.

1. *Are you fully insured?*   With insurance, you get what you pay for. It's sensible to get alternative quotations for assessing the value of your objects, but don't be underinsured – it's not worth it, for if anything does go wrong, most insurers will lessen the settlement in proportion. Given the volatility of the art market, a revaluation every few years, taking recent prices into account, is advisable; these prices, rather than the price you paid 10 or 20 years ago, are what it will cost you to replace the items with something comparable. Revaluation should be considered about once every three years or on a 'roll-over' basis, revaluing a third of a collection each year over a three-year cycle.

2. *Reducing the premium*   If you baulk at paying the full cost, you can choose to be your own co-insurer for a certain proportion of the risk. You can choose either to pay a percentage of any damage – for example, 20 per cent, thus paying only 80 per cent of the normal premium, or to pay the first, say, £500, of any claim yourself.

Excluding the risk of theft from your policy but staying covered for 'natural' damages like floods and fires greatly reduces the premium but also reduces peace of mind. It is highly inadvisable for expensive items.

3. *Common sense precautions*   What minimises the risk of loss also, not surprisingly, reduces the insurance premium. As far as theft is concerned, it pays to instal burglar alarms if you collect expensive items, and to have them maintained and tested. There is a 'protection maintenance' clause in most policies. Also, lock doors and windows!

It sounds obvious, but don't hang your most valuable painting in the room below the water tank, don't leave ceramics on the shelf which the children brush past on their way in from the garden, and don't leave valuable-looking objects by the window on the ground floor, especially if you look straight out on to the street – they can sometimes be just too tempting! Within reason, sacrifice display to safety.

4. *A safe?*   That said, exhibiting or using valuable objects in your own home is one of the delights of owning them; if you buy fine furniture, silver or porcelain you are in a sense buying a whole way of life.

To many people, therefore, the idea of depositing much loved items in a bank safe is anathema. But if you are worried about keeping very valuable things in full view at home when you are out, one compromise is to have a safe in your own home where objects can be stored when you are away for the weekend etc; even if your home is burgled, thieves will have some problems getting at it.

A bank safe buys peace of mind and, if you are going abroad or buying chiefly for investment purposes, is often the best solution (though even super-secure safes and vaults have been burgled). Keeping works of art there certainly reduces insurance premiums, but check that the objects are covered when in transit to and from the bank.

5. *Insurance in transit* Take care, too, that objects are insured in transit from the dealer's shop or auction house to your home and if you are moving them from one country to another, that the premium includes door-to-door transport rather than merely the journey by air or ship.

If you leave pieces with a restorer, check that they are covered, either by his policy or by yours.

6. *A museum?* More public-spirited than a bank safe is to keep your works of art in a museum. Don't assume because you don't own a Van Gogh that no museum would be interested; museums can welcome items worth just a few hundred pounds. The risk of theft and fire is greatly minimised and, what's more, the museum usually pays the insurance.

Making good the damage

If the worst comes to the worst, and your item is damaged, you will have to decide when to cut your losses and what to try to salvage.

'Loss adjusters' are appointed by the insurers to assess the extent of the damage, thus ascertaining your claim for depreciation in value. If the item has already been damaged before, this probably won't be enormous; if this is the first damage to something previously in mint condition, then it will; the first chip to the Sèvres vase, in other words, could be very damaging; the second proportionally much less so.

If something is much damaged, it can be taken as 'constructive total loss' – the insurers pay you as if the piece had been lost, and then try to sell it, keeping anything they make on it.

If your work of art is stolen rather than destroyed, you are compensated as if it is lost for good. If it turns up, you can arrange with the insurers to buy it back if you wish. Again, the volatility of the art market comes into play; if the piece has appreciated dramatically, you will have to negotiate a fair price which takes this into account. Most insurers are sympathetic, but such problems highlight the importance of finding a specialist insurer. These include the Fine Arts Division of Rich Industrial Insurance Brokers Ltd (31 Davies St, London W1) and Sneath, Kent and Stuart (Dorriston House, 21-25 Earl St, London EC2).

ART AS AN INVESTMENT: THE PROS AND CONS

For

- Assets appreciating in most cases much faster than inflation. Sotheby's Art Index averaged 18 per cent annual growth since 1975; 31 per cent in 1987 and 39 per cent in 1988.

- Assets appreciating much faster than inflation; potential for large capital gains.
- International marketability. Works of art are a powerful international currency which is cushioned against local downturns and exchange rate fluctuations. They can boast of a cosmopolitan appeal which nationally-quoted equities can never hope to match, and can be traded all over the world, which makes them ideal for the expatriate investor. Telephone and postal (commission) bids are accepted practices.
- Security – from the knowledge that art has been traded for centuries, and from salerooms' guarantees on authenticity, and dealers' buy-back guarantees, which include a minimum rate of growth and a 'redemption date' of the investor's choosing, but to which he is not tied.
- Control for the private investor. You know exactly where your money is invested – you are looking at it, sitting on it, pouring coffee from it – and you need knowledge and interest to buy well. This makes a concept like insider dealing a nonsense in the art market, while the international reputations of the salerooms would suffer irrevocably from any whiff of dishonesty.
- For UK taxpayers, the possible benefits of being assessed for capital gains tax, with a £3,000 chattels exemption per transaction, rather than income tax.
- Investment possible at any level. Over half the works of art sold at auction each year fetch under £1,000, and most sectors of the art market – including Old Master paintings and prints, watercolours, European and English porcelain, books, scientific instruments and antique veteran and vintage cars – offer scope to investors with £5,000 or less initial capital.
- Pleasure over and above financial gain.

Against

- No dividends.
- Problems with liquidity: it may take several months to convert a work of art into cash – the auction rooms take a lead-time of three months – and it is impossible to sell in parts.
- Long-term nature of the investment: it is not advisable to keep a work of art for less than around seven years, and many investors expect to hold a piece for 10 or 20 years. Buyers like works which are 'fresh' to the market and have spent a respectable period in a private collection.
- High maintenance and insurance charges.
- Higher dealing expenses than in the conventional markets – the salerooms charge a 10 per cent commission to buyer and seller, and dealer's mark-ups are often as much as 100 per cent.

3 BUYING AND SELLING ANTIQUES

It is well known what a middle man is:
he is a man who bamboozles one party
and plunders the other.
Benjamin Disraeli

One gives nothing so freely as advice.
Rochefoucauld, *Maximes*

Unless you are very adventurous, you are probably going to buy and sell through a middle man. Traditionally, that means a dealer; more recently, the auction houses have become a viable alternative for the private buyer. Your choice will depend on what you collect, how long you have been collecting it, whether you happen to come across a dealer you get on well with and how confident you feel.

THE RISE OF THE AUCTION HOUSE

Christie's, some say, was put on the map by the French Revolution, when the French nobility fled with what treasures they could and lived off the proceeds after they had been disposed of at auction. Since the eighteenth century, the auction houses have come a long way, but London has always been the centre of the antiques world; today it remains the Mecca of dealers worldwide, although there are now as many important sales in New York. Both Christie's and Sotheby's have co-ordinated their London-New York activities with all the precision of a military exercise, and no other international auction house begins to approach the scale of their operations, or the level of their profits.

There has been much grumbling about the way the salerooms feed off art-historical research, carried out in academic penury, and yet give nothing back. Recently, they have responded with a series of free exhibitions – in 1988 Sotheby's Childhood Exhibition and Christie's Camden Town Exhibition, for example – but their critics miss the fact that the auction houses are more or less the best museums in the world. Where else could one find top quality exhibits which change regularly and can be handled freely? One of the most surprising features of the saleroom to the newcomer is the haphazard and informal array, or disarray, of priceless goods; bidding for a porcelain jug one sits on a Regency daybed and is looked down on by Dutch burghers and English aristocrats waiting to be sold.

That gives any collector who lives within visiting distance of London a head start, for there is no better way of getting your eye in than viewing some of the best pieces around. Even if you have no intention of bidding, it is worth adding your name to the mailing lists of the major salerooms and going along to some auction previews in your collecting area. The price lists also give a good idea of the value of your own collection.

But why not bid? Over the past 20 years, the public face of the salerooms has changed enormously, and from being primarily a source of wholesale supply to dealers, they are now winning ever increasing numbers of private buyers. There is no doubt that their approach is a lot more friendly than it used to be, and an effective public relations machine, while laying bare a lot of the mysteries beneath the auctioneer's hammer, has got across a double message: that art is big money, but that there is plenty affordable by the moderately well off, and nothing exclusive about the salerooms which sell it.

More than anything else, profits bring publicity, and no one needs to watch the television programme *The Antiques Roadshow* for longer than a few minutes to learn why the art market – still, after all, a remarkably small and exclusive sector of the economy – arouses such interest, as well as picking up a few disagreeable hints about human nature. For, in nine cases out of ten, the glint in the eye of the owner really appears not when the beauty or authenticity of the family heirloom is being extolled, but when a price tag is attached to it. You can understand why media attention given to record-breaking sales like the Van Gogh *Sunflowers* or the Rossetti *Proserpine* attracts an equal measure of new sellers and new buyers, both wooed by stories of investment wonders, straight into the salerooms. Twenty years ago trusted dealers would have held their hands as they dipped gently into the shallowest waters of the art market.

As they moved into the limelight, certain saleroom activities have attracted grievances, such as the practice of keeping confidential the reserve price, but nothing has aroused more rancour than the salerooms' enormous turnover (a combined total of £1.5bn from Christie's and Sotheby's in the 1987-88 season). When two minutes' work at the podium selling *Sunflowers* or *Irises* earns a few million pounds in commission, eyebrows start to be raised, and the profits earned by the dealer, the traditional villain of the piece because of his high mark-ups and potential ability to fleece the less knowing, look much less exorbitant.

But this does nothing to minimise the accessibility of the salerooms, which have in recent years managed to encroach upon traditional dealer territory in building up personal contacts with collectors. Experts are now eager to hear of private collectors' special interests, and will keep an eye open for suitable pieces.

Dealers remain the auction rooms' largest suppliers and their biggest customers, and if you bid, the chances are that you will be bidding against a dealer. In some trade-dominated sectors – which tend to be the traditional collecting areas like Old Masters or silver, the odds will be much higher. In the vital market area, Impressionist and Modern paintings, private buyers have the edge in the salerooms, and at the top price levels here dealers report the grave indignity of recognising their clients at auction and being unable to keep up with them during bidding; they have to add on their profit margins when it comes to reselling.

Buying at auction is usually, though not always, cheaper – usually, because of the dealer mark-ups which buyers face otherwise; not always, because the frantic competition of saleroom fever can push prices to levels unimaginable in the cool light of a dealer's shop. Some examples of this happening at sales of contemporary prints in New York are quoted in Chapter 5.

Auctions are, however, the best way of testing the strength of a market or the interest in a certain subject; one reason why their supply will never dry up is that trustees executing wills are virtually forced to go to public auction to avoid the charge of not achieving a good price through a dealer. As the prices achieved at auction are made public, with none of the secrecy associated with the activities of a dealer, it is the saleroom activities which tend to be used as a marker of the health or otherwise of the art market. Prices quoted in this book are mostly those fetched in the salerooms; expect to pay more if you buy through a dealer.

Although it is the best guideline available for the price of objects whose value lies in the fact that they are unique, a price fetched at auction is by no means a watertight evaluation of the worth of an item; it simply means that on one day one person was prepared to pay that price for that object.

WHICH SALEROOMS?

The old cliché had it that Christie's was the gentleman's saleroom and Sotheby's was more concerned with vulgar trade, but if that ever contained a germ of truth, the distinction is long since gone. There is little to choose between the two grand and glittering salerooms, vying with each other for splendid pieces and splendid profits. As both now dominate the second hub of the commercial art world, New York, sellers can be sure that if a piece is deemed to do better there, both salerooms will ensure that it makes the journey.

As Christie's and Sotheby's have both been established for so long, it is hard to see their positions of supremacy challenged, especially as both are developing increasingly go-ahead approaches, refining the speed and smoothness of their services. In the summer season of 1988, the two fought each other over Impressionists from the Clore collection, sold because their owner had suffered substantially on Black Monday, and Christie's won by promising to sell the paintings within a few weeks rather than the more normal three months. Increasingly sophisticated financial services are now available too, and it looks highly likely that the still anonymous buyer of Van Gogh's *Irises* is paying Sotheby's by instalments.

Lower down the market, Sotheby's and Christie's are well established too. Twenty years ago, they would direct sellers with more humble wares down the road to Phillips or Bonhams, who were only too keen to help. But in the 1970s they realised there was big money in small fry, and both opened offshoots to their West End salerooms where cheaper pieces could be given special attention.

The best known of these is Christie's South Kensington, one of the most exciting and vibrant salerooms in the country. In areas with a great price range of items like Old Masters, watercolours and silver, the lower end of the market is handled here; prices for Old Masters tend to fall between £500 and £5,000, for example, while a lot of watercolours sell for under £200. Christie's South Kensington is also home to the lower profile departments like toys or ephemera, to slightly offbeat sectors and to new areas like topographical paintings, where quality is variable and top prices can exceed £60,000. There is a lot of run-of-the-mill property, but this finds a ready market as furnishings for the well-heeled residents of Kensington who drop in on their way home from work. Its High Street front attracts buyers who would be less likely to pass through its exclusive main office in King Street, while its central location ensures that dealers and foreign visitors are regular customers.

Everyday property, mostly furnishings for new homes on show in room settings at prices some department stores would be hard put to match, are sold at Sotheby's at Conduit Street. With a much less independent image than the Christie's offshoot, it is geared to the private buyer – many sales take place after work at 5.30pm – rather than the trade. It does a quick turnover; vendors do not receive pre-sale advice or catalogues, and the date of the sale is fixed at the time of the initial agreement to sell. Sotheby's secondary efforts have been more ostensibly focused on its two regional salerooms in Chester and Billinghurst in Sussex, which have seen some superb sales of the middle range and house a few specialist departments including guns and fans.

Meanwhile, Phillips and Bonhams, the number three and four London salerooms, have fought back. Phillips is less grand and formal than the big two, and may appeal to some collectors for that very reason, but it does sell works at the very top of the market as well as in the lower and middle range. It achieved its first £1m lot when a Matisse was sold there in June 1988. Its main salerooms in Blenstock House handle items from £25 up, though the bottom range is sent to general sales of furniture, ceramics and pictures at its branches in Bayswater (the W2 saleroom) and Marylebone. In 1988 Phillips acquired a six storey building at 101 New Bond Street – the old Phillips headquarters, from 1797 until they were destroyed by fire in 1939, were at no 73 – and plans are underway to open there, linking the new premises to the present main saleroom at Blenheim Street, in the 1988-89 season.

In some specialist areas like Doulton ware and toy soldiers, Phillips outdoes its bigger rivals. Bonhams, which concentrates on middle and lower range items, has also tapped the special interest market in its sales of specialist genres – sales of flower paintings held to coincide with the Chelsea Flower Show, for example, or erotic art at Bonhams are always guaranteed a good turnout. Bonhams, which offers a friendly, fast service and includes a wine bar and coffee shop at its Montpelier Street premises, appeals more to private buyers than to the trade. The Montpelier Galleries hold the more exciting sales where records – for example, for the work of ceramicist Lucie Rie in 1988 – are sometimes achieved; run-of-the-mill sales of furniture are held each week at the Chelsea Galleries.

Regional salerooms

Where Phillips has really scored over the others is in its large network of regional salerooms, which is continually expanding and currently numbers 20. These days, provincial auction houses, though less glamorous than their London rivals, are not quite the poor relations they used to be, and given the scarcity of quality goods throughout the market, are places which London and international dealers cannot afford to ignore.

Phillips is here up against thousands of independent regional houses, many of which double up as estate agents, holding sales of works of art with any frequency from once a week to once every six months. Their catalogues are less detailed than their London counterparts, but once proved reliable they attract London visitors regularly, and occasionally, in the case of the good regional houses, achieve record prices. In the autumn 1988 season, one of the best known houses, Lawrence of Crewkerne, established a short-lived record for Philip Wilson Steer when a portrait of a young girl fetched £134,200 just weeks before a similar work by this artist went for £187,000 at Sotheby's.

Buyers may hope to find a bargain unnoticed in a less specialist sale, but there is good reason for selling in the provinces too. Many dealers reckon they pay over the odds at a provincial sale for the simple reason that they have had to travel to get there and don't want to come away empty-handed. The scarcity factor also comes into play, with objects which might be dwarfed by similar or more glossy pieces in London looking very spectacular and unusual in isolation. Objects of regional interest, such as locally made furniture or prints and maps of particular districts are very likely to do better outside London. But like any auction house, a regional saleroom's prosperity depends on its expertise and reputation, and if it feels that a piece it is offered would be less successful in the provinces, most will suggest a London saleroom, and some will organise the transfer.

It varies from saleroom to saleroom, of course, but the London contingent at a sale can be as high as 50 per cent, and its influence ensures that while trends are not set in the provinces, they are quickly followed. There's no point in getting a day return to Brighton or Carmarthen in the hope that the newest collectable in Bond Street will still be selling in a job lot at a tenth of the price. Dealers make a point of scouring the regional salerooms in the hope of just such a lot, or of something that has been miscatalogued. A few are successful – one of the Old Master rewards for the dealer known as Buffy 'Hoover', because he cleans up the provincial sales, is described in Chapter 4 – but mostly pieces are correctly catalogued. If a catalogue whets your appetite, however, local salerooms can be a marvellous source of pieces for a collection. And for the vendor, selling locally is easier, more convenient, and usually the cheapest course to take.

Bargains for the buyer may yet be round the corner, however, as a result of a legal battle fought at the end of 1988 in which a Guildford auctioneer, Messenger May Baverstock, was deemed negligent in selling two pictures of dogs for £840. They had been expected to fetch less, but someone saw the chance of making a fast buck, and they subsequently resold at Sotheby's for £90,000, catalogued as the work of George Stubbs.

This raises a whole range of questions about authenticity and the eye of the beholder – one Stubbs expert is less sure about the dogs than Sotheby's – and also has some far-reaching consequences for the investor. For while even a major auction house can make mistakes (see below), it has the funds to compensate vendors who have lost out, and do so promptly and without a fight. Some smaller houses, however, will be more worried by the ruling; those which are primarily estate agents may consider dropping the antiques wing of their operations altogether, and at the very least, many non-expert firms will be more wary about catalogue entries, which will be briefer and more general. For the buyer who knows what he is doing, this inevitably means more chance of finding a bargain.

The country house sale

For a glitzy day out of town, the certainty of a good time and the remote possibility of a bargain, nothing beats the grand, sad old country house sales, when the entire contents of an estate is spilled on to the rostrum in a marquee in the grounds. With the possible exception of the sometimes reluctant seller or a former owner's heirs, everyone loves these sales. Experts from Christie's and Sotheby's descend in droves to catalogue the property, buyers lap up the glamour, and local residents who would not normally attend a sale turn out to bid for a piece of nostalgia.

The lots are normally spread over several sessions and two or three days, divided roughly by sectors – furniture, paintings, silver – but not by quality, which varies much more than in the saleroom. The giant catalogue usually sells out early, so it's worth going on the first day if you're not over fussy about what, if anything, you are bidding for. Some buyers venture to these sales in the hope that hasty cataloguing and, possibly, the absence of an expert, will have overlooked a masterpiece. In fact, nostalgia tends to send prices sky-high, and seeing furnishings in their natural settings rather than cluttered together in the saleroom can do wonders for their sale-ability; moreover, a superb provenance is physically apparent, and pieces from a collection usually do better than individual items, with buyers prepared to pay for the love and care with which they have been amassed. As a result, experts warn collectors against trusting record prices reached at country house sales. Sometimes, though, the sudden appearance of a bulk of material in an international sector can raise interest enormously, where one piece might have gone unnoticed. This seems to have been the case at the massively successful sale at Great Tew Park, organised by Christie's in May 1987, where prices for furniture by the Regency maker George Bullock rocketed, and have moved on to a higher plateau in subsequent London sales.

The major London auction houses are now keener than ever to value large estates, clearly hoping to stumble across undervalued treasures even if the rest of a property turns out not to be unexciting. With the number of quality works ever diminishing, buyers should take their cue here, for it is in the old English country houses that an abundance of top pieces, with impeccable provenances, are to be found.

BUYING AT AUCTION

As the telephone bidding at the two Van Gogh sales in 1987 illustrated, distance is no object for the committed buyer. But telephone bidding, a glamorous alternative for those who cannot attend the sale but want to bid in person, is only viable if the expense of the item justifies it. For sheer élan, there is no substitute for going to the sale yourself. If you are shy about bidding, going as a non-buying spectator to a few sales should cure you, and since the introduction of the 'paddle' system at Christie's, most of the mystique and intricacies of bidding at auction have been felled with one blow. Sotheby's is now also introducing paddles.

In exchange for your name and address, you are given as you enter a numbered 'paddle' which you raise when you wish to bid. A couple of lots on, the sale is registered on the computer, payment is made and you can leave with your purchase.

Bidding procedure

At other salerooms, most buyers simply raise their hand or catalogue when bidding; once the auctioneer has accepted their first bid a nod of the head is usually enough to continue bidding. If your bid is successful, you will then be asked your name if you are unknown to the auctioneer. Very little winking or scratching of the left temple goes on, although it is inevitable that regular buyers, especially dealers, and their particular interests will be familiar to an auctioneer, and they will probably need to do less to establish initial contact with him.

If you are a new bidder, it is possible that you will not be noticed as soon as you want to be; it is quite impossible that a blink of the eye will land you up with a priceless piece of Ming for which you will have to mortgage your house. It is probably the speed with which the auctioneer picks up genuine signals that has created this fear among new bidders, but it is the ultimate horror of the auctioneer to knock down a piece to someone who cannot afford to pay for it, and in fact if you are unknown to him and *do* hope to make a substantial bid, you should draw yourself and your credit (for example, a bank reference) to his attention before the sale.

For the auctioneer is a master of ceremonies here, juggling bidders against the reserve, deciding whose bid to accept and controlling the size of the increments by which bidding is advanced. These do not vary in a standard sale, but if you are bidding for a very expensive lot, you may try offering a smaller increment, which should be accepted if there are no other bids.

An auctioneer usually accepts two bidders who bid alternately, but he is aware of other interested parties and turns to them as soon as one of the two original bidders drops out. Before he brings the hammer down, he always asks if there are any more bids, so there is no fear of an item being knocked down to a rival for less than you would have been prepared to pay.

If your bid is successful, you pay the 10 per cent buyers' commission (plus VAT)* that has now been introduced in all the major London salerooms – Christie's South Kensington in 1986 was the last to resist – and in many regional houses.

Commission bids

For no extra cost, you can leave with the auctioneer a commission or order bid if you cannot be at the sale or prefer not to bid. Catalogues, printed a month in advance of the sale, include estimates for each item and a bidding slip at the end. Absentee bidders state the maximum they are prepared to pay for a lot and the auctioneer then executes the bid 'as cheaply as is permitted by other bids or reserves'.

In practice, the fate of a commission bid is usually decided before the sale. Where two or more such bids exist for the same lot, only the highest reaches the auctioneer's podium. If two bids are equal, the one which has arrived first is given preference. Sometimes commission bids look like 'phantom' bids which the auctioneer is simply inventing to raise the price. Even more misunderstood is the practice, so-called, of 'taking bids off the wall', which the auctioneer must resort to if he has only one person bidding

*Footnote: prices given in this book include the buyer's premium where applicable.

for a piece on which there is a reserve. In this case, he must call out bids on the *vendor's* behalf until the bidder reaches the reserve or drops out, in which case the object is bought in. Like most legitimate business activities, both practices are open to abuse, but most auctioneers are scrupulously honest. Any evidence of crooked dealing would irrevocably damage the reputation and well-being of the saleroom, and of the whole market. There has certainly been a great deal less evidence of crooked dealing in the art market than of insider dealing on the post-Big Bang stock market.

If you leave a commission bid, or if you instruct a dealer or an agent to act on your behalf – you will have to pay commission to him as well as to the auction house – be sure that you are clear about your maximum bid, for nothing is more annoying than feeling you have lost a piece because of a misunderstanding. This is where the 'plus one' bid comes into play. For example, if your maximum bid is £1,000, it is possible that the object is sold for £1,000 but not to you. If bidding has, from your point of view, got off on the wrong footing, your bid may have been accepted at £850, a rival's at £900, yours at £950, with the prize going to him at £1,000. If you are bidding in person, you would be likely to try one more bid; if you are absent, it is worth giving your maximum as '£1,000 plus one', so that your agent has flexibility to make one last bid *over* your maximum. That way, you ensure that if the piece is knocked down to someone else, it is at least at a sum you are not prepared to pay.

Bidding strategy

Bidding strategy is not the same as buying strategy. The latter, covered in detail in Chapter 1, has to do with responding to movements in the market, building up a collection, and trading up lesser pieces for better ones, and is in the long term more important. The former governs your behaviour at auction, and needs to be a combination of priorities well thought out in advance and quick responses to an auctioneer who covers on average 100 lots an hour. For a newcomer, the most stunning point about an auction is the speed, and it is worth attending a few sales without intending to buy just to gather the confidence to keep up.

'Psychological' approaches – coming in at the end as a new bidder rather than being in from the start, for example – are advocated by some, but their efficacy has never been proved. Most auctions are run-of-the-mill, even tedious affairs, which seldom merit subterfuge or secrecy, but some bidders enjoy playing coded games, if only for their own satisfaction. Some, for example, have a letter-number code in which they jot down prices and possible bids in their catalogue. If you don't want them to read yours, adopting a nine-letter word with no duplicated letters, such as 'introduce', and using 'x' as '0' for ease of reference, gives you an instant code – £250 is NOX, £700 is UXX. I must add that I have never used any such thing, and never felt the worse for it.

THE CATALOGUE

In an ideal world, by the time you get to the auction, you will have examined the lots which interest you at the pre-sale viewing, and you will know the catalogue backwards. Deciphering catalogue codes is in itself an art; the most important rule to remember is that the auction house is appointed to act for the vendor, and will do all it can to make a lot look attractive without misleading the buyer.

If you are buying at the major salerooms, you need to interpret the catalogue titles before you can even get to the right sale. Middle or lower range works of art are not described in catalogues headed, as perhaps they might be, 'run-of-the-mill' paintings, or silver, for example, but either 'fine' pictures, silver etc, or simply 'Victorian pictures', or 'Continental silver'. Top quality pieces appear in sales of 'Important' Victorian paintings, English silver, etc. Within the catalogues, buyers will notice a huge difference in the level of cataloguing: for the 'important' sales, a single lot description can take two pages, and virtually every lot is illustrated. There is less detail, though still illustrations for most pieces, in less important sales, while at Christie's South Kensington and less important sales at Phillips, for instance, only a few items will be illustrated and lot descriptions kept to a couple of lines. This is where errors can occur, and the knowledgeable can strike lucky, but it is often at this level that the new collector enters the fray, and can be misled himself. Chapter 4 highlights the difference in cataloguing between a top range and a middle range furniture sale, and shows that dates used are very precise, and if a piece is not dated or attributed there could be something suspicious – a later reproduction, or additions that mean the piece will never really be considered authentic. Where appropriate, catalogues explain the use of expressions like 'attributed to', 'circle of' and 'manner of'. Salerooms use broadly the same terms, but not all terms carry the same meaning at all auction houses, so it is as well to check them at each new saleroom you visit.

Estimates

Each lot described in the catalogue carries an estimate, which is usually a price range indicated by a lower and a higher figure. At under £100, the range is seldom more than £10 or £20 (ie an item is estimated at £50-60), but more expensive objects have a wider range, and it is not uncommon for, say, a painting to be estimated at £50-80,000. Prices for the rarest and most valuable works are the hardest to estimate (their very rarity means there is little to compare them with), and potential buyers are advised 'Refer Department', where some suggestions of the expected price will be given to serious buyers. At this end of the market, estimates can be many millions of pounds out – both *Sunflowers* and *Irises* sold for twice as much as was widely expected – but even for more ordinary objects estimates can be far from accurate, and the salerooms do not assume infallibility here.

In some sectors, particularly those where recent bad times have stayed in collectors' memories, such as silver, conservative estimates are a good ploy to keep vendors happy when they get more than anticipated, and generally to suggest a buoyant market. On other occasions a recent and dramatically successful sale in a sector can boost estimates to unrealistic levels which then fail to be attained a second time round, although basic conservatism usually means that upward pressure on estimates rarely follows just *one* strong sale. But dips or surges in any area or in the market as a whole can make estimates, fixed in advance, unrepresentative. And though saleroom experts are experienced, they are generally working in much wider fields than the collector, whose private estimate on objects in his own narrower area may therefore be more valid.

On the day, the wind can blow either way. Bidding at auction, as at bridge, has much to do with temperament as well as with resources, and there are bidders who overstep their self-imposed limits every time. Flexibility of bidding, though, is one of the advantages of attending an auction yourself, and also one of the advantages the private buyer has over museums, whose bids are fixed in committees weeks in advance.

Don't give up the idea of bidding for an object because of its high estimate; you may by chance be the only bidder, and pick it up more cheaply than you think. Conversely – and this is where bidding strategy overlaps with buying strategy – one of the most pressing pieces of advice given by collectors and experts alike, and arising out of bitter experience, is to be prepared to pay over the odds for something you want badly, because you will kick yourself afterwards if you don't. Most collectors have favourite pieces they claim to have paid 'too much' for, but the chances are that someone else will be prepared to do the same, and remember, top quality pieces have consistently been shown to appreciate faster than any others. Moreover, if you want something to complete a set, it is worth paying over the odds for it because its value is greater to you than to other collectors.

SELLING AT AUCTION

Religious paintings do not set an auctioneer's heart on fire, so it was understandable when a rather gruesome one – St Lucy presenting her eyes, which she had plucked out to put off an unwanted suitor, to the Holy Family – was estimated at a Sotheby's valuation day in Bournemouth at £400 in the summer of 1987. The owner, whose grandfather had bought it at an auction in 1930 for £5, sought a second opinion at Phillips, which identified the painting as a work of the little-known sixteenth century Bolognese master, Annibale Carraci, and sold it to an American dealer for £847,000 in December 1987.

A similar story could be told against any auction house, and though mistakes are unusual, the lesson to the prospective seller is that it pays to shop around the salerooms. Their verdicts on value, authenticity and the chances of finding a buyer should roughly tally. It does *not*, however, pay to shop around the dealers, especially if you end up trying to sell at auction. Dealers will seldom buy at auction works they have been shown but not offered by a private client. They will consider that they suggested a fair price at the time, and will be reluctant to show interest a second time round. The market likes new, fresh works, and dealers are an incestuous bunch who know very well who has already seen what. One sad 'dealer-soiled' casualty was the fabulous Burne-Jones *The Prince Entering the Briar Wood*, which had never been published until it appeared in Christie's catalogue for a sale in November 1987, but was bought in at £520,000. The reserve price must have been ludicrously over-optimistic, but one reason why bidding did not go higher was that the fresh picture was not fresh at all by the time it got to Christie's, having been seen by just too many dealers along the way.

These two stories illustrate something of the risks and the rewards of selling at auction. The temptation is strong because, given dealer mark-ups, you are likely to get a better price at auction (though the buyer will pay less); moreover, unlike dealers, who work for both buyers and sellers, auction houses are unambiguously on the side of the consignor, and are honour-bound to get the best possible price for him.

A saleroom will give you a free valuation if you take the item you wish to sell or, if it is too bulky, provide a photograph – if necessary an expert will then come to your home to value the object. The major auction houses have numerous regional and international offices, and will send their valuation experts anywhere in the world, on any mission.

If you decide to sell, a form will be filled in describing the article, its valuation, details of the insurance and your name and address. Your object will then be stored until a suitable sale, for which it will be catalogued and given a lot number. You must pay, according to size and use of colour, for any illustrations you want included in the catalogue, and for the insurance on the item while it is stored in the saleroom.

The reserve price

To safeguard you as the vendor, a reserve price, a guaranteed minimum below which the object will not sell, is agreed for most high quality pieces before they are consigned for sale. The figure arrived at is what both you and the saleroom consider a 'realistic' price, and remains confidential between you, although the buyer can guess that it is almost always somewhat lower than the lower estimate which appears in the catalogue. If you insist on too high a reserve the saleroom may decline to act for you, judging that it will waste everyone's time if, as it expects, the figure is not reached. With top quality works, which are anyway the most difficult to value, it is possible that an expert will take a gamble and accept a higher reserve than he would have liked, in order to secure the commission.

If your piece sells, you will pay the normal seller's commission, unless you are selling something very expensive, in which case the saleroom knows that if it does not lower the charge, it will lose the work altogether. Vendors' charges at the four major London salerooms are shown in the chart opposite.

If your object is unsold because there are no bidders, or the reserve is not reached and it is 'bought in', as the salerooms euphemistically term it (the house 'buys' it on behalf of the vendor), you will still have to pay a small commission. Sometimes hasty contact with the vendor can persuade him, after his piece has failed to sell, to accept a lower figure, and then the object may be sold immediately after the sale, away from the glare of publicity, though usually for less than the figure at which bidding stopped. Such negotiations were especially necessary in the sales immediately following the Stock Exchange crash in October 1987, when the reserves fixed far ahead in the days of booming stock markets no longer looked sensible in the subdued mood of autumn. At Sotheby's Old Master sale in December 1987, for example, a Dutch interior by Pieter de Hooch was bought in at £290,000 but sold after the sale for £280,000. The market

Vendors' charges (per cent of hammer price)

	Under £500	Under £1,000	Over £1,000	Withdrawn	Unsold	Special sectors	Insurance
Christie's	12.5%	12.5%	10%	10% of reserve	5% below £500, 2.5% above £500 based on bought in price plus expenses	Wine 10% through-out	1%
Phillips	12.5%	10%	10%	10% of reserve	£10 + VAT if reserve fixed by Phillips; 10% if reserve insisted on by vendor	Stamps 10% through-out	1%
Sotheby's	15%	15%	10%	10% of middle estimate plus expenses	Up to 7.5% below, up to 5% above £1,000, based on bought in price plus expenses	Wine: 10% over £500 15% under £500 stamps, coins, medals: 15% throughout Cars: 10% throughout	1%
Bonhams	12.5%	10%	10%	10% of reserve	3%		1%

judges the strength of a sector, though, less by the top prices fetched at a sale than by the percentage of unsold lots, and if a piece is bought in, especially if it is something significant, it may weaken the entire sector. It certainly makes it more difficult to sell at another sale or to a dealer.

Reserves are fixed at least three months in advance because selling at auction is a lengthy process. You need do little after consigning your object except idly peruse the catalogue and wait for a cheque in the post, but you often have to wait a long time for the sale to take place, and after that you have to wait for the buyer to pay the auction house. Cataloguing will be slow, and though in some sectors auction houses hold sales every week, in others a suitable sale may be six months away. An auction house concerned about its reputation, moreover, will consider carefully whether it is the best place to sell the object, and though you will feel you are getting a good service, a transfer across the country or even across the Atlantic will increase the delay. Factors for the individual to take into account when deciding what sort of auction house to approach are considered below.

The ring

One hazard which any potential seller should be aware of is the notorious practice of the 'ring', when a group of dealers within a sector get together before an auction, agree to bid on a piece in collusion with one another to keep the price low, and then auction the object themselves after the sale, splitting the difference between the price fetched at their own auction and that fetched at the public auction among the members of the ring. The salerooms are trying hard to eliminate rings, but they do still operate. For two or more dealers to agree to bid as one unit for a piece is however perfectly legitimate, if they inform the auctioneer of their intentions, and this practice is growing as works of art get increasingly expensive.

THE ROLE OF THE DEALER

Using expertise to buy advantageously in any market is considered fair dealing, and there will always be those who are so good at it that they will turn it into a profession. As antiques become bigger business, the market grows more sophisticated and international, and the financial risks and rewards increase, and so a successful antique dealer needs to be a uniquely versatile character.

Ideally, he is both of this world and above it. He has a scholarly love for his subject, but brings to it the added piquancy of knowing just where it stands in market terms. He may have made a small fortune proving a doubtful attribution – such are the fruits of wisdom – but until the right moment comes again, there are cards that he will keep close to his chest. On the other hand, he will give freely of his knowledge to the collector, to whom he can be the guiding light in starting, refining or upgrading a collection. He has an infallible eye, a near-perfect memory, and he can spot a fake at 10 yards. But he will never use his skill to sell you one, and, you have to hand it to him, the profit he makes from his mark-ups seems a fair return for all that risk taking and getting of wisdom.

Thus the paragon. But they do exist, and may serve a collector all his life. As developers of public taste, they are influential on a personal as well as a general level. If they have been influential in forming a collection, they are likely to know where the collector's taste is going, and what will appeal to him at each stage of his collection and his budget. Some are not above a benignly patronising attitude to their clients – one of the most famous, Joseph Duveen, sold the same 'beginner' painting, some instantly appealing erotic nymphs by Bouguereau, to his new customers for years. As soon as one tired of its slightly sickly naughtiness, and expressed an interest in higher things, he willingly bought it back and sold it on, at a profit, to the next budding connoisseur.

Single-handedly, a dealer can develop a sector out of what looks like thin air. Duveen did this rather unscrupulously with Gainsborough, whom he persuaded his American clients to be the greatest Old Master they could hope to acquire. This is patently not true, and when the artificial prices Duveen had created crashed, Gainsborough took a long time to recover. It is in the nature of a dealer's job, however, to use judgement and foresight to promote an area he believes is undervalued. Buying in an inexpensive sector which suddenly takes off is the dream of all collectors; dealers with a talent for taking the public's aesthetic pulse, as it were in advance, can sometimes bring it about. Dealers build up stock very gradually, and can collect fine examples of a school or a genre relatively cheaply for years before showing them at a fair or an exhibition and thus, if they are lucky, raising public interest – and prices – enormously. The dealer David Messum launched the painters of the Newlyn School this way; their work doubled in price in a few years and is still selling strongly in the salerooms. Occasionally, an unscrupulous dealer puts up a colleague or a friend to bid up prices on a sector he wishes to see rise, but this is rare, and prices so artificially achieved seldom last.

There is nothing to stop a private collector trying to do this, like David Messum, the honest way, but dealers have time on their side, and can choose exactly when to buy and sell. Ironically, in some sectors their best profits come not from high mark-ups and quick turnover but simply from capital appreciation on works that over a few years became suddenly fashionable. That, though, is a happy by-product for the dealer, who must aim to make his profit like any middle man, by buying low and selling high.

When asked about their mark-ups, dealers are quick to point out that they too have to make a living. While it is hard to refute this, it is also hard to see why it entails the frequently seen mark-ups of 50 or 100 per cent or more on works bought at auction which appear a few months later at fairs. Since the Stock Exchange crash, though, profits have been slimming down, and the middle-range dealer has not had as easy a time in 1988. Mark-ups depend on the individual dealer and his sector; where turnover is high, they can be as low as 10 per cent, which can make the saleroom's 20 per cent commission look very mean. On slower sellers, often expensive pieces, mark-ups could be as high as 100 or even 300 per cent. Against this must be set the risks that dealers take when buying at auction on behalf of their clients, and the fact that they have, unlike the saleroom, no guarantee of a quick or even a long-term turnover of stock. And since they have had to pay the 10 per cent buyer's premium at auction, one of their biggest sources of supply is no longer as cheap as it was.

BUYING AND SELLING THROUGH A DEALER

If you sell through a dealer, you will probably get less for your object, but you should get the money instantly, rather than a minimum of three months after consigning the object, and you will not risk its being bought in – and therefore being less saleable next time round – at auction. If you buy through a dealer, you are likely to pay more than you would at auction, though there are exceptions – the de Heem which fetched $6.6m at Christie's New York after a dealer had failed to sell it at $4.25m (see Chapter 3), for example – but you have not only the security of a well-conditioned authenticity, but, in most reputable cases, a guarantee to buy back the object at a fair price should you tire of it. Some dealers also let you try out objects in your home before you commit yourself to buy.

It is more leisurely and altogether more relaxed than frantic saleroom viewing and bidding. A long-term dealer-collector relationship is mutually worthwhile, for dealers can advise on refining a collection and take back pieces which are sold in order to upgrade a collection. A further safety net is that reputable dealers do not buy on commission, so they have risked their own cash on anything they offer you and must be prepared to do so again. A reputable dealer will offer a buy-back guarantee with, according to his confidence and the state of the market, a certain growth percentage. This makes a good dealer one of the safest ways to buy in the art market, and many will find the premium charged worthwhile.

In leaner times, more dealers will buy and sell on commission; if you are selling, it is not a good idea to offer the dealer a piece on commission only, for you will be the only sufferer if it gets stale in his shop, and he will have less urgency in shifting it than other pieces he has actually paid for. If you are buying, try to ascertain whether a dealer does acquire goods on commission; it may indicate that he has less confidence in what he is offering you than he should.

Choosing a dealer

Many dealers have been established for centuries, have vaults full of fine art which they keep for years, and have advised families on acquisitions and sales through generations. Their reputations are assured, as are their profits, but new collectors might find them a little pompous. In the end it comes down to personal rapport; the big dealing houses have several departments and a large staff, and whether you hit it off with the expert in the relevant section is chance. But visits to several antique shops and casual chats should ensure you find a dealer you trust. *The Guide to Antique Shops of Great Britain*, published annually by the Antique Collectors Club, should be useful. If you feel hassled to buy, or to leave if you clearly do not intend to buy, then the dealer may be interested only in a quick profit, but what is lucrative to a good dealer is in the last resort what is beneficial to the collector: a relationship which can develop over years of custom. A dealer knows that if he fleeces you on your first visit, you will realise it soon enough, and never return.

The British Antique Dealers Association and LAPADA

If a dealer belongs to the British Antique Dealers Association (BADA), which has 400 selected members, or the London and Provincial Antique Dealers Association (LAPADA), which has around 750 members, you can trust that he has been vetted for fair dealing, and you can appeal to the associations if you feel you have been treated wrongly. The comparatively small numbers indicate the high standard required by the association. Founded in 1918, BADA is the oldest antique dealers association in the world, and has been influential since its beginning in achieving tax concession on works of art. It also helped set up the Confederation Internationale des Negociants en Oeuvres d'Art (CINOA) in 1935, an international association consisting of national federations and associations representing the art trade in member countries. Membership of either organisation indicates respectability and the potential protection of customers. CINOA, rather loftily in view of the profit involved, says a dealer 'serves a cultural mission by distributing objets d'art which he identifies through his experience'.

But in some specialised collecting sectors dealers seldom belong to BADA; Harriet Wynter, for example, is the only dealer in scientific instruments who is a member, but that does not mean that all the others are sharks. In other specialised sectors dealers have their own associations, and you should look into how carefully members are vetted and how significant membership might or might not be. It is very easy, for example, for a bookdealer to join the Provincial Booksellers Association; the Antiquarian Booksellers Association, on the other hand, is a highly respected body whose members are rigorously scrutinised before being admitted and serious book collectors in search of a dealer can trust its recommendation.

Trust your own judgement

When it comes to buying or selling through a dealer, most people will have some confidence in their own judgement of human nature, bearing in mind that as with shopping in a department store, cheapest does not always mean best. Consumer rights go some way towards protecting buyers if they are badly treated. If you buy what the dealer *knows* to be a fake, you can be compensated, but so much in the art market is opinion, and so little can be done if the dealer you have paid £5,000 for a writing bureau simply disappears before delivering it, that the old maxim of *caveat emptor* should always be borne in mind. The onus is on the buyer to inspect an object rigorously and to obtain written as well as verbal descriptions, including the date, of anything he buys. That said, most dealers are knowledgeable, honest, friendly and relaxed, and many name the sociability of their profession as one of its chief pleasures. Visiting many of their shops, whether to buy or to browse, is a delight.

Don't be put off by the risks of mistakes, for salerooms can also get things wrong (although if they do, there will always be someone – buyer or seller – who stands to gain; a dealer can lose out by his own mistake, but he can gain personally as well).

In recent years, efficient saleroom publicity and regular newspaper and TV coverage, together with the sheer range of items handled by the salerooms, has meant that dealers have been eclipsed by the massive ascent of the auction house. New wealth finding its way into the art market, moreover, has seen no reason to defer to age and experience, and new collectors have simply bought what caught their fancy. Steadier and seasoned collectors or collector-investors cannot really complain about the havoc this sometimes causes, for in the art market overall fashion calls the tunes, and one only needs to look at the see-saw fate of a sector like Victorian paintings to recognise what an arbitrary mistress she is. Nonetheless, sectors which bound ahead on injections of new wealth are not stable, for new wealth is fickle, and will divert its funds to the Stock Exchange or a divorce case with few qualms. Once gained, dealers tend to keep their clients, while salerooms see a faster turnover of customers as well as of goods. It is the collector, buying at whatever level, building up and refining his collection, often with the help of a dealer, who is the backbone of the art market. While dealers serve this clientele, they are unlikely to go out of business, and the wheel of the art market will go on spinning.

ANTIQUE FAIRS, MARKETS AND CLUB

A contented antique dealer is a rare specimen, and his chief complaint, when he is not musing on saleroom hype, is of the lack of good quality pieces. This is uttered frequently, and most incongruously in the midst of some glitzy art fair like the Grosvenor House, when all around top quality items jostle for pride of place and price tickets in six figures are common.

Such occasions are not heartening to the bargain hunter, and all but the most affluent collectors are likely to hesitate at the steep prices, but any collector will find a visit, and his admission fee, worthwhile for the sheer array of fine and important objects on show. Again, English collectors are lucky that London plays host to the world's most prestigious antique fairs.

Rivals in glitziness are the Grosvenor House Fair, organised by BADA each June, and the Burlington House, held at the Royal Academy each September until 1988, but to be held in a new venue – the Royal College of Art – at a more sensible time for the antiques trade, in November, for 1989. Both are exclusive, with all goods vetted carefully for authenticity and quality, and both give dealers a chance to show their mettle and to attract new, or potential new customers. Both include a great many objects priced over £100,000 and quite a few at over £200,000. The Grosvenor sets out to attract the flashily rich, and does so very successfully; the Burlington responds with a more international repertoire – foreign dealers are banned at the Grosvenor – which ensures a broader scope of goods on display and attracts international buyers. Paintings tend to dominate here; furniture is at the forefront at the Grosvenor, but both are strong on the bedrocks of the art market – paintings, furniture, ceramics and silver – which attract most collectors. Some pieces surface again at the Burlington after being shown at the Grosvenor, for sales are not everything here, and follow-up visits to a dealer's shop can be as valuable for both dealer and collector. For buyers on the look out for new sources of supply, a day at the fair can be more profitable than several tours of the West End, and once a useful contact has been made, prices back at the shop may be less steep.

Fewer than 100 exhibitors squeeze into these spaces, and through the exclusive vetting committees of the Grosvenor or the Burlington House fairs. At the fair at Olympia, held annually in June, almost 300 exhibitors are packed into two levels, and prices start at £50 or less, although the top end of the market is also well represented. Collectors of the middle range may find bargains, and will certainly find interesting objects here. Olympia is a cheerful, buoyant fair; along with the twice-yearly Chelsea Antiques Fair (in March and September) it is one of the most popular of the middle-of-the-road antiques fairs. These seem to increase in number each year; they are widely advertised in local papers and calendars of fairs appear in trade magazines. Out of London the most important fairs are the British International Antiques Fair in Birmingham, held annually in April, the

West of England Antiques Fair in Bath, held each May, and the Northern Antiques Fair in Harrogate, held each September.

Also increasingly popular are specialist fairs like the World of Watercolours and Drawings or the International Ceramics Fair, and, a first timer in 1988, the Twentieth Century British Art Fair. These are also listed in the press, and important national events are listed in the relevant chapters below. They are indispensable events for the serious collector, if only to see what is on offer and to assess prices.

One reason for the popularity of the antiques fair is the speed with which a buyer can flit from dealer to dealer, comparing quality and prices while saving on footwork. Antique markets offer similar benefits on a permanent or semi-permanent basis – the length of a dealer's lease varies – and, as rents and rates on central London properties soar, a stall at a market rather than a move to the country is the recourse of many dealers.

Not that these markets are homes of the down-at-heel – far from it. Upmarket, specialist dealers in paintings or ceramics, for example, take space at one of the posh London emporia whose dealers seldom change, and use them as a base for travelling to fairs up and down the country. These are exclusive haunts where there is little chance of anything going cheap – where two or more dealers are gathered together, they tend to buy from each other until the object reaches a realistic market price – but plenty of quality. The top ones in London are the Bond Street Antique Centre, the Chenil galleries in the Kings Road and Grays Market in Davies Street in the West End. Not quite in the same league, but less formal and imposing, and very lively, is Camden Passage in Islington.

For something closer to a market than an emporium, Alfies off the Edgware Road and Antiquarius in Chelsea are among the most vibrant; there is more Art Deco than Ming here, and plenty of scope for those interested in the cheaper collectables like antique clothing or jewellery, and perhaps some chance for the bargain hunter. He, however, should really get up early and go to the trade markets where prices are low and bulk buying common. In London, Bermondsey has a particularly high standard of goods and a quick turnover, and offers superb opportunities for those in the know in a huge range of sectors from scientific instruments to English furniture.

As a kind of market by post, membership of the Antique Collectors Club gives collectors superb buying and selling facilities through the Club's monthly magazine *Antique Collecting*. This publication has the largest list of 'For Sale' items of any antiques magazine, and also the best-informed, most astute and wittiest commentary on prices. It is indispensable reading for collectors at all levels, and also guarantees that members will be kept informed of the latest superb reference books published by the Club on a variety of collecting subjects. Membership of the ACC is divided into regions and local club meetings take place.

TRANSPORT

Transporting works of art is expensive and risky, and experienced road haulage companies and shippers are essential. Dealers and auctioneers should be able to recommend local firms. Remember to check what is and what is not included – especially insurance – when you ask for quotations.

Insurance for transportation by road or sea is higher than by air, which is generally considered safest. It is also most expensive, and impractical for bulky or heavy items. The problem with transporting goods by sea, however, is the possible delay, particularly with those services which are anyway infrequent.

However you decide to move your works of art, expert packaging can be arranged, through a dealer or auction house, and is essential. It is also important if goods are being sent in the post. The Post Office publish a guide to the transportation of valuable goods, and it should be noted that the insurance cover limits are very low.

Every cosmopolitan collector's nightmare is to land himself with something in a foreign country which he is unable, literally or legally, to get home. It is therefore vital to find out well in advance the import-export regulations in the relevant countries. Few sets of national regulations are the same, so the general advice here must be backed up by specific research.

IMPORTS AND EXPORTS

Antiques over 100 years old are imported into the UK free of duty and VAT. An import licence is not required, but you must provide documentary evidence, in the form of an 'antique' declaration, and an invoice describing the object and its age. If this is not accepted by Customs, it must be supported by a certificate of age from a dealer.

Also exempt from import duty and VAT are items coming into the UK to be sold. VAT is deferred against the importer's VAT registration number and then collected from the purchaser when the piece is sold (such pieces are marked in auction catalogues to indicate that VAT is payable by the buyer). If the piece doesn't sell, no VAT is paid.

Original works of art sold or given away by their creator (or his estate) before 1 April 1973 are exempt.

Items sent from one EEC country to another are also exempt if accompanied by forms showing that all taxes have been paid. Importing goods into other countries varies, but works of art imported into the following countries are not charged duty if accompanied by a BADA certificate of antiquity:

Australia
Bahamas Islands
Brazil
Canada
Cyprus
Iceland
Jamaica
Lebanon
New Zealand
Nigeria
South Africa

Getting objects out of countries is generally harder than getting them in, with some countries notoriously tight-fisted about letting out any works of art. Italy, with probably more valuable works of art within its borders than anywhere else, does not allow any export. France has a record of being difficult, as the Commission des Beaux Arts often swoops in to buy, for the benefit of a French museum, any item destined for foreign shores, at its declared value. This effectively means that museums in France acquire top pieces without having to compete in the open market – they simply have to match the highest bid, not exceed it.

Export laws in the UK are relatively lenient. There are no restrictions on the export of works of art less than 50 years old; pieces over 50 years and valued at under £16,000 are covered by an Open General Export Licence which can be obtained from the Dept of Trade and Industry, Export Licensing Branch, Millbank Tower, Millbank, London SW1, tel 01–211 3115.

Problems arise with more valuable pieces if they fail the so-called 'Waverly criteria' which the Dept of Trade Export Reviewing Committee use to satisfy themselves that a piece may leave the country. If it is considered to be of outstanding aesthetic or national importance, an export licence may be withheld. Usually, a specific time is allocated within which a British institution must find the money to buy the object; if none can manage it, the licence is given. Although in theory similar to French law, licences are rarely refused in the first instance, whereas in France they are refused constantly. Details on export duties and taxes are available from the Dept of Trade and Industry, Tariff Section, 1 Victoria St, London SW1, tel 01-215 7877.

4 PAINTINGS: THE INTERNATIONAL MARKET

Buy old masters. They fetch a better
price than old mistresses.
            Lord Beaverbrook

Those who think that they might now be
millionaires if only their grandfathers had
not bought the Barbizon school should set their
minds at rest. In 1900, when a Van Gogh
could have been had for £50, your grandfather
would not have known where to look for one.
            Gerard Reitlinger, *The Economics of Taste*

OLD MASTERS

'Their time will come', is the defiant war cry of the Old Master picture dealers. 'Wonderfully cheap and authentic', they boom, 'repay endless contemplation'. 'Irresponsible', they say, each time an Impressionist painting breaks another record, and they go on to mutter about the busy trade of twentieth century life which prevents people from having the *time* to enjoy a symbolic Dutch still life or a dreamy Italian madonna.

Wandering off Bond Street into one of their shops, the walls heavy with centuries of oils in their massive gilt frames, many unimaginably large for a modern sitting room, time does seem to stand still and it takes the amateur, at least, a while to unwind into these richly detailed and allusive works. Unfortunately for the dealers, this is one reason why prices, as well, are not moving as fast as they could, and why the Old Master market looks positively sluggish in comparison to the rise in prices for the instantly appealing Impressionists and Modern pictures. In the important autumn sales of the 1988–89 season, second rate Impressionists like Sisley and Fantin-Latour were fetching over £1m with hardly an eyebrow raised, while a couple of contemporary American artists casually topped £3m – Jasper Johns going on to reach almost £10m – yet the salerooms were astonished when a magnificent Guido Reni, recently discovered and fresh to the market, exceeded its derisory £70–100,000 estimate to fetch £825,000.

Once the key sector, Old Masters are now one of the most overlooked areas of the art market. The gap between them and the Impressionists has been widening for years, although there are those who live in constant hope of a revival waiting just round the corner. In 1984, Sotheby's Old Master Index rose by 38 per cent, giving credence to the reappraisal theory, but since then, and especially in 1987 and 1988, the rise of the Impressionists has been inexorable. Figure 4.1 tells the story.

Traditionally, wealthy new collectors look to Impressionist paintings first. They are easy to enjoy immediately, a lot of the images are famous and familiar, they are highly decorative and, not too large, they will grace

Fig. 4.1: Sotheby's Old Masters v Impressionists indices

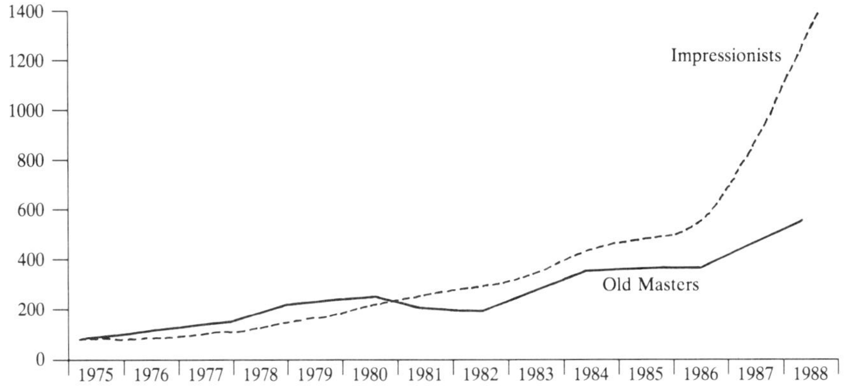

Source: *Sotheby's Art Market Bulletin*

any home. Later, some collectors may tire of what they perceive as superficial glitz, and turn, either backwards or forwards, to something more demanding – to the more scholarly Old Masters, whose subject matter and symbolic content require more time and research, or to the complex abstractions of the Modern and contemporary schools.

The market for Old Masters

In January 1988 a vast and sumptuous still life by Jan Davidsz de Heem became the most expensive Old Master ever to be auctioned in the United States. Christie's drooled over this most vainglorious of all Dutch *vanitas*, lovingly cataloguing the array of pomegranates and the pink lobster, looking alluringly out of a blue and white Ming vase, the silver and the shells, the discarded musical instruments, all supposed to teach onlookers a strict lesson and send them off in search of less worldly pleasures.

One of them, on the contrary, paid $6.6m (£3.7m) for the picture, a particularly lavish outlay in view of the fact that the painting had been offered by a dealer in London in 1987 for $4.25m. The feverish price escalation here echoed some of the excitement more usually generated in Impressionist and Modern sales, and suggested that perhaps the long-awaited Old Master revival was about to start. Such still lifes, swimming with sumptuous and extravagant images, seem almost guaranteed to bring on an attack of saleroom giddiness in the way some Impressionist pictures have done in the past.

The day before, another de Heem had established a short-lived record of $2.53m, and 11 other works from an important private owner sale, the Guterman collection, had also achieved record prices. Within just 48 hours, sale of Old Master paintings in New York reached $32m (£17.8m), and private buyers, not usually a strong element at Old Master sales, were out in force.

In another sector, a spate of record prices would produce a crop of sellers eager to benefit from a buoyant market, and, in turn, new buyers responding to the quality of the goods available: witness the Impressionist spiral. But a crucial weakness in the Old Master market is that there just are not enough top quality pictures in circulation for this to happen, and all the very best ones have long since disappeared into museums. This is one reason why it is unfair to compare prices with those fetched for the Impressionists, where top works are still in circulation. And it goes further than this, for the trouble with the Old Master sector is that collectors, put off because they know they will never be able to acquire the very best, refuse to compromise on the second rate and simply don't bother with the sector at all. Thus when a masterpiece does come up, there are very few people in the market for it – hence the problem with the de Heem in London. And in London in December 1986, another casualty was a pair of portraits by Frans Hals of some Dutch burghers, which were bought in at £1.4m and £1.6m. Two of the finest and freshest Old Masters seen for years, experts and the seller alike knew that the quality and condition meant they were worth more than that – Frans Hals, unlike Renoir, is not a frequent visitor to the saleroom.

The subject matter

One problem is subject matter. Attractive still lifes, preferably of flowers or fruit rather than dead birds, are in. So are pretty young girls, and officers in uniform. A Reynolds portrait of a man, for example, might fetch £5,000 – a derisory sum for a work by one of the greatest portraitists – but a portrait of a young woman, set in a decorative landscape, would go for nearer £1m. And it was the gleaming military uniform of Lieutenant Colonel Jonathan Bullock that pushed a Gainsborough portrait through the £1m barrier – it fetched £1.1m – at Christie's in the 1986-87 season.

Out, though, are religious subjects, difficult mythological scenes, or portraits of stodgy noblemen long sunk into oblivion or consigned to a footnote in a history text book. This is unfortunate, because these were the subjects which were most frequently commissioned by patrons of old, but these days, as one auctioneer said ruefully, 'no one wants a martyr', although a madonna will sell a lot better than a crucifixion. Nor, generally, do people want to go off to research the meaning of the painting they have just bought in a dictionary of classical legends, and they are unlikely to relish the prospect of some pompous merchant, glowing with newly rich status, staring out at them from the walls of their living room.

A quick browse around the preview of a typical sale of important Old Masters at Sotheby's in July 1988 shows what collectors are up against here. Among the religious contingent,for example, there is a quite dramatic Salvator Rosa, *Jonah and the Whale*, which could almost be a secular work and doubles its top estimate to sell for £126,500. But otherwise, the tone is militantly sombre, and the prices correspondingly low. A *Massacre of the Innocents* (estimate £15-20,000) is £6,600; *The Beheading of John the Baptist* manages £11,000, and a copy of Rubens' famous *Descent from the Cross* is £39,600. A moving *Jerome in the Wilderness* by Leonardo Monaco makes £374,000, three times its estimate, but it is very early (around 1400), which probably accounts for the price.

And no one wants two magnificently rich and intense works, *St Francis Receiving the Stigmata* and *An Ascetic Saint*.

The top lot at the Sotheby's sale was an unusual Canaletto, *The Redentore in a Capriccio Setting*, which made £440,000. The sort of Old Masters which strike delight into an auctioneer's heart are the familiar Canaletto gondoliers or the Brueghel skating scenes which adorn Christmas cards; they are bright, lively and highly decorative; their subjects are immediately comprehensible, they would not look out of place in a modern home, and they sell. A fine and typical group of carousing peasants, *A Wedding Feast* by Peter Brueghel the Younger, for instance, fetched £451,000 in 1980 and resold just four years later, not usually a risk worth taking, for £660,000, a good return by the standards of any market. The Dutch and Flemish still lifes and genre paintings are among the most popular of all Old Masters. Greatly favoured by dealers, there are a massive number of them around, but always impeccable in detail and precision – the guild system operating for painters in Holland in the 16th and 17th centuries ensured this – they make a very safe investment.

Alternatively, an auctioneer will smile on the obviously enjoyable and escapist paintings of the French eighteenth century, notably by Boucher and Fragonard. Their sugared sexiness – lolling shepherds and enticing cupids – amply compensates for historical or mythological themes, and they too are technically superb. They have also managed to find favour with Japanese buyers.

But in a period when decorativeness is more prized than ever, so much of what was painted before 1800 has become thoroughly alien to modern taste, and the skill and subtlety and tenderness of the Old Master artist, his breadth of reference and academic scope, go unnoticed when set against the bold and direct images of Impressionist and Modern art. Add to that the ailing, sometimes faded condition – restorable with care, time and money, but hardly helpful to a buyer going on first impressions – of many Old Masters, and it becomes a bit clearer why the Mantegnas and Rembrandts come cheaper than the Monets and Van Goghs.

The importance of attribution

In Impressionist and Modern sales, dealers have been largely unable to hold out against the impact of the private collector buying directly at auction. Old Masters, though, remains a natural sector for dealers to exercise their specialist skills and they are far more necessary to the private buyer here than for someone buying later works. Dealers can gradually cultivate a client's taste for some of the scholarly, academic works whose strong points are hardly instant gratification, they are knowledgeable about condition, and they can tread the minefield of fakes and copies in a market where every second painting is attributed to 'the school of', 'the circle of' or 'a follower of'.

New buyers especially feel happier with firm attributions, and the hazy history of a lot of Old Masters is a further discouragement to many to dip into this field. But for the speculator willing to do a bit of research, maybe as a hobby, this is where the potential lies, for art historians are constantly rewriting the value of other people's money by reattributing works, either up or down the scale, to different artists.

At Sotheby's July 1988 sale of important Old Master paintings, a quarter of the 80 lots were catalogued as 'school of', 'studio of' etc, and among the others there was tell-tale evidence of a history of disturbed identities. A seventeenth century still life by Isaac Soreau was offered along with a certificate from 1978 attributing it to Jakob van Hulsdonck; a work by Caracciolo was sold with a label attributing it to Caravaggio, and a group of monkeys and exotic birds painted in the seventeenth century, which had fetched $1,000 as the work of Jan Weenix in 1949, made £126,500 when the hand of David de Coninck was identified 40 years later.

When the lesser and middle range Old Masters are sold, less than a third of the works may be attributed to known artists, and dealers regularly buy at the cheap end in the hope of proving dubious attributions. At Sotheby's in December 1987, a seventeenth century Dutch *Portrait of a Girl* was catalogued as by Jan de Bray, but the curator of Dutch and Flemish paintings at the Metropolitan Museum in New York believed it to be by Thomas Willeboirts Bosschaert, and Chaucer Fine Art paid £20,900 as against an estimate of £4-6,000 for it.

One dealer, nicknamed 'The Hoover' (because he 'cleans up'), makes a habit of scouring provincial auctions for wrongly attributed paintings; an obscure portrait he picked up for £187 at Sotheby's in Chester reappeared at Christie's a few months later, in November 1987, where it resold, complete with proven name tags for the artist (Sebastiano del Piombo) and his subject (Pope Clement VII), for £418,000. This sort of thing just cannot happen with later works, whose provenances and authenticity are beyond question, but with many Old Master artists working from studios or employing skilled apprentices in workshops, maybe signing their work to pass it off as their own when time to finish a commission was short, certain attributions are very difficult to make, and can be undone by further research. Moreover, in the sixteenth and seventeenth centuries no one thought twice about copying the work of a great master and selling it, merely as a copy and with no intention to deceive. The trouble is that some copyists, tricksters or not, were so good that modern experts have been bewildered, and a painting long held to be the 'original' is sometimes downgraded to a copy when a 'better' or more convincing 'original' makes an appearance.

Equally, a painting can be upgraded, as happened when a work by Annibale Carraci, a little-known sixteenth century Bolognese artist, was valued at a Sotheby's valuation day in Bournemouth at £400 but sold at Phillips for £847,000. Even the second round of experts who saw the painting at Phillips nearly got the attribution wrong; in the catalogue the work was attributed to Sisto Badalocchio, a follower of Carraci, but Phillips changed their minds a week before the sale and contacted potentially interested dealers.

Fortunes have been made and lost this way, and reattribution is a hazard anyone collecting Old Masters must accept. It can happen at any level of the market, though the Carraci was a typical case – a great master, but one whose works surface infrequently. Reattribution tends, though, to plague the works of lesser artists more, where, however, it also does less damage, for often reallocation from one obscure seventeenth century artist to another will not alter the price at all. This is an important point that new buyers, who are often starting to collect in the very areas where reattribution has less of an effect on prices, sometimes fail to grasp.

Price trends

At this end of the spectrum, Old Masters are being sold at what seem give-away prices, but then at all levels they seem almost ludicrously cheap. Of the 230 Old Master paintings offered by Sotheby's in July 1988, almost half were under £15,000, and almost a quarter under £5,000; only 13 made more than £100,000. This offers plenty of scope for anyone prepared to do a bit of research and maybe take a punt on a little-known artist.

The best chance for Old Master pictures is that a small stock, which currently seems to deter buyers, will eventually work in the market's favour. It is possible that when the number of high quality Old Masters still in private hands is massively reduced, prices will soar as collectors compete to secure the last few. A two-tier market, with some stickiness at the middle and bottom, has already begun. According to Sotheby's Art Index, Old Masters have performed erratically of late (see Figure 4.2), with lacklustre results in 1985-86 but quite reasonable returns in 1987-88. But it would require a revolution of taste for Old Masters to catch up with Impressionists this century.

Fig. 4.2: Old Masters Index — annual % change

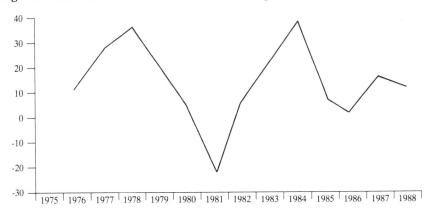

Source: Sotheby's Art Market Bulletin

THE RISE OF THE IMPRESSIONISTS

'If I sold only good paintings I should starve', Renoir once said. Though never cheap, Impressionists do vary enormously in quality, allowing collectors to dip into the market at differing price levels. Moreover, a prolific output from artists like Renoir means that while supply is diminishing fast enough to spur collectors on, there are plenty of works, all of unquestionable authenticity and provenance, to enable a comprehensive collection to be formed, and plenty around to exchange and trade up.

This is one reason why record-breaking Impressionist sales are able to build so successfully upon each other, bolstering up the confidence which has been at the heart of this mighty market for the last few years.

In December 1986, Monet's *Rue Mosnier aux Paveurs* broke the record for an Impressionist picture when it was knocked down at Christie's for £7.7m, and in that autumn season £80m was paid in London alone for Impressionist and Modern works.

With this bullish backcloth, there could not have been a better time than March 1987 for Van Gogh's *Sunflowers* to appear on the market. Immediately after selling it for nearly £25m, Christie's were offered another Van Gogh. *Le Pont de Trinquetaille* sold in June 1987 for £12.65m, giving it a short-lived record as the second most expensive painting sold at auction. Along with the *Rue Mosnier aux Paveurs*, it appeared in December 1987 on the walls of the Zurich Kunsthaus, the traditional repository of works owned by rich Swiss collectors. Maybe the buyers didn't want to risk savouring the works at home, or maybe both were bought by the same consortium of buyers. Either way, it looks likely that one eye at least was on the investment potential.

But *Le Pont de Trinquetaille* was not all. Three months – more or less the minimum time lag between commissioning works for auction and the appearance at a sale – after *Sunflowers*, Christie's and Sotheby's were awash with Impressionist paintings, and at the end of the 1987 season, Impressionist sales were up 55 per cent on the previous year.

The salerooms held their breath to see whether the performance could be repeated. There was a little flutter after the Stock Exchange crash: a couple of Renoirs were unsold, and there were even murmurs that Degas' *Les Blanchisseuses* at £7.48m in November 1987 could have gone higher in happier times, although nobody could really say that about the sale of *Irises* for $53.9m. Signs of trouble, though, came with the sales of lesser Impressionists, which remained about 30 per cent unsold in the winter of 1987; these will be an almost certain casualty of another slump on the stock exchange.

The Stock Exchange crash hastened on what would almost certainly have developed in any case – a flight into quality and the clear development of a two-tier market. In the top tier, regular estimates of over £1m still appear daunting in the catalogues, and it is hard not to be wary of the inflation of the Impressionist currency when a Renoir is bought in at £1.4m and a Monet, estimated at £1.8 – £2.5m in the catalogue of the Alan Clore collection in June 1988, is unsold at £1.7m. So buoyant is the present mood, though, that hardly an eyebrow was raised when a telephone bidder paid over £7m for a Van Gogh, *Romans Parisiens*, which Christie's sold on behalf of a Swiss collector in June 1988, and the record £3.85m fetched in the same sale for Monet's *La Maison Bleue, Zaandam*, barely lasted into the next month before it was eclipsed by the £14.3m fetched by *Dans la Prairie*.

Monet was clearly flavour of the season in the autumn 1988 sales: *Le Pont Japonais* made £6.05m, *Le Pont du Chemin de Fer à Argenteuil* was £6.82m, and one of the 47 versions of the *Waterlilies* made £5.72m, going to a new home in Japan via the department store Seibu. Seibu also took east a Renoir *Head of a Girl* for £1.98m.

MODERN PAINTINGS

It was another Tokyo department store, Mitsukoshi, which in the same season paid a record sum for a twentieth century work of art. Picasso's

A gap in the markets: Canaletto's The Churches of the Redentore and S. Giacomo, Venice, *one of a pair, made £682,000 in Christie's Old Masters sale in December 1988* . . .

while Monet's Le Pont du Chemin de Fer à Argenteuil *made ten times as much – £6.82 million – at Christie's Impressionist sale in November 1988.*

Fig. 4.3: Sotheby's Impressionists -v- Modern Paintings indices

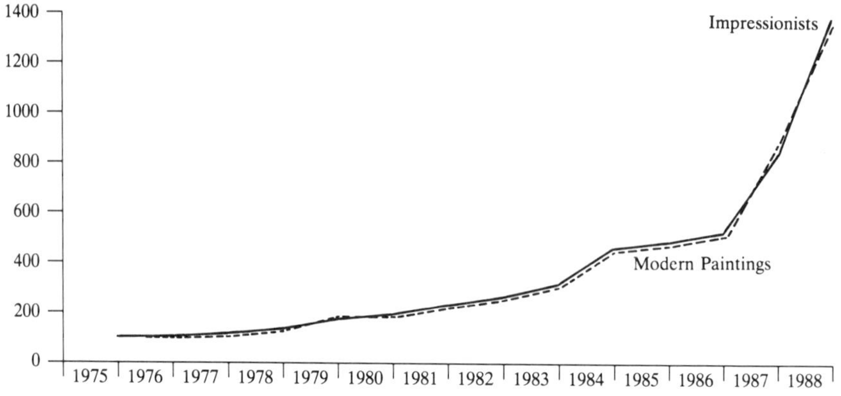

Source: Sotheby's Art Market Bulletin

Acrobate et Jeune Arlequin was knocked down for £20.9m, the third picture – a Cubist work fetched £8.5m and *Maternité*, from the much sought-after Blue period, was £13.67m – to break the record for his work within just one month.

As Figure 4.3 shows, modern art, boosted largely by American buyers, has been level-pegging with the Impressionists all the way; the 1988 season rounded off to record growth rates of 65 per cent for the Impressionists and 63 per cent for the Moderns. Among very rich American buyers, modern and contemporary art has long been considered as prestigious as famous Impressionist images. In the autumn of 1988, enormous prices, including a smattering of extraordinary records in New York, pushed contemporary art on to a new plateau. The record for a work by a living artist was broken twice within a month when Jasper Johns' *White Flags* made $7m (£3.9m) only to be overtaken by the same artist's *False Start* at $17m (£9.4m). Both fetched more than the most expensive Old Master ever sold in the United States.

London, which has lagged behind New York in this sector, is starting to show signs of catching up, and although records for living British artists are much more modest – £352,000 for Hockney's *A Neat Lawn*, for example, or just £28,600 for a Patrick Heron – this is an exceptionally exciting area for collectors at present, with plenty of room for the market to go higher. The investment prospects for modern and contemporary British artists are discussed in Chapter 5.

NINETEENTH CENTURY PAINTINGS – A NEW MARKET?

Rising or waning, the status of Old Masters and Impressionist and Modern paintings as an international currency looks assured. Sandwiched between them are nineteenth century paintings, where demand has always been more locally based.

Sotheby's index of nineteenth century paintings has aways looked rather tame (see Figure 4.4) although the mutually exclusive demand for most of its components makes it the least representative of the indices, as violent swings in one local market can mask steady movement everywhere else. In

1986, for example, the index actually fell, largely because the booming orientalist market in which the Arabs were big buyers collapsed along with the oil price.

Fig. 4.4: Sotheby's Fine Art indices

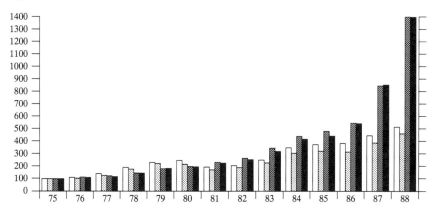

Source: Sotheby's Art Market Bulletin

Key ☐ Old Master Paintings
▓ 19th Century European Paintings
▓ Impressionist Art
■ Modern Paintings

Waxing rich on the international merry go round, the salerooms have in recent years tried to get some nineteenth century paintings along for the ride. The result has been some carefully engineered promotions to international status of areas which have always had a more or less exclusively national following.

The first and most famous to go was Scandinavian paintings, which took off well, no doubt helped by the exhibition *Dreams of a Summer Night* at the Hayward Gallery in 1986. For a couple of years, prices soared, but they are now levelling off, indicating that what is more or less an artificially induced demand can only go so far. There is no doubt that at the top end of the market, collectors are far wiser – and take home far more interesting works – spending six figure sums on the best of the Scandinavians rather than on third or fourth rate Impressionists, and it was largely this that drew in collectors in the first place. If the Impressionist market ever comes unstuck, it will be the lesser pieces which suffer, while the top end of any market is safe in the long term.

In the sales of Scandinavian art in the spring of 1988, high prices were paid for stunningly decorative works by the top artists. A portrait by Carl Larson of his wife fetched £264,000, and Anders Zorn's painting of two girls in a wood fetched £495,000, though even this seems cheap compared with some Impressionists.

It is too late to jump on the bandwagon now, and a sign that the market might be nearing saturation was that of the 500 or so works offered for sale, around 25 per cent remained unsold and most of those which did sell went back to Scandinavia.

The same season saw reasonably successful specialist Spanish sales, but disastrously, a specialist sale of late nineteenth and early twentieth century Viennese paintings was almost 50 per cent unsold, suggesting that there is a limit to the extent by which a marketing department can create a market. Investors who are not looking for a gamble should beware of following any market that has suddenly declared itself open for international business; long-lasting rises in price for a sector usually begin more subtly. It is sadly parochial, but those who stay at home are likely to see bigger returns, with British art being one of the most buoyant sectors of all.

5 19th AND 20th CENTURY BRITISH ART

> The British public has always had an unerring taste for
> ungifted amateurs.
>
> John Osborne

Will your grandchildren curse you for buying Alfred Munnings instead of
L S Lowry? Or will they stare, bemused to discover in the attic an
innocuous little picture of children on the beach by someone you think was
called Dorothea Sharp, which you admit to paying several thousand
pounds for many years ago? Maybe they will sit at your feet to be told
about a gloomy goddess, sexy in a reluctant sort of way, by a Victorian
painter who tarted up mythological subjects, which you always liked but
which cost nearly £1.5m back in the 1980s, or perhaps they already sit at
your feet to hear about that same goddess which you could have bought for
£357 in 1926, if only you had thought of it.

Victorian and modern British pictures are sectors which call for historical perspective. In 1851, Prince Albert complained about the 'tyrannical
influence' of the Great Exhibition: 'the works of art', he said, 'by being
publicly exhibited and offered for sale, are becoming articles of trade,
following as such the unreasoning laws of markets and fashion.' In the next
century, never was the tyrannical influence more dramatically exercised
than against Victorian, and later modern British paintings. In the last 20
years, both have undergone a revival which is probably unequalled in the
rest of the art market. There are still bargains to be found, but so large are
the sums paid in these areas that even collectors who have never wavered
in accordance with fashion are forced to acknowledge that buying these
pictures is an investment as well as a pleasure.

INVESTMENT HISTORY

Lauded in their own day, and patronised by the newly rich status-hungry
industrialists of the nineteenth century, the Victorian painters fell from
grace almost as soon as the twentieth century was into double figures. They
stayed in the doldrums for more than half a century, getting less and less
fashionable by the decade, their gushy moralising and morbid sentimentality earning the contempt of art historians and collectors alike.

It seemed a relentless downward spiral. Sir Lawrence Alma-Tadema,
one of the most eminent of the Victorian neo-classicists, was paid £5,250 in
1904 for *The Finding of Moses*, which resold in 1935 for £861. Seven years
later it dropped to £273 and 10 shillings, and in 1960 it was £252. *The Roses
of Elagabalus*, which was £105 in 1960, started life in 1888 at £4,000.

The decline and rise of the Victorians

The Pre-Raphaelite Brotherhood and their associates, who took anything up to six painstaking years to complete a work, commanded enormously high prices in the nineteenth century, especially after Ruskin championed their cause. The dealer Agnew paid Holman Hunt £11,000 for ownership and the right to reproduce *The Shadow of Death* in 1874, while Burne-Jones, whose name was linked with the Brotherhood although he was not a member, received £5,775 for *Love and the Pilgrim*, a medieval allegory, in 1898. In 1933 you could have bought it for £210, and in 1942 it was bought in at £21.

Another Burne-Jones, *The Prince Entering the Briar Wood*, was bought in in 1987, this time for a ludicrous £520,000 (see Chapter 1). In the meantime, Victorian art had seen an about-turn in fortune, sparked off in the 1960s when interest was aroused by its technical virtuosity and extraordinary attention to detail, about which there can be no dispute, whatever you think of the end result.

There were some headline-catching leaps in price in a very short time, and suddenly Victorian paintings were all the rage. One painting which changed hands four times between 1950 and 1982 was *Ophelia*, a very popular Victorian subject, in the version painted by another later follower of the Pre-Raphaelites, John William Waterhouse. In 1950, the work managed a mere 20 guineas; in 1968 it caught the start of the revival and made 420 guineas. Just three years later, in 1971, it was 3,000 guineas, but when it resold in 1982 it fetched £75,000. In just over 30 years, the painting rose in price well over 3,000 times.

High prices, moreover, were achieved almost exclusively through British demand. Foreign collectors have never got excited about these strange, obsessive images and figures, many of them inspired by the reading of some very British authors – Walter Scott, Tennyson – and showing the influence of English-rooted ideas like those of Ruskin, Carlyle and the Oxford Movement. Although the Pre-Raphaelites travelled to Italy and were keen on Dante and, most of all, the artists of the early Italian Renaissance, their brand of medieval revivalism is unlike anything produced abroad, and foreign collectors have tended to see them as a footnote in the history of art.

One long-time lover of the Victorians was L S Lowry, who explained in 1956, 'as a student I admired D G Rossetti and, after him, Madox Brown. The queer thing is I've never wavered, they're my two favourite artists still'. In 1964 Lowry bought what he considered to be one of Rossetti's finest paintings, the portrayal of William Morris's wife Jane, with whom Rossetti was infatuated, as Proserpine, Empress of Hades. Lowry paid £5,250 for it – its obvious quality and the mesmeric charm of the sultry goddess suggestively eating her way through a symbolic pomegranate saved it from the derisory prices paid for some of its contemporaries, and was a good advance on the £357 it had cost in 1926. And it proved the wisdom of backing your own taste, for when the painting was resold in 1987, it fetched £1.43m, the record for a Victorian picture, and more than 200 times more than it made in 1964.

The same year as *Proserpine* fetched £5,250, another stagey Victorian picture, *Contradiction – Oberon and Titania*, by Richard Dadd, whose

Rossetti's sultry portrait of Jane Morris as Proserpine, *which fetched £1.43m, the record for a Victorian picture, at Christie's in November 1987.*

best work was painted when he was insane, sold for £7,000; it resold in 1983 at Sotheby's for £550,000. On a similar scale, Tissot's *Bunch of Lilacs*, £7,350 in 1975, made £81,000 in 1982. Tissot, whose favourite models were children and pretty women, particularly his striking Irish mistress Kathleen Newton, chose his subjects from aristocratic diversions like boating parties and was extravagantly detailed in his portrayal of fripperies like silken gowns and picnic hampers. Even in 1983 examples of his work could be found for £10,000, but they now average around £100,000 and Tissot is among the most popular of Victorian artists. *A Fête Day in Brighton* sold in New York in 1988 for $962,500 (£509,259). For any collector who finds his records of nineteenth century hedonism complacent or unstimulating, there are hundreds relieved at the absence of the maudlin sentiment or moralising tendency of the Pre-Raphaelites, and it is difficult not to be swayed by his decorative power.

The Victorians also had a penchant for melodrama, and this too has bolstered up prices; it certainly contributed towards the £780,000 paid in 1983 for a painting of the fatally doomed looking couple in Millais' evocative *The Proscribed Royalist*. Prices like this, and of course for *Proserpine*, which more than doubled its estimate, bring Victorian paintings one step closer to Old Master status, and prices in six figures are becoming increasingly common, for supply is scarce – partly because of the time taken to complete a painting and also because many sold to industrialists in the north of England, and have disappeared into museums in these areas.

A lot of Victorian paintings now make familiar and instantly recognisable images, and there is no doubt that a large number of new buyers were drawn towards them in the 1960s and 1970s, pushing up prices not just for the well-known Pre-Raphaelites and neo-classicists but also, in a knock-on effect, for the huge number of paintings at the lower end of the market.

Performance of Victorians and Moderns compared

Another knock-on effect, however, occurred when a perception that Victorian art was 'too expensive to collect' took root, and interest shifted to modern British pictures, which date roughly from 1880 and encompass a lot of the decorative themes which made the Victorians so appealing in the first place. The curious result has been that modern British pictures can now be more expensive than their illustrious predecessors, which they have, since the early 1980s, in some cases overshadowed. In time, however, this is bound to right itself; technically, the earlier period is generally more assured, and this technical expertise will always be in its favour in any long-term readjustment of relative prices. Against this, some earlier works suffer from questions of 'genuineness', which few modern paintings do.

Buyers looking to invest in these areas should balance these factors carefully. Rises for modern British pictures have been staggering in the last few years partly because they were so hugely undervalued in the 1970s, and they are likely to go higher. Among Victorian artists, the best work by the best artists is no longer affordable by most people – Tissot, the classicists Alma-Tadema, Lord Leighton (£286,000 for a long-lost painting of a Sybil, a female prophet, at Christie's in 1987) and George Frederick Watts,

Poynter, Rossetti, Burne-Jones, the Pre-Raphaelite follower John Mel-huish Stradwick (£121,000 for some lute-playing damsels gazing into a medieval middle-distance in the nostalgic *In the Golden Days*, in the same sale) – all have fetched huge prices. But almost *because* they *seem* so unaffordable, and thus discourage collectors, works by some of them are still available at well under £50,000 and in this period of levelling off, are a good investment given that they can be expected to catch up in price over the next decade or so. Portraits by Burne-Jones and Lord Leighton sold in the last couple of years for under £25,000, and are a much safer bet than the equivalent sum spent on some currently fashionable modern pictures. On the other hand, there are modern artists still to be discovered selling at under £5,000, and plenty of steam left in that market. Both sectors offer the collector a wide choice, and the development of the modern British picture market was consolidated in October 1988 by a good turnout, both of dealers and buyers, at the first Twentieth Century British Art Fair at the Cumberland Hotel, although it was mostly the cheaper pictures which sold. It is more important than ever to stick to good quality works for investment purposes, however.

VICTORIAN PAINTINGS

Hundreds of thousands of artists managed to make quite a decent living in Victorian England, mainly by a sort of 'formula' painting in which a theme once offered successfully was reworked again and again. As a result, although there are obvious variations in the quality, for a broad base of professionally expert Victorian paintings, what determines price is not so much the artist as the subject matter. At this level, the market wants safe, familiar works by hands that have painted numerous similar pieces – rarity is a disadvantage. Thomas Sydney Cooper, for example, did well early on from some paintings of sheep and cows, spent most of the nineteenth century – he lived from 1803 to 1902 – repeating them, and now sells for between £2,000 and £3,000, sometimes more for an exceptional work. A Cooper painting on a different subject, which in another market might have been sought after as unusual, turns out to be much harder to sell than a familiar theme.

The lesson here is, keep to the straight and narrow, and your paintings will appreciate gracefully and steadily. There is a solid base of British collectors prepared to pay between £500 and £5,000 for a regular supply of landscapes, marine views and paintings of children and animals. The sepulchral end of Victorian sentimentality – dying children with angels hovering overhead – is not the sort of thing a private collector wants in his home, but the sunny end is easy and unchallenging and has exactly the decorative content whose appeal has been growing over the last two decades.

Landscape and marine painting

Landscape painting reached its zenith in Victorian England, and more landscapes are sold at auction than any other type of picture. Price is determined partly by location – top sellers are the Highlands and the Lake

District, anywhere along the Thames, certain coastal resorts like those in North Yorkshire, and well-known scenic areas from abroad, notably the Alps and the Mediterranean coast. But a lot of Victorian landscapes simply recollect the pleasure of rural tranquillity in some very British but otherwise indeterminate part of the countryside; wooded river scenes, the sun setting over rolling vales, highland lakes and mountain streams, and farmyard domesticity, are among the most popular. Price is determined by the composition of the landscape – the more there is to look at, the higher the price. Thus 'a shepherd and his sheep by a stream in a wooded landscape' or 'a wooded river landscape with cows watering and a church beyond' are likely to fetch more than simply 'a wooded landscape' or 'a view of the moors'. Figures, animals or cottages help the price; value is also enhanced by dramatic elements *in situ* – a lock or a mill, a mountain or a fallen tree.

Two works of almost identical size by one of the better-known artists in this genre, Benjamin Leader, were sold at Christie's in November 1987. The first, *On the River Conway, North Wales*, was a beautifully mellow composition crowded with the ever-popular cattle semi-submerged in a stream – always a good selling point, notwithstanding the fact that lesser artists painted them thus to avoid depicting the feet, which are the most difficult part to draw – a stone cottage set in a wood, some pretty female figures, including a mother and child, in the foreground, and rolling hills in the distance. This epitome of the rural dream, suffused by sunlight – another good selling point – fetched £22,000; the second Leader, *On the North Welsh Coast*, a view of sea, sand, a handful of barely visible figures, and a great deal of sky, managed a mere £4,400. Although the bleak splendour of the North Wales coast is superbly captured, there simply is not enough going on in the painting to sustain the sort of interest generated by a fuller composition. Nevertheless, the quality of the work was high enough to secure a price well above the average for a wooded landscape or farmyard scene, hundreds of which sell for around £2,000. That makes a record achieved for Leader at Bonhams a year later – £57,200 for the popular view of Goring on Thames – all the more remarkable.

One peculiarly English cousin of the landscape is the marine painting, which is in much shorter supply and therefore tends to command higher prices. They are getting scarcer and prices are rising considerably, with the best sellers those produced in the first half of the nineteenth century. As with other subjects, 'formula' painting comes into play here: artists developed a talent for painting ship portraits, and sometimes even perfected just one type of scene – Thomas Rose Miles, for example, stuck to moonlit views of stormy seas, now fetching between £1,000 and £2,000. Although the painting of ship after ship appears monotonous to the uninitiated, connoisseurs drool over the composition and over details like flags – an American flag fetches the best price – and there is no denying the extraordinary technical skill of artists like John Wilson Carmichael, the brothers Thomas and James Butterworth, or Clarkson Stanfield. A good work by these artists commands over £10,000, pushing up prices in the lower range. This is good news for collectors who have bought paintings at between £750 and £2,000, but should not tempt buyers to go lower than that. So coveted are marine views that even an untalented artist can command a couple of hundred pounds for a poorly painted ship, tossing on

The Victorian landscape: the more there is going on, the higher the price.
Benjamin William Leader's busy On the River Conway, North Wales,
made £22,000 at Christie's in November 1987, while . . .

the same artist's bleak On the North Welsh Coast *was just £4,400 at the*
same sale.

a dubiously rough wave, but these are for the marine addict rather than for anyone thinking of investment.

Children and animals – the irresistable combination

The third ingredient in the staple diet of the Victorian picture collector, paintings of children and animals – preferably children *with* animals – is doing better than ever. Typical of the genre is Arther John Elsley's *The Favourite of the Litter*, in which a little girl stands on a ledge by a fountain and caresses the puppy in her arms, while other dogs look up beseeching the same treatment. This painting fetched £8,250 at Christie's in 1987; other titles indicative of the mood of much of the sale included *Boys will be Boys* (some children chasing animals in a farmyard), and *Best of Friends* (a cat snuggling down, apparently content, in the paws of a dog five times its size).

Even more than with landscapes and marine views, tastes here have little to do with fashion or art-historical opinion, and just as sex will always ensure a buyer for a good nude, so unbridled sentimentality will also secure a healthy price for a family of dogs or rabbits. Such is the pull of the decorative in the 1980s, however, that artists like Arthur John Elsley have doubled in price in less than five years, and enthusiasm shows no sign of waning. Prices continue to run beyond all expectations – a group of wide-eyed animals, *Foxhounds and Terriers in a Barn*, by John Emms, for example, exceeded its £3-4,000 estimate to sell for £15,950 at the Christie's sale.

Although collectors who bought over the last decade are able to trade up, many lovers of, say, Horatio Henry Couldrey, or Edgar Hunt, will find that, as for Elsley, prices are eluding their pockets – two wonderfully luminous Hunt paintings of chickens fetched nearly £10,000 each in 1987, for example. One alternative – and this applies even more significantly to lovers of landscapes and marine views – is the watercolour market, similar in subject and lower in price; another is to search out, from the host of Victorian artists selling at auction, likely candidates. to benefit from the inevitable knock-on effect. There remains some competent work available at under £2,000, and auctioneers have noticed an increasing tendency among private buyers to take a punt on a picture simply on the basis of an appealing subject. The market has done particularly well as a result of broader trends in the 1980s, and has capitalised on the revaluation of the top Victorians, but such is the nature of the landscape and animal genre that there should always be a body of collectors with a few thousand to spend, irrespective of a change in the cultural mood or in the Stock Exchange.

MODERN BRITISH PICTURES

It is almost impossible to write about this sector without feeling that one has, somehow, missed a boat which one never quite realised was sailing. No matter what picture one chooses, it seems, there is someone on hand to explain that only five years ago it cost a tenth of the price. Sadly, that is no guarantee that in five years time it will cost 10 times as much. All we know is that the mixed bag called modern British paintings, which starts around 1880 and continues more or less through to contemporary works, has in the 1980s shown more consistently dramatic rises than any other sector of the art market. Sotheby's major November sale in 1977, for example, totalled £176,000; the equivalent sale in November 1987 totalled £1.6m. The rise of individual artists varies but many have soared. Typical cases quoted by Sotheby's include a portrait by Sir William Rothenstein (£1,540 in March 1976 and £24,200 in March 1986), and a still life by Sir William Nicholson (£1,760 in November 1977, £30,800 for a similar work in November 1985). At the same time, certain areas within this sector have appreciated so fast that others begin to look undervalued, for all the talk of the revival. It is here that the shrewd investor can still cash in on the boom.

Traditionalist paintings

Modern British pictures began fetching high prices when buyers could no longer afford the decorative, easy Victorian oils which became increasingly and then prohibitively popular in the 1970s. Certain dealers, notably David Messum, saw the potential of later works which had something of the same flavour, and their promotional efforts paid off handsomely. The paintings they promoted were not really modern at all, but what is termed 'traditionalist', and what sells them is decorative appeal.

Buyers new to the art market generally avoid the abstract and complex and go for easy to appreciate subjects which in this sector means views of well-known and loved English places, especially coastal resorts and scenes and fashionable resorts abroad, and all the trappings of Edwardian elegance – ladies with hats and parasols, family outings in the barouche – which many people look to as a 'golden age'. The *milieu* celebrated here is not much different from the affluent idylls of Tissot and his contemporaries. Sneered at in the years after the Second World War, when there was anyway little money around to invest in paintings, homages to the rich and fashionable are now back in favour. Typical of the trend is Sir William Orpen, popular in his day (1878-1931) as a portraitist of the *belle monde*, but still selling for around £500 in the 1970s. By the early 1980s £5,000 was more usual, but in November 1986 an exceptionally pretty example of one of Orpen's favourite sitters, entitled *The Blue Hat*, fetched £137,500 at Christie's in King Street (see Chapter 2). In the same week a more modest portrait of another pretty young girl, *Young Ireland*, fetched £37,500 at Christie's South Kensington, an illustration of the price gap between the top and the middle range of an artist's work, but in itself also a marker for Orpen's reassessment as a significant artist.

Traditionalist paintings, cosy, familiar works tinged with the undeniable, rose-coloured hue of romance, but less sentimental than the Victorians, are still the hard core of any sale of modern British pictures and the area where the auctioneer can relax, certain of eager demand. But those artists who first became expensive maybe five or seven years ago are just beginning to seem, as might be expected after the initial rush of enthusiasm, a more sophisticated form of buying, with premiums paid for top quality pieces, and prices for the rest levelling off, though at a 'level' undreamt of 10 years ago.

The Newlyn School

The Newlyn School, which sparked off the whole sector, are the obvious example. Contemporary with the later Impressionists, whose works they had seen abroad, the Newlyn painters, led by Stanhope Forbes, settled in Newlyn, Cornwall, in the 1880s, and painted *plein air* scenes of day-to-day life for the next four decades.

Few of these artists were ever thought important while they were alive, and in the 1970s their bright and cheerful works fetched a few hundred pounds each. Now prices of over £20,000 are not unusual, even for lesser and later Newlyn painters like Harold Harvey, who painted Cornish cottages and fishing boats, and Dorothea Sharp, whose pretty, bright pictures of children cavorting on the beach typify the lure of this world where the sun always shines.

Several critics believe these sorts of prices – Harvey's *A Test of Strength* fetched a staggering £55,000 at Phillips – are overcompensating for past neglect, and with auction sensations spreading the news of saleability, there is some fear that supply may soon outstrip demand. For artists like Sharp, signs of a two-tier market crept into Christie's sale of important modern paintings sale in March 1988, when a couple of average Sharps, *At the Seaside* and *Children by the Sea*, fetched £7,920 and £7,700, a slightly more unusual example, *Children Paddling*, made £17,000, and an exceptional and atypical painting, with, for once, no sign of a coastline, *Children and Striped Rug in a Field*, was £30,800.

If the Newlyn School does peak, the top quality works will hold their own, and it will be the second rate which suffers. Rather than spend a few thousand pounds at this level, new buyers could look around for similar works by artists outside the Newlyn School, where prices have further to go. An example is Frederick William Jackson, whose paintings of the North Yorkshire coast predated the Newlyn coastal scenes and are in the £2-5,000 range. *Runswick Bay, Yorkshire*, made £4,180 at Christie's in 1988.

Another highly appreciating Newlyn artist is Henry Scott Tuke, whose male nudes lounge healthily in meadows and on beaches and have greatly appealed to buyers recently. *Sunbathers*, for instance, fetched £2,640 in March 1978; a comparable piece in size and subject, *Comrades*, made £22,000 in November 1987. It is possible that Tuke will go higher, but again, an alternative would be the work of similar artists, cheap now, but whom buyers might turn to as Tuke becomes too expensive. As an example, Christie's South Kensington suggest John Shirley Fox, whose *Naked Youth Reclining in a Field of Cow Parsley* resembles Tuke's approach but fetched just £480 in November 1986.

Scottish painting

But even if prices do fall back, or at least stop rising, the Newlyn School showed there was money in much forgotten modern British art, and that message did not go unheeded among the proponents of other, previously neglected schools. One group to become similarly fashionable is early twentieth century Scottish artists. Like their English counterparts, the vigorous works of the Glasgow Boys (the Scottish Impressionists) and the

How much further can prices for modern British pictures go? An unusual Dorothea Sharp, Children and Striped Rug in a Field, *made £30,800 at Christie's in March 1988 . . .*

a more typical example was just £7,700 at the same sale. In the 1970s neither would have exceeded £1,000.

Scottish Colourists (the avant-garde artists active from the first years of the twentieth century to the 1920s), did not begin to shoot up until the 1980s, and this sector still has some way to go. International interest is developing, but the bulk of demand comes from private Scottish collectors, who are likely to form a stable collecting base to support the market in the future. Sales are usually held in Scotland.

Something of a landmark was reached for these artists in December 1986, when Christie's Scotland devoted an entire and very successful sale to the work of the four Scottish Colourists, Samuel John Peploe, Francis Campbell Boileau Cadell, George Leslie Hunter and John Duncan Fergusson. Their works are bright, bold and very attractive; they painted mostly still lifes of flowers or luscious coastal scenes with a Mediterranean flavour. Peploe is the best known, and his *Japanese Vase and Pink Roses* fetched the top price of £40,700. Another Peploe still life of pink roses in a white vase, which had sold at Christie's Scotland in 1979 for a record £13,500, fetched £38,500 at the 1986 sale, tripling its price within seven years.

In February 1988 a sale at Sotheby's in Glasgow confirmed that this sector is still going strong, with prices far outstripping estimates. The top price here was for a two-sided Peploe still life of geraniums and roses (£68,200 as against an estimate of £20-30,000); £28,600 as against an estimate of £8-12,000 was also considered good for a Cadell still life, *Marigolds*, while *Tangier*, a watercolour by Joseph Crawhill, one of the Glasgow Boys, fetched £57,200 (estimate £10-15,000).

However, these prices look modest in comparison with those fetched later in the year. At Sotheby's Gleneagles sale in August 1988, the dealer Richard Green paid £214,500, over twice the estimate, for a Cadell, and in December 1988 Peploe's portrait of a favourite model, Peggy MacRae, sold at Christie's for £506,000 – a record for a Scottish picture and for any work of art sold at auction in Scotland. The estimate was a conservative £60-100,000. Such prices can only boost an already buoyant market, and for anyone who can still afford it, this is a sector to move into quickly.

Famous names

Although the general trend for modern British pictures is a relentless upward swing, it is the activities of buyers of very different tastes who will affect, say, prices for Munnings and prices for Lowry. Figures 5.1-5.6 below show the average auction prices over the decade 1977-87 for six of the best loved and most instantly recognisable English artists of the period. The annual figures, dependent to some extent on the chance of what comes on to the market, are erratic, but over the decade a steady upward movement is clear for all the artists. As in any market, the top works by each artist have performed better as an investment than the average; Lowry, for example, shows very slow rates of growth but *The Thames at Whitehall*, which fetched £5,720 in 1977, increased by an average 17 per cent per annum to sell in May 1987 for £24,200.

Buyers new to the market are often surprised how cheaply a familiar image by Lowry or Stanley Spencer can be bought. In 1986 both artists averaged around £6,000; the leap for Spencer was largely caused by the

Fig. 5.1: L.S. Lowry — average auction prices (£,000)

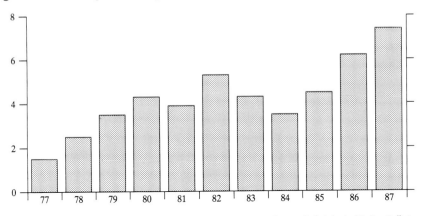

Source: Sotheby's Art Market Bulletin

Fig. 5.2: David Hockney — average auction prices (£,000)

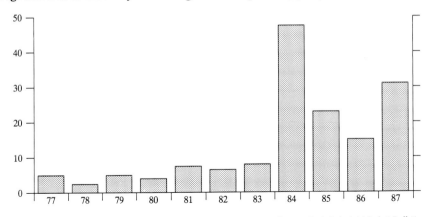

Source: Sotheby's Art Market Bulletin

Fig. 5.3: Sir Alfred Munnings — average auction prices (£,000)

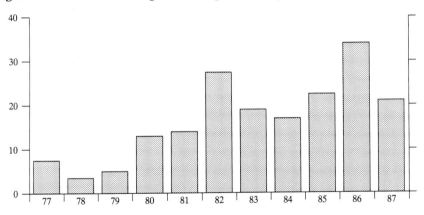

Source: Sotheby's Art Market Bulletin

Fig. 5.4: Sir William Russell Flint — average auction prices (£,000)

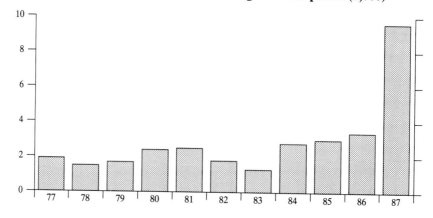

Source: Sotheby's Art Market Bulletin

Fig. 5.5: Sir Stanley Spencer — average auction prices (£,000)

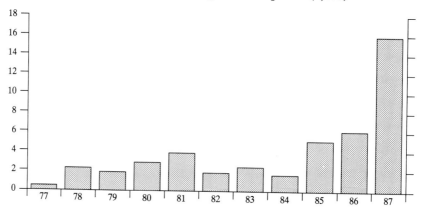

Source: Sotheby's Art Market Bulletin

Fig. 5.6: W. R. Sickert — average auction prices (£,000)

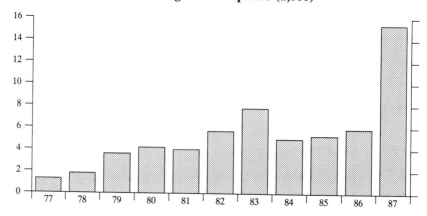

Source: Sotheby's Art Market Bulletin

sale of *The Coming of the Wise Men* in May 1987 for a record £82,500. That record was left far behind when in November 1987 Sotheby's sold Spencer's *Christ Preaching at Cookham Regatta* for £429,000.

So far, Lowry has been less lucky; the huge supply of his works depresses prices, or perhaps his 'matchstick' men and women and primitive urban images are sadly out of tune with the taste for the expansively decorative, and look odd among much modern furnishing. But some experts believe prices have moved so slowly that a revival could be round the corner, and at Christie's in 1988 a small painting, *The Factory Gate*, fetched £11,200, way above its £3-5,000 estimate.

Worlds away are his near contemporaries Alfred Munnings and Montague Dawson, whose Edwardian country estate charm – marine views and portraits of the aristocracy and, more particularly, their race-horses – look custom-painted for the newly rich. Their work is quint-essentially English, recalls an all but lost world, and this may be why a following for it is gradually developing in the United States. Munnings' *The Start at Newmarket: Study No 4* fetched $1.21m in New York in November 1987, an auction record. There is little prospect of Munnings' appeal faltering in the long term, and as one of the few English artists to win favour in the American market, he must be a good investment.

Munnings is technically superb but hardly innovative or original, and what sells his paintings is their subject matter. Subject matter is behind the enduring success of another contemporary, Sir William Russell Flint, the best known painter of nudes this century. The eternal appeal of Flint's images, and his brilliant draughtsmanship, makes it hard to foresee a day when his popularity will decline. In 1986 the average price of around £3,500 was within the reach of many a modest collector, with the record, £35,200, paid in March 1986 for *The Judgement of Paris*, not putting Flint utterly out of British bounds. That record still holds, but the 1987 average soared because a large number of top works sold, boosting the market at all levels. Flint is becoming increasingly expensive, and even sketches and drawings can now command over £2,000 – *Studies for Suzanne and the Elders*, for instance, fetched £2,200 at Christie's South Kensington in 1987. And a gloriously summery painting depicting three clothed young ladies, *Souvenir al Compiegna*, which epitomised everything that is decorative and appealing about traditional British art, fetched £11,550 at Christie's in March 1988.

GOING FOR THE LESSER-KNOWNS

The prospects for Flint, getting more expensive but still with room to move higher, look good. In a sector as vast and as prone, in sudden small areas, to sudden take-offs, as modern British art, the danger is to jump on the bandwagons that have already started rolling very fast and, mesmerised by recent rates of appreciation, to pay high prices just as a levelling off sets in. It would be far more lucrative to attend auctions and see who is beginning to get noticed, where the first little tremors of a price rise may be lurking, and the saleroom experts are still finding works by many artists they have never heard of coming in to be sold. There are some marvellous works by artists who five years ago were virtually obscure, and some of these are excellent candidates for investment. At Christie's March 1988 sale, for example, there was a nude as enticing as any of Flint's by Arthur Royce Bradbury, which fetched a well-earned £10,450 and could go much higher, and for those on the look out for attractive landscapes, a selection of works by an artist just recently come into prominence, Edward Seago, were a good buy. Two views of the Seine made £8,800 and £11,000; a warm and evocative *Shrimp Boats, Ostend*, was £4,400, and a poorer *Sunset* was £1,980, showing that buyers are discriminating here.

The knock-on effect is very pronounced in this field, and as one school or artist slips beyond widely affordable price barriers, another, lesser-known, name is bound to be waiting in the wings. Anyone who spotted Wilfred de Glehn, a friend of Sargent's, in the early 1980s when he was virtually unheard of, would have recouped their investment many times. De Glehn painted Sargentesque landscapes, views of Venice and portraits of women, and as Sargent has become prohibitively expensive – £187,000 for *Santa Maria della Salute, Venice*, at Christie's in 1988, for instance – to many who like his works, de Glehn has come into his own, commanding prices of between £25,000 and £40,000. An exceptional and very pretty work showing three sisters in a garden in Normandy, looking for all the world as if they had just finished a tennis match offstage during a Noel Coward play, made £71,500, but if de Glehn continues to follow Sargent up the ladder he should remain a good investment even now.

Modernist paintings

The brave investor, however, will look beyond easy traditional paintings like these to some of the lesser-known modernist artists, more difficult and intellectual but ultimately perhaps more rewarding. The best known are probably Stanley Spencer and the Camden Town Group, led by Sickert, who is one of the best loved of all twentieth century English artists. His *Facade of St Marks, Venice*, fetched a record £96,800 in May 1987, which is why the average price for his works (see Figure 5.6) shot up from under £6,000 in 1986 to nearly £16,000 in 1987. A great deal of good work is still available at under £10,000, and a few more prices like the one in May should increase confidence in an already steady market. High prices have also been paid for other members of the group in recent years – £30,800 for *The West Street, Dieppe*, by Charles Ginner, in May 1985 (the same painting made £12,100 in June 1979), and £26,000 for *Behind the Blind* by Spencer Gore in May 1986.

But less familiar modernist painters have been well and truly eclipsed by some of their traditionalist counterparts, and given that many were much more significant artists, a readjustment looks likely, which means prices have some way to go.

In November 1987 an important work by Glyn Philpott fetched a record £39,000, and there was much excitement at Christie's in March 1988 when a very seductive painting, *The Entrance to the Tagada*, far exceeded this at £94,600. Though well established now, prices for Philpott, as for Sickert and Spencer, should still have some way to go – a good Sickert, *Chicken*, seemed cheap at £27,500 at the same sale when compared to the hefty sums paid for the Sharps – and there are many other modernist artists now underpriced who could go the same way as the recently unknown Philpott.

I would watch out especially for Duncan Grant's Bloomsbury work, which is still available at around £3,000; Ivon Hitchens, who hovered at around £5,000 for years but zoomed up to over £9,000 with *Windy Countryside* and *The Lodge Gate*, at Christie's in March 1988; £39,600 for a colourful still life at Sotheby's in May 1988, and – the good work no doubt enticed out for sale by these encouraging prices – £50,000 for *White Gladioli* in the autumn of 1988. Buyers are clearly discriminating between the average and the outstanding, both here and in the work of another name to watch, Winifred Nicholson – flower paintings *White Lily, Corinth* and *Sun Haze* were just under £3,000 each at Christie's in March 1988, but *Vermilion and Mauve*, a lovely example of the style estimated at £3-5,000 at Christie's more run-of-the-mill sale in July 1988 was £20,350. Both artists should have some way to go yet, as should Paul Nash, a war artist who painted scenes from both wars. At £6,820 and £5,280, *The Ridge, Wytschaete*, from 1917, and *Different Skies* 1939, both sold comfortably over estimate at the Christie's March sale, and Nash is typical of the sort of modernist artist who is stimulating without being off-puttingly complex.

CONTEMPORARY PICTURES

Also worth watching are some contemporary British artists who appear at modernist sales. America has left Britain looking like a poor relation when it comes to contemporary art, and for a British artist to have any chance of achieving the sort of six-figure sums regularly paid in the New York salerooms, he must break into the US market. A few have done so – most famously Hockney, but also Freud, Bacon, R B Kitaj, Howard Hodgkin and Michael Morley, and these are now heavyweight international names which appear in sales of contemporary rather than exclusively British art. But a number of good established British artists who will be found each year on the walls of the Royal Academy Summer Exhibition also appear at auction quite cheaply, and should be good buys. Always instantly recognisable, for instance, is Carel Weight, whose *Walkers in a Park* was £2,640 at Christie's March sale. Other names include Ruskin Spear and Patrick Heron.

If you are *very* plucky, you could try galleries like The Young Unknowns Gallery, which promote the work of young living artists. Those who bought their David Hockneys (see Figure 5.2) and Bridget Rileys years ago are now patting each other on the back, but buying little-known contemporary work is the biggest risk of all, for you are not gambling on a fixed body of work, by which an artist's reputation will rise and fall, but on a living entity: the artist himself. You have to take a guess not just at the market's response to his work in 20 years time – difficult enough – but at what his as-yet-unproduced work will be; whether it will be good enough to make your early example priceless, or so mediocre that he – and the work that you have bought – will vanish unvalued into obscurity. If your judgement is vindicated, the rewards are large – for example, an early Hockney, *The Room, Tarzana*, sold for £500 (Hockney got half that) when it was painted in 1967; in 1987 it fetched £260,000 at auction. But for every Hockney there are hundreds of young art school hopefuls who never make it.

New interest in the modernist British school: prices for Ivon Hitchens hovered around £5,000 for most of the 1980s, but in 1988 suddenly soared. Bracken Field *was £40,700 at Christie's in November 1988.*

One of the thrills of buying work by new young artists is the sense of being in at the start, of history in the making. The paint barely dry on the canvas before it hangs on your wall, these fresh-from-the-studio pictures have little immediate secondary market at auction; they must bide their time. A few artists are beginning to sell new works directly through the auction houses, though the sale of contemporary art is largely confined to galleries. For the buyer, contemporary art, like most other art, is usually cheaper at auction. The very new artists, however, who could offer hope of the greatest profits, will not be well known enough to be represented, and galleries, and the Royal Academy Summer Exhibition – go on the first day or to a preview, because the good works tend to sell immediately – are the places to look.

In a new development, which suggests that British contemporary art is an area which could become even bigger business, Christie's South Kensington is mounting the first ever sale of 'new' art by a London auction house. The salerooms have traditionally been reluctant to offer new contemporary work, as unsold pieces can have a drastic effect on a young artist's reputation and morale. For the brave speculator, however, Christie's 'New Contemporaries' sale at the Royal College of Art in March 1989 will include work by around 20 young, and as yet unestablished, artists at prices estimated to be within the £100–900 range, is not to be missed. If it goes well, it is likely that new young artists will be able to charge rather more for their work, as they already do in the United States.

The permanent youth of the contemporary art market is one of its biggest attractions, especially to younger buyers, who prefer to explore areas other than those collected by their parents. The signs are that in Britain, traditionally a laggard in this sector, collectors – and the galleries vying for their custom – are increasing in number, and that a market that has always been something of a fringe affair might be about to come on to the main stage.

6 WATERCOLOURS

> He used to say that he had known profiteers during
> the war, who bought a few Birket Fosters so that
> after dinner, armed with a big cigar, they could take
> refuge in contemplating them and having a good cry.
> A C R Carter, *Let Me Tell You*

Like the soppy bits of Dickens, the unashamedly sentimental watercolour will always have its following, and none are better loved than those of the later Victorians. In the first volume of *The Economics of Taste*, published in 1960, Gerald Reitlinger notes scathingly that the market for Myles Birket Foster 'seems to flourish towards the end of wars'. Collectors in the nostalgia-hungry 1980s have taken him to their bosom too, embracing also with unprecedented enthusiasm his rival in nursery rhyme innocence, Helen Allingham. When her cottage gardens became dauntingly expensive – they are now at least £4,000 apiece – the salerooms began to lap up the floral fancies and pastel prettiness of contemporaries like Lilian Stannard, Beatrice Parsons and Louise Rayner, famous for her idealised townscapes. As they too get dearer, new names appear, for demand continues unabated. In the late 1970s these pictures were cheap and cheerful at under £100; now few fetch less than four figures. Surprises like the £10,000 paid at Christie's South Kensington in 1987 for Charles Green's *In The Brickfield*, which looks as if it was drawn to illustrate a Thomas Hardy novel, have made watercolours one of the most vibrant of the lower priced markets, attracting hundreds of new collectors each year.

INVESTMENT HISTORY

In the 1950s, when the watercolour market first began to recover the ground lost since its collapse in the 1920s – David Cox's *Ulveston Sands*, for instance, managed £787 in 1955 after selling in 1924 for £1,596 – names like those above were virtually unheard of, and even works from the 'golden age' of watercolour painting, the late eighteenth and first half of the nineteenth centuries, could be picked up by the portfolio for a price in single figures. These became expensive in the 1970s, and at the same time interest in the late Victorian school started developing as an offshoot of the success of Victorian paintings, with buyers migrating from the chocolate box oils into the cheaper but similarly decorative watercolour sweeties. For the 'formula' of a well-tried, not to say well-worn, subject, holds true here too, and what these artists have in common is a specially sickly overlay of schmaltz which distorts any individual landscape and makes every cottage garden look identically picturesque. Beloved of the rich Victorian industrialists, who were busy rendering their reality more and more remote, they have thrived off the recent demand for the decorative. Yet as early as

1846 the *Connoisseur*, on a visit to a watercolour exhibition at Pall Mall, looked at the works of Copley Fielding, currently appreciating fast, and decided that they were 'composed more with reference to their effect in a drawing room than close resemblance to nature'. Never mind, concluded the reviewer, they are 'so beautiful we don't care whether it is natural or no'.

The 'cottage garden' genre

Modern buyers clearly agree and there is still plenty of steam left in the Victorian school. Between 1985 and 1988, prices for some previously little known artists more than doubled, and the upward trend continues. The cottage gardens of Henry John Sylvester Stannard, for example, were under £1,000 in the mid 1980s; they now average around £2,500 and are pushing even further ahead. At Phillips in April 1988, a fine and typical example, *Children outside a Cottage*, was £4,400 and in Phillips July 1988 sale a much less interesting example, *At Thurleigh, Bedfordshire*, with chickens rather than children in the foreground, was £4,950 (estimate £1,200-1,800). Lesser-known Stannards like daughter Theresa and brother Alexander Molyneux are also featuring at auction, but this is beginning to be a discriminating market and though Theresa has found favour, Alexander Molyneux is much less skilled and prices do not approach that of his more illustrious relations. *A Country Cottage* and *A Quiet Stretch of River* at Phillips in April and July 1988 each made £660, and it is hard to imagine him catching up.

Victorian watercolour painting was something of a family business, with the Stannards and 'Garden' William Fraser and his relatives forming two particularly large tribes; Caroline Paterson, sister of Helen Allingham, also sprang into prominence in 1987 when *Cats Cradle* topped £10,000 at Phillips. Helen Allingham's own cottage garden pictures are now hugely expensive. Interiors by her are rarer, and a very fine one showing two children and their governess in an elegant Victorian study exceeded its £6-10,000 estimate to fetch £39,600, easily a record for Helen Allingham.

That shows that there is life beyond the cottage garden, which is music to most dealers' ears. At the risk of biting the hands that feed them, dealers have a not very secret contempt for cottage garden banality, expressed in the term 'jolly hollyhocks', and they have been hoping for some time that the range of the average collector's taste will widen to take in other works which still remain affordable.

The interest in the cottage garden has diverted attention from one of the other major watercolour themes, the view from abroad. Many Victorian watercolourists followed their predecessors from the eighteenth century on some form of the 'grand tour with sketchbook', and many of the results seem cheap compared to the tamer views churned out by their contemporaries back home. At just over £4,000 at Phillips in 1988, Ernest Arthur Rowe's stunning view of *The Pagoda, Villa Inercia, Capri*, was highly attractive, and at £2,640 the crowded bustling landscapes in William Purser's companion pieces *Constantinople* and *The Sweet Waters of Asia* seem good value, while John Salmon's view of the most popular of all watercolour scenes, *Canal, Venice*, must have been a bargain at £1,040.

The range of prices for watercolour: Turner's The Grand Canal with Santa Maria della Salute *which fetched a record £440,000 at Phillips in April 1988 . . .*

Back among the cottage gardens and the pastoral English views, though, investors are probably surer of a good return, for there is no sign of interest tapering off. An undistinguished view of Hurstbourne in Hampshire, with some sheep, by Robert Angelo Kittermaster Marshall, made over £1,000 at Phillips in 1988, and another little-known artist, John White, made £2,200 (estimate £500-800), with *A Walk through the Cornfield*. A Hector Caffieri, *A Young Girl in a Meadow*, which would have made a few hundred pounds in the mid 1980s, was £3,520 and another artist who has recently sprung to prominence, Carlton Alfred Smith, fetched over £5,000. Both these artists may well go higher; another name to watch is Arthur Hopkins, and, at his best, Hercules Brabazon Brabazon. Eventually this sector will peak, and when demand levels off, it will be the owners of the second rate who will have problems selling on. The best, here as elsewhere, should hold its own.

Earlier watercolours

One result of the recent popularity of the Victorians is that price differentials between the 'jolly hollyhocks' school and the acknowledged masterpieces of the watercolour genre from the earlier period are being eroded, for though mostly still more expensive, the latter has seen nothing like the same rate of appreciation in the past decade. Investors in search of quality should take a look at the subtle, understated landscapes of the

and a typical Victorian composition, William Stannard's A Summer Border, *£1,750 at Phillips in July 1988.*

1750-1850 period, with their delicate play of light and shade, their pure and restrained use of colour, and the outstanding draughtsmanship of these artists, for there is bound to be a readjustment as the cottage gardens threaten to catch up and overtake.

Some, to be sure, are rather stiff and unnatural, lacking the easy flow – or gush – of their successors, but they present no difficulties of theme or subject, and tend to celebrate views which are either familiar or highly decorative or both. Elegant rather than pretty, it seems only a matter of time before they are widely recognised as the perfect adornment for the tasteful middle class home with a several-thousand-pound gap on one of its walls.

At a typical Christie's sale of watercolours from this period in November 1987, only 10 per cent of the lots fetched over £4,000, and only two lots over £10,000. Among those which did were views of Paris by Frederick Nash (£9,900 against an estimate of £2-3,000 for a view of the Boulevard des Italiens, with the Parisian *beau monde* strolling in the foreground), James Holland, David Cox Junior, and Thomas Shotter Boys; a couple of watercolours of the Loire Valley by William Callow, and some classical English landscapes – William Daniell's view of Windsor Castle from Eton, John Varley's Westminster Abbey and Edward Dayes' Winchester Cathedral, and, among several pictures by James Ward that far exceeded expectations, Harlech Castle (£7,700, estimate £1,500 to £2,000) and Melrose Abbey (£6,600, estimate £1,000 to £1,500).

These are typical names, and typical views. The same artists crop up again and again at watercolour sales; those mentioned above, along with Edward Lear, one of the best loved watercolourists, John Sell Cotman, Richard Bonnington, Peter de Wint, Samuel Prout, John Frederick Lewis, famous for his eastern views, David Roberts, whose views of the Holy Land are much sought after and have appreciated well in recent years, and William Turner of Oxford, are the staple diet of the later eighteenth and first half of the nineteenth centuries. In a medium ideally suited to the mellow tones of landscape, other subjects are rare, though a fine and immensely detailed interior by Holman Hunt, *A Woman in Jacobean Dress reading on a Window Seat in the Interior of West Hill House, Hastings*, was one of the best sellers in the November 1987 auction, fetching £9,900. Its sale may have been prompted by the astonishing £25,300 paid at Sotheby's in February 1987, against an upper estimate of £5,000, for the same artist's evocative *A Girl Reading a Letter by Lamplight*, from the collection of John Witt, who wrote a book on Holman Hunt.

THE FUTURE FOR THE MARKET

Such pieces are a real find for the watercolour collector, and one place to look for them is the annual World of Watercolours and Drawings Fair, held every January at the Park Lane Hotel and a runaway success, with bargain hunters queuing round the block, since its launch in 1986. Most works fall within the £1,000 to £5,000 range here, with the top dealers turning out the lower end of their stock which may go up to £10,000 or £20,000 or more. This, though, will get you something rather more unusual than a 'jolly hollyhocks' picture, which the organisers of the fair are trying to reduce in number to gain more variety. Overall, though, the interest generated by the middle range at the fair is a sign of the buoyancy of the watercolour market, and this would be a good place for new collectors to start deciding what appeals. Among the traditional British watercolourists – and this is one of the most solidly British sectors of the art market, with collectors confident that here at least is one area where the British have always excelled – only Turner is more or less out of bounds for the average collector. He fetches five and sometimes six figure sums, with a record of £440,000 paid by a German industrialist at Phillips in 1988 for an important view of Venice.

The watercolour market is one of the easiest to dip into, and one of its strengths is the frequency with which new collectors, attracted by the chance of acquiring work of the highest quality for as little as £2-3,000, are recruited. However, the balance between the different periods works itself out, it is difficult to go wrong when buying watercolours by familiar names. Even in the short term the profits to be made here may still be enormous, and there are many other watercolourists still waiting to be discovered, as the dealer who failed to sell the Caroline Paterson *Cats Cradle* for £45 in his Norfolk shop discovered when he took it along to Phillips.

If the earlier works do re-establish their prominence, they will have a long way to go, but it seems likely anyway that they are underrated. In this market, however, safety lies in the large and ever growing number of collectors and in the diversity of their tastes. It also lies in the high quality of a lot of the work, and in the fact that there is still much research –

inevitably attracting further interest and pushing up reputations – to be done in an area which only began to be taken seriously, by a few lucky aficionados, in the 1950s.

The only warning to new collectors, then, must be to look very carefully at the condition, especially of the earlier work. Many watercolours from the late eighteenth and early nineteenth centuries have suffered with time; make sure what you are buying has not lost its fresh colouring, and once you have bought it, keep it out of direct sunlight. Once blue – the first colour to go – has turned to mottled brown, a watercolour's value is inestimably reduced, and it will be hard to sell. Also watch out for foxing, brown marks which come with age to the pages of books as well as watercolours; if caught in time, they are quite easy to get rid of, but once allowed to develop they too can render a picture worthless.

7 PRINTS

You stay here, and I'll bring the etchings down.
Cartoon caption by James Thurber

The famous line 'Come up and see my etchings' dates from the 1920s, the heyday of print collecting in Britain. It sounds even more of a euphemism today because prints have become something of an abstruse and rarified taste, the stuff for connoisseurs. In the 1920s, they were nothing of the sort: it was common to buy prints rather as one bought shares, and it was even more lucrative.

A revival of Old Master prints at this time encouraged interest in contemporary printmaking, and soon etchers like Arthur Briscoe and Gerald Leslie Brockhurst were all the rage. Colnaghi's, then the major London dealer in prints (sadly, their print department closed at the end of 1988), published editions of 200 prints at around £200 apiece, and sold out within a week – many of the buyers simply slipped off to Christie's with their purchases and pocketed huge profits after each auction.

But it was a market created almost wholly by investment, an artificial boom. It is easy to see why this happened, for of all the sectors of the art market, prints can be clearly understood in financial terms. They come in limited editions – which means they are easy to collect but there is no fear of the market being flooded – but, unlike almost any other sort of art object, they are not unique. Within certain narrow margins, therefore, it was possible for a collector of contemporary etchings in the 1920s to treat a print like a share certificate – if X got £100 for *his* print, he could say, then *mine*, in the same edition and in similar condition, must be worth that too.

But riding on the crest of a share certificate wave only went so far, and the print boom collapsed along with everything else in the Wall Street Crash of 1929. Prices sank to pitiful levels, and remained in the doldrums for decades. Arthur Briscoe's *Clewlines and Buntlines*, for example, which sold for £100 in 1926, was £2 in 1955; his *On the Main Yard* made £3 in 1931. And Old Master prints, which had provoked the enthusiasm for contemporary etchings in the first place, sank just as deeply – the average price for a Dürer print at auction in the 1930s was £10.

WHAT IS AN ORIGINAL PRINT?

Without doubt, a big attraction of Old Master prints is the possibility of owning an original piece by an artist whose work in any other medium would be unaffordable. But what does an 'original' print mean, when the very definition of a print includes the fact that it is one of several produced in the same edition?

For anyone dipping into the market, to be sure you are buying an original print is the first step. Scholars still argue over certain ambiguities in the definition, but they are generally agreed on the following. An original print is produced when an artist works directly on to a matrix – a woodblock or a copperplate – and then transfers the image on to paper as a print by means of a printing press. After a certain number of impressions, the plate wears down, and obviously each impression is ever so slightly weaker than the one before – hence the difference in quality between an early impression, which is strong and rich in detail, and a late one, which can be worth a mere fraction of the price. 'Burr' is the smudgy effect found on early impressions as a result of drypoint etching, and is highly sought after as proof that the image is an early one.

Between certain impressions, moreover, the artist sometimes made changes to the plate, altering the 'state' of the prints before and after. To explain this, a print from a plate which was altered twice will be described either as 'first state of three', 'second state of three' or 'third state of three'.

To avoid the danger of selling prints made from plates altered by someone other than the artist, reputable dealers stick to prints produced within an artist's lifespan or immediately afterwards, when they continued to be 'in the hand' of the artist, ie from a plate he and no one else had worked on. That does not, however, exclude the work of printmakers who reproduced as prints the paintings and drawings of other artists.

Before modern methods of photomechanical reproduction reduced the concept of a print to suggest a mass-produced copy of a Renoir oil which every first year undergraduate buys from Athena, such reproduction prints were skilful works of art for which the printmaker was given full credit. Although a Rembrandt etching reprinted in the eighteenth century would never fetch as high a price as 'the real thing', some other reproductions are very expensive and much sought after. They appear in catalogues as, for example, Jean Etienne Liotard: Sleeping Venus *after* Titian, indicating that Liotard has reproduced on a plate Titian's painting, and then made a print from it. Those prints are originals by Liotard; prints produced from a plate created by Rembrandt but reworked by a later follower after his death are, by contrast, basically forgeries – they are purporting to be something they are not (the work of Rembrandt alone). That is why dealers restrict themselves more or less to prints produced within a printmaker's lifetime; they guarantee their prints to be genuine, and will refund your money if they are proved otherwise.

OLD MASTER PRINTS

The story is instructive, not just as another example of how prices can go down as well as up, but in explaining the present low prices in the Old Master print market. Interest revived in the 1960s, and was consolidated in the 1970s, when regular auctions were resumed. But even though appreciation over the past 20 years has been healthy – around 10 per cent a year – prices started from such a low base in the 1960s that prints still have some catching up to do. Growth rates, moreover, have been nowhere near as exciting as for other sectors of the fine art market. While paintings, watercolours and drawings have all, at some stage in the period 1960-85, taken off dramatically, prints remain the poor cousin of the graphic arts, the one sector where it is possible to build a good and interesting collection on a relatively modest outlay.

*Original, affordable
works by the Great
Masters: Dürer's* The
Vision of the Seven
Candlesticks *was
£1,650 at Christie's in
November 1988 . . .*

Old Master prints are so specialised a market that it would be a brave
new collector who set off straight to the saleroom to sift through the
thousands of prints which turn up at auction. A dealer is more important in
this field than for the other fine arts; he can train your eye and fill you in on
historical context, and the niceties of condition, state and impression – a
minefield for the unwary – as well as advising on building a collection on
the basis of printmaker, period or subject (for example, views of London).

The market for Old Master prints

Old Master prints date roughly from the mid fifteenth to the early
nineteenth century, and many of the greatest artists working in this period
experimented with and refined the art of printmaking. Neglected for so
long, there is no shortage of supply even from the earlier centuries, and
prices reflect this.

£1,000 is the average auction price for a print by Dürer, considered by
most experts to be the father of printmaking at least in northern Europe –
Mantegna holds a similar position in the south – and by many its finest
artist and technician. Rembrandt, alone reckoned to be in their league,
fetches an average £2,000 a piece. At the top end of the scale, though,
Dürer prints change hands for over £100,000, and a couple from the
Chatsworth collection, the most important collection of prints ever

Rembrandt's Christ
crucified between
the two Thieves *was
£1,320 at the same
sale . . .*

auctioned, made over £200,000. From the same collection, which Christie's
auctioned in 1985, a Rembrandt made nearly £600,000, the record for a
print, and a Mantegna £350,000.

But in the salerooms or in dealers' catalogues there are always examples
from the lower range, and both Rembrandt and Dürer were prolific
printmakers. The quality of the impression often explains the otherwise
incomprehensible difference in price for these artists. A fine early example
of Rembrandt's *Abraham's Sacrifice* with the much prized burr was £12,100
at Sotheby's in June 1988; a later impression, still good and with some
burr, was £7,150. Other Rembrandts in the sale ranged from £495 to
£5,500, with a vast range of subject matter, for Rembrandt was as lively
and tender a master of genre as of religious scenes.

After Dürer, Rembrandt and Mantegna, the best known printmakers
are Jacques Callot, Canaletto, Goya, Adrian van Ostade, and Piranesi. All
were prolific, which is one reason why so much material remains available
at under £1,000. Prices span a huge range, but even fine early impressions
can be found cheaply. An excellent buy in Colnaghi's winter 1987
catalogue, for example, was a beautifully warm and delicate print of *The
Smoker and the Drinker* by van Ostade, a master of Dutch genre; this very
fine impression of the very rare second state – of which there were just 10
impressions – cost £950.

Appreciation of all these artists should continue at growth rates of at
least 10 per cent per annum, with the top range rising faster. What

determines price between the three figure and the six figure sums are a number of factors including rarity, the quality, richness and detail of the image, and the condition, impression and state of the print. The set of 80 plates from the fifth edition (1881-86) of Goya's *Los Caprichos* sold for £3,850 at Sotheby's in 1988; in the same sale the same 80 plates from the third edition (1868), very good and good impressions, with some burr, made £14,300.

The most expensive print at Colnaghi's in the winter season of 1987 was a uniquely important work, a Madonna by Cima da Comegliano from 1460-70, pre-dating even Dürer. The plate originally engraved by Cima wore out through over use, and although another set of impressions was made two centuries later from a retouched plate, this was the only surviving print from the earlier period. Priced at £30-40,000, it is a good example of how rarity can push up prices.

Even in this relatively academic field, there are crazes which suddenly boost prices. A recent one is for the superb Dutch mannerist Hendrik Goltzius, whose prints sold in boxes for around £1 in the 1950s and 1960s and whose best work now commands £20,000 or more, although devotees can still find prints at under £1,000; £770 for *Mars and Venus Surprised by Vulcan* at auction in 1988, for instance, in a good impression, but has the fault of being trimmed just within the platemarks.

Equally, there are genres which are ludicrously undervalued. Eighteenth century prints *after* Fragonard and Boucher have been popular for years – Colnaghi's at the end of 1987 offered a very fine one by Louis Marin Bonnet, one of the first to discover an effective method of imitating pastel drawings, of *Tête de Flore* after Boucher, in an exceptionally fine impression for £7,750 – but sixteenth century prints after Raphael and Michaelangelo look correspondingly underrated, and could be an area to buy while prices stay cheap – good impressions can be found at present for £2-3,000.

Although this is generally a steady sector, there are artists or areas which can suddenly shoot up in popularity, helped perhaps by a romantic story or simply an attractive image. James Barry is a typical case. Born in Cork in 1741, he pursued the lifestyle of a flamboyant radical, got himself elected to and then expelled from the Royal Academy, and produced some highly charged romantic prints which until 1985 seldom changed hands for more than £40-50. His work is rare, and when it suddenly became popular in the mid 1980s, prices shot up to around £2,500-3,500 – a thoroughly menacing but instantly appealing *Discovery of Adam and Eve* cost £2,450 in 1987, and could be expected to fetch between £3-4,000 in 1988, as enthusiasm for Barry sends prices higher and higher.

As with any sudden upward movement, the temptation is to get on the bandwagon before it is too late. But a good impression of an attractive image by someone less well known is a far better buy than a mediocre impression by Rembrandt which costs two or three times as much. A wise collector will look to the hundreds of still cheap Old Master printmakers who might become widely popular in the future but should at any rate hold their own. A few names to look for include Stefano della Bella – *Portrait of a Man* sold in 1987 for £80, while a fine early impression of the rare first state of *The Holy Family with St Elizabeth and St John the Baptist* from the collection of Prince Liechtenstein was £595 – Giulio Bonasone (£495 for

Time in 1988), Jan van de Velde, Lucas Cranach, Giovanni Tiepolo, Giovanni Jacopo Caraglio and Giovanni Benedetto Castiglione. But there are hundreds more in this very underdeveloped sector, with prices starting in the £100s and much good material available at around £500-2,000. At the sale of the British Rail Pension Fund's Old Master prints, considered a very fine collection (it made £2m), well over 10 per cent of the lots sold for under £1,000. But the old maxim of buying the best you can afford was borne out in the sale of Old Master prints from the collection of a Swiss steel maker, Dr Albert Blum. His collection, amassed during the slump of the 1920s and 30s, was regarded for quality and variety as one of the finest to be seen in 20 years. It fetched $5m (£2.8m) in New York in 1988, with less than 1 per cent bought in.

Museum buying started comparatively late – in the early years of this century – and though it is now an active force, curators still tend to go for big names, leaving much to be discovered by private buyers. One of the reasons why connoisseurs love prints is as historical or documentary evidence, and it is probable that in the next 10 years prints will be more closely related to their historical context. Until a few years ago, few monographs bothered with them; now they cannot do without them, and as the connection between printmaking and the other fine arts is shown more strongly, a better place, and a higher price, should be established for prints in the market place. And as art historians run out of well-known subjects to research, they are turning to lesser figures, inevitably boosting interest. Some of the prints in the £500-2,500 range could turn out to be very lucrative investments.

The drawbacks

The downside for prints is that they will always be subtly rather than instantly appealing, and that they are not easy to choose and buy. Unless you are very careful, delicate contrasts of black and white are lost among the bright splashes of modern decor, and few people have the time to study the background and technical details which make printbuying a pleasure. Yet walking into a print shop and saying 'I'll have that one' simply doesn't work. In addition to complexities of state and vastly differing qualities of impression, the print market has various fetishes about condition. The major obsession is with margins – a print with full margins is worth twice as much as an identical one that has been trimmed. This opens up the market to the forger, who will add on as many margins as he can. In 1984 a buyer at auction was convinced enough to pay £42,000 for a Rembrandt *Roman Landscape* whose margins were later found to have been added on, reducing the value by half.

That again puts the case for trusting your money to an experienced print dealer. If you do, you are unlikely to go wrong, and there is no fear of the market reaching saturation point. It is even possible, though unlikely, that in the next 10 years the knock-on effect will come into operation in favour of Old Master prints, and collectors who cannot keep up with paintings, watercolours and drawings will turn to this underrated sector. But this is not a place for the speculator. It is more probable that prints will remain an acquired, quietly academic taste. For all their graphic skill, intensely rich and detailed images and their technical virtuosity, they lack immediate impact. But scrutinised over years of familiarity, they yield new depths and new details, a gradual revelation of the artist at work. That is why collectors and art historians will always feel passionately about them, and that, given the number of prints still up for grabs, should ensure a healthy market.

MODERN PRINTS

Old Master print experts talk disparagingly of the 'so-called' limited edition of modern prints, and there is no doubt that they have a point. While Old Master prints are limited by historical fact – only a certain number of impressions were made, and by no means all have survived – modern prints are limited by human intention, and numbered obsessively so that collectors know what they are getting. For the simple truth is that the modern printing press could effortlessly supply unlimited numbers of any impression it wanted. Although strictly speaking an original print is one made from a plate on which the artist has worked directly, and a print created by photomechanical methods is considered a reproduction, some printmakers use the photomechanical process in the actual production, and it is very hard to distinguish precisely between the two.

While purists complain that modern limited editions are artificial, this does not greatly trouble most buyers, and the bold colours and dramatic subject matter of twentieth century prints, as well as much less difficulty over condition, have put them well ahead of their black and white counterparts in the Old Master department. In the United States especially, they are riding high on the back of the success of Impressionist, Post-Impressionist and contemporary paintings, and auctions are packed, standing-room only affairs.

What determines the price of a print is the artist, the quality of the image, the size of the edition and, related to this, the rarity of the work and the involvement of the artist in the printmaking process. The importance of this last is becoming increasingly obvious when assessing why certain works have over the last 10 years done so much better than others. Jim Dine and Jasper Johns, for example, are both known to masters of the printmaking process and closely involved at every stage, and their work has soared in recent years; Johns' print of two American flags, *Flag 1*, produced in an edition of 65 in 1973, made £153,118 at auction in the autumn 1988 season. On the other hand, the later prints by Salvador Dali are known to have been produced in a very dubious way – Dali is believed to have signed the paper before the impressions were even made. It is no wonder that buyers are unenthusiastic about the large numbers available, and easy to see why such large editions were produced.

The modern print market

Modern prints are a more volatile market, but they do have the same pull as Old Master prints in that they offer many collectors a chance of owning works by artists who in other mediums would be quite out of reach. Works by the six classic modern printmakers, Picasso, Chagall, Miro, Matisse, Braque and Rouault are all to be found for under £2,000, and

and Chagall's Auto-portrait au Vente Noire *was £2,200.*

some are under £1,000. At the other end of the scale, six figure sums are not uncommon for these artists; it all depends on the image and its rarity. Take prices for Chagall, one of the most prolific of all printmakers, at Sotheby's major sale in 1988. Only one print was under £1,000 (£990 for *La Tour de David* from 1979) but in the £1-5,000 range there were a lot of fine images of quintessential Chagall themes – *Acrobatic Woman Circus Rider* (£1,265) from 1959, *Trapeze Acrobat with Bird* (£3,850) from 1967. *The Four Seasons, Chicago* was £7,480 (a proof before the letters were added) and £5,500 (with the letters), and a set of 42 plates from the *Daphnis and Chloe* series was £165,000. At every level, this holds something for the buyer wanting an 'original Chagall', and that is one reason for the market's buoyancy.

But even in the top range, there are still fortunes to be made – such is the fanaticism of the print market, especially in New York. Just weeks after the Stock Exchange crash in 1987, for example, two telephone bidders pushed the price of a rare Matisse, *Jazz*, to $410,000; five years earlier the print had fetched $70,000. And in the same sale a Renoir lithograph from 1900, *Enfants Jouant à la Balle*, made $80,000; the print in similar condition was $60,000 six months earlier.

Renoir, Matisse and Chagall are all pretty and accessible. More abstract modern masters like Braque and, to some extent, Miro, are showing less rapid appreciation. Prices for Picasso vary enormously, with the early etchings in the suite depicting the life of some circus artists the most popular, and the late prints from the 1960s the least, although if a revaluation of later Picasso, as suggested by the Tate Gallery exhibition in 1988, gets under way, this could change. At present the edition of 250 steel-faced by the dealer Ambrose Vollard are most popular, with famous images like *Le Repas Frugal* going from strength to strength. £50 in the 1950s, the going rate was around £20,000 by the mid 1980s, with one in New York fetching an astonishing $100,000 at the end of 1987.

British prints, still smarting from the blow of the 1930s, are much more affordable. Whistler, who started the craze off in the first place, is still easy to find for under £1,000, and one of the most famous etched images from the 1930s, Gerard Leslie Brockhurst's *Adolescence* was £2,310 at Sotheby's in 1988. A David Bomberg made £2,530, and a Graham Sutherland etching from 1924 was £1,045, twice its lower estimate. As the reputations of artists like Bomberg improve both at home and abroad, British prints might experience a knock-on effect of rising prices.

What attracted investors to the print market in the 1920s remains one of the eternally comforting things about buying a print: the knowledge that some other people, but not *too* many, have paid a similar sum for roughly the same work of art. Contemporary prints, of course, are more of a gamble, though this is one of the most flourishing sectors of the entire art market at present. Japanese interest – the Japanese are especially keen on pop art – has staved off any adverse effects the 1987 crash could have been expected to have on a sector much beloved of American Yuppies.

The top names here will always be bought by collectors who appreciate that contemporary printmaking is an art in itself, rather than a series of vibrant and powerful images not quite as vibrant and powerful as in contemporary paintings. The top-selling trio are Jasper Johns, Roy Lichtenstein and Jim Dine, all of whom stimulate the sort of fever pitch bidding for which New York salerooms are famous. Lichtenstein's pop art from the 1960s (see Chapter 1) is among the most sought after, and does much better than his later works. At the end of 1987, *Sweet Dreams, Baby!* from 1965 made $20,000 at Sotheby's and $22,000 at Christie's; six months earlier it had fetched $7,000. And *Huh*, from 1976, made $4,250 at Sotheby's; the identical print was available across the road at dealer Pat Caporaso's for $2,800, another example of casual buying, as for the Longo which was $6,500 at auction and $4,500 across the road at dealer Brooke Alexander.

Contemporary prints will always attract speculators because the possibility of making a killing in a very short time is just too tempting to resist. The sort of hour-to-hour appreciation that fuelled the market in the 1920s, when collectors hopped round the corner to Christie's after calling in at Colnaghi's to buy a print hot off the press is still known in New York today. Diebenkorn's *Green*, for example, was published in 1986 in an edition of 60 by Crown Point Press, and sold for $15,000; an etching made $42,000 at auction in 1987.

But the market in London is much more sober, and it is also possible to pay less at auction than at the publishers' – a print can need decades in the secondary market before it becomes more valuable than when new, so salerooms can be a good hunting ground. The old trick is knowing the contemporary printmaker who is on the way up to fame from the one on the way down to obscurity. Many prints never match their opening prices; prices for most Andy Warhol prints, for example, continue to drop, while others, like David Hockney, have performed well and are steadily increasing; a set of six *The Weather Series* from 1973 made £39,600 in 1988. As with all contemporary art, it is a matter of putting your money where your eyes are – not for those with unsteady nerves.

8 ANTIQUE FURNITURE

> Lady Kitty: I think it's a beautiful chair. Hepplewhite?
> Arnold: No, Sheraton
> Lady Kitty: Oh I know. *The School for Scandal.*
> Somerset Maugham, *The Circle*

> Gentleman do not buy furniture. They inherit it.
> Douglas Sutherland, *The English Gentleman*

THE INVESTMENT RECORD

Since 1975, an average piece of English antique furniture has seen an annual appreciation of 20 per cent. That means that what cost £100 in 1975 could sell in 1988 for £1,005. As Figure 8.1 below shows, that is a lot more than an equivalent amount invested in the stock market. Even before the October 1987 crash, an average piece of English antique furniture was a more lucrative investment than the average stock market investment, which at best equalled it; since October 1987 English furniture has been shown to be far safer as well. And as Figure 8.2 shows, recent growth rates have been exceptionally high: 34 per cent from 1986 to 1987 and 32 per cent from 1987 to 1988. A piece costing £566 in 1986 would now be worth almost twice that. And if you had bought before 1980, that will have amply compensated for the brief slump at the beginning of this decade. The pattern of Figure 8.2 bears out the old wisdom of the art market – be prepared to ride out the bad times, and never buy with the intention of making a profit in just a few years. You may be lucky, but you will not always be. Compare, for example, the price rises in the three year periods from 1980-83 (sluggish) and from 1985-88 (buoyant). In any 10 year period, however, such variations are ironed out.

These figures are based on the Sotheby's English Furniture Index. Another monitor of antique furniture prices comes from the Antique Collectors Club (ACC), whose analysis of a representative sample of middle range furniture was published in 1968 as the first *Price Guide to Antique Furniture*. An annual update (price £2.50 from the ACC) has been published ever since, and the figures provide an invaluable guide to what has been happening to prices over the past two decades.

The ACC conclusions are very similar to the results demonstrated by the Sotheby's figures. The ACC Index shows an annual rise of 17.5 per cent per annum over 20 years; the slightly lower figure is due largely to the severe economic slump in the UK, which badly affected sectors of the art market dominated by British demand, and antique English furniture along with everything else. This plays no part in the Sotheby's Index, based at 1975, which is correspondingly more influenced by the high rises in the last three years.

According to the ACC, a piece of furniture which cost £100 in 1968 would now be worth £2,200 in 1988, which no one should complain about

Fig. 8.1: Sotheby's English Furniture Index/FTA All-Share Index

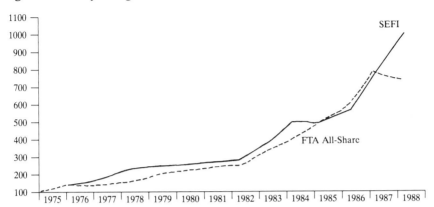

Fig. 8.2: Annual % change Sotheby's English Furniture Index

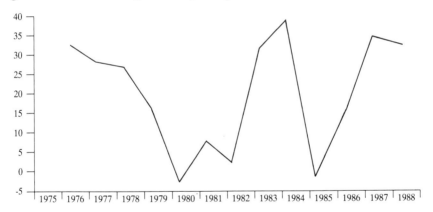

either. The ACC Index is especially valuable because it breaks down the figures into eight sectors, according to the type of furniture. A piece of early mahogany, at £2,809, has done rather better than the average; a Victorian piece, at £1,898, has performed slightly worse. Figures illustrating each sector of the ACC Furniture Index appear below (Figures 8.5-8.11). If you had bought well, however, you would have done better than any of the indices show: one astonishing example quoted in the ACC *Price Guide* is a bergere chair, which rose from £30 in 1968 to £2,150 in 1988 – three times the already buoyant average of the Index. Other examples in the *Guide* include an oak coffer (£40 in 1968, £650 in 1980, £1,500 in 1988), a mahogany dining table (£474 in 1968, £4,250 in 1980, £17,500 in 1988) and a Victorian walnut davenport (£55 in 1968, £700 in 1980 and £1,600 in 1988).

What all the figures prove is that good antique furniture is an asset which hardly ever goes down in price, and if it does, does so by a very small amount, and for a very short period of time. It is a stable market, backed by an unusually large dealer presence – around 80 per cent of stock at auctions is bought by dealers – and by a strong base of private collectors. American interest has pushed up prices, but the enormous body of national collectors – there are over 11,000 members of the ACC, the majority of whom are interested in fine furniture alone – and the dealers, mean that this market is not subject to the sort of volatility that often develops when American buyers enter the fray. The English furniture sector is about as far away in spirit from the vagaries of the financial world as it is possible for an established and sophisticated market to be.

The status of furniture within the art market, as well as prices, has risen over the past two decades, and as it has achieved greater prominence, it has come to be seen more as a work of art and less as an elaborate extension of the carpentry trade. As Figure 8.3 shows, among traditional alternative investments of the art market, it compares favourably with all sectors except the mega-media stars, Impressionist and Modern art. Looking at Figure 8.4, it is worth bearing in mind that until 1986 English furniture showed higher rates of growth than Impressionist and Modern art. Sotheby's Art Market Index by sector, drawn in graphic form in any of the five years preceding 1986, would have closely resembled Figure 8.4, not Figure 8.3. The upshot is that what has changed the pattern are two exceptionally buoyant sectors which have shot ahead. What has remained the same throughout is the steady growth of English furniture, and its healthy position in the art market.

Note, by the by, that French furniture, unquestionably more delicate and decorative, shows only half the capital growth of its English equivalent. Without wishing to put you off if you are set on it, it should be said at

Fig. 8.3: Sotheby's Art Index by sector (1988)

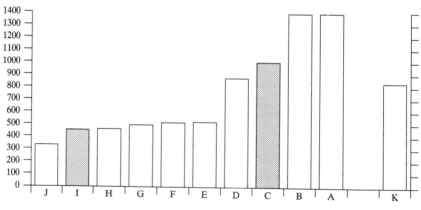

Source: Sotheby's Art Market Bulletin

Code: A Impressionist paintings; B Modern paintings; C English furniture; D Chinese ceramics; E Continental ceramics; F Old Masters paintings; G English silver; H C19th European paintings; I French & Continental furniture; J Continental silver; K Aggregate

Fig. 8.4: Sotheby's Art Index by sector (1986)

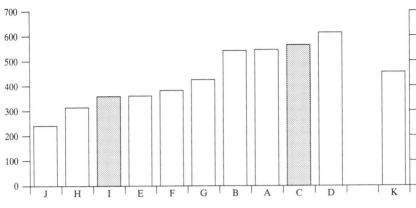

Source: Art Market Bulletin

Code: A Impressionist paintings; B Modern paintings; C English furniture; D Chinese ceramics;
E Continental ceramics; F Old Masters paintings; G English silver; H C19th European paintings;
I French & Continental furniture; J Continental silver; K Aggregate

once that French furniture is a trap for the unwary and, since the eighteenth century, has been a closed door to all but the very rich. It is the most beautiful furniture in the world, but so ornate – not to say effete – that it would look odd in the average twentieth century home, and with many pieces fetching six figure sums, and some – for example a mother of pearl and polychrome boulle marquetry bureau, sold at Christie's in 1987 – over £1m, perhaps that is just as well. Anyone wishing to indulge should consult specialist dealers and attend a great many auctions before committing valuable sums.

THE PROSPECTS

Like any market which has performed well over the long term, English furniture's best selling point is its record. In the explanation of its success lies the proof of its underlying strength, and optimism about the future.

A dealer-dominated sector with a strong home base of collectors is an investor's dream. Professional people earning steady incomes have been collecting furniture for decades, and for generation after generation. Yuppies have diverted money made on the Stock Exchange and Americans have swooped in when the exchange rate has been favourable, but that solid collecting base has never been threatened or eroded. People buy antique furniture because they like it. What they are really buying is a way of life, or at least objects that are enjoyable to live with for years. You may trade up pieces, but that is unlikely to be because you have tired of them. Furniture does not pall in the same way as paintings can do, and a collection of furniture will probably be added to as often as it is exchanged. Demand, in other words, shows no sign of diminishing.

Towards the lower end of the market, it is all the more reliable because the impetus to buy has an extra edge. At this level, antique furniture is cheaper than the modern reproductions in the department stores. It is extraordinary that anyone *does* buy in the department stores, when for the same money you can not only get an authentic object but one that will go up in price rather than down (to second-hand status). Those wise first time home furnishers who have seen this particular light are buying not luxury items but quasi-essentials – most people would agree that finding something to sit on and eat off comes before filling the gap in the wall. As a result, this end of the furniture sector is not just an alternative home for funds otherwise destined for porcelain, silver, gilts, shares or underneath the mattress, but an alternative to something that would have to be bought anyway. And collectors who start at this level are likely to graduate to higher things, either by trading up or as their incomes increase.

Supply and demand

While demand rises unabated, it is the common complaint of dealers that supply is drying up. That wail, amid well-stocked shops, has been heard for years, and is nothing new – there are, of course, plenty of fine pieces still around. On the other hand, it *is* harder to find them. Provincial antique shops are not the founts of quality and bargains that they were 20 years ago, and as prices rise, and dealers become universally expensive, markups increase. They have to, because expensive pieces sell more slowly. So the in-and-out costs of buying and selling are likely to rise further.

The auction houses, however, have managed to capture a good chunk of buyers at the lower end of the market, and it is a sign of the growing general interest in antique furniture that both Christie's and Sotheby's now have a clear two-tier market. Christie's sell their lower range at South Kensington, while Sotheby's have a special retail outlet in Conduit Street where antiques are arranged as 'home furnishings' in room settings, and sales are held at 5.30pm. The trade turns up to the important sales in the day, and private buyers flock in after work.

One effect of the public's raised consciousness is that there is less selling. Houses are no longer emptied into an auctioneer's hands when a relative dies; families tend to hang on to old furniture, either because they like it or because they know how scarce and valuable it is becoming.

One reason for the scarcity is undoubtedly the dollar-pound depths in the mid 1970s and the early 1980s, when for visiting Americans auction houses and London dealers took on some of the allure of the bargain basement. Much has been shipped away, and much is still to go, for Americans have few antiques of their own, and what eighteenth century furniture they do have is prohibitively expensive.

Surplus money in the mid 1980s led to a burgeoning of the property market and of the upper end of it in particular. This was the heyday of the interior decorator, called in to kit out London pads for company letting at thousands of pounds a week. The interior decorator has made his mark in many sectors of the art market, but has been perhaps especially active in the antique furniture market, both in pushing up demand and in tilting interest towards the decorative rather than the authentic. Most of all, he has widened the awareness of collectors, and as better-informed buyers exercise more choice, a greater distinction between quality and inferior pieces should develop. It started to do so even before the stock market crash, particularly in some other sectors of the art market, notably paintings, and is now doing so in the furniture market.

New research – a boost to the market

For all the growing interest, English furniture remains something of an under-researched field. It is true that more French furniture is signed than English, and this has always acted against the prestige of the home-grown product. Much English furniture sold at auction is catalogued by reign or period (George II, early Georgian), though Chippendale, the most famous English cabinet maker, usually left accounts at the house where he worked.

But there is a growing academic interest in the work of individual English cabinet makers, and a work published in 1986, the *Dictionary of English Furniture Makers 1660-1840* (see Bibliography) has demonstrated how many English pieces are signed. This seminal work should slowly affect prices as the mark and styles of individuals become known. It is a scholarly but valuable book, of use to the private collector as well as dealers. Christie's had one copy specially bound with a blank sheet every 10 pages to fill in the names of furniture makers yet to be discovered and researched – a sure sign of the importance to the market of this academic movement. And two Christie's experts, Hugh Roberts and Charles Cator, are working on a study of two lesser known cabinet makers, Mayhew and Ince. When research like this is published, there is bound to be at least a gradual and possibly a dramatic effect on both reputations and prices.

The sudden fashion and surge in price for Regency in general and Bullock in particular after the Great Tew Sale in 1987 (see below) shows that once the furniture market hits on something, it does not easily let go. Yet 20 years ago no one had heard of Bullock. There must be many Bullocks in the wings in the 1980s, and every chance that the furniture sector has a long way to go. Its status in the art market continues to be enhanced, but the fact is that top pieces of furniture are still fetching a fraction of the price of second or third rate paintings. Over the long term, that should be adjusted, leaving current furniture prices with a great deal of room for movement.

THE 'AGES' OF ENGLISH FURNITURE

'Superior in straightforward simplicity and fascinating reticence to the furniture of other countries' is how Percy Macquoid trumpeted the qualities of antique English furniture. Written at a time when scarcely a piece of English furniture exceeded £500, Macquoid's *History of English Furniture* (1904-1908) was a seminal work of research which established a prestigious place for English furniture in the antiques map. His arguments in favour of the homegrown product are still gaining ground, and his taste in English furniture has until recently retained a profound effect on the market; indeed, it is still to be felt.

Macquoid was in at the start of a widespread lambasting of the century that had just been left behind, and his virulent attack on Victorian taste had its parallels in the fine arts market – Edwin Long's widow accepted £130 in 1908 for a work her husband had refused to sell for £5,250 in 1891, for example. Believing what followed to be beneath contempt, Macquoid divided furniture up to 1820 into four categories – 'the age of oak' (1550-1660), 'the age of walnut' (1660-1720), 'the age of mahogany' (1720-1770), and the period 1770-1820 which, 'inspired by affectation for all things classical, combined with curiously unbalanced taste, can best be described as "the composite age"'. When Volume 4 was published in 1908, 'the composite age' had been upgraded to 'the age of satinwood', but it remains the least satisfactory of Macquoid's categories.

'With the close of the eighteenth century, originality and real beauty in English furniture ceased', wrote Macquoid, and for more than half a century collectors believed him. As a result, for many purists 'antique' English furniture still means Georgian furniture, but revaluation of the later periods, spurred on perhaps by the diminishing supply of eighteenth century pieces and backed by research, is under way. Regency furniture was the great discovery of the 1980s, and prices have zoomed ahead in the last five years, the decorative look being much in demand. Victorian furniture had a short-lived renaissance in the 1970s, but though it continues to gain respect, it has shown a much less exciting performance since then. But it is nowhere near the doldrums that Macquoid left it in.

Macquoid's research is being supplemented, but his first categories, denoting the type of wood most widely, but not exclusively, used by cabinet makers in each period, have stuck because they are so expressive of the ages described. Figures 8.5 to 8.10 show the Antique Collectors Club Furniture Index broken into sectors by period. Mahogany is subdivided because the quality of early and late pieces is very different – the latter, along with Regency furniture, would have been part of Macquoid's 'composite age'. At auction, catalogue entries would generally describe walnut as 'Queen Anne walnut' or 'George I' walnut, early mahogany as 'George II mahogany' and later mahogany as 'George III mahogany'. Figure 8.10, Country furniture, refers to a specialised sector of simple, solid provincial pieces – mostly chairs, tables, chests – which continued to be made in oak and elm throughout all these periods. Prices are not much higher than those for reproduction furniture, for the strong rustic style is not greatly in keeping with the present trend for the decorative. But as Figure 8.11, which compares the performance over the past 20 years of the seven areas, shows, there is still a lot of steam left in the country market. But prices are low enough for a new collector to buy good quality pieces.

As any country house sale proves, no collector needs or should stick to any of these sectors – the great jumble sale, as experts fondly called it, at Great Tew in 1987, brought forth pieces ranging from every conceivable period which had nestled comfortably together for centuries – lots 125 to 147, for instance, the last two dozen lots of the first session, included a Charles II oak gateleg table (£495), a George I walnut side table (£7,480), a George III mahogany dining table (£16,500), a Regency rosewood library table (£20,000), and a late Victorian secretaire bookcase (£2,640).

Most collectors are furnishing homes smaller than Tew Park, and some consistency is probably a good idea, both aesthetically and for investment. Walnut, mahogany and Regency pieces, however, have always coexisted happily, though each different wood has a very individual character which a new collector will soon find instantly recognisable.

Oak furniture

Oak, the 'vernacular' wood used mainly in the first half of the seventeenth century but up to 1800 in the country, is coarse grained, warm and homely. Typical pieces are gate-leg tables, chests and dressers, often with heavy

Fig. 8.5: Growth of oak furniture 1968-1988

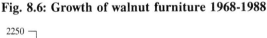

Source: Antique Collector's Club Antique Furniture Index

relief carving. Furniture was merely functional in the seventeenth century, surfaces were often roughly finished, and because of this oak has never been considered as sophisticated as later woods. Phillips Antiques at Auction survey for 1988, however, suggested that 'the fortunes of seventeenth century oak may be ready for revival', and there are signs that this is beginning to happen. A lot of good oak pieces are still available, for the indestructible quality of the wood meant that much has survived; unfortunately much, too, was discarded because the style was for so long undervalued. In the eighteenth century oak pieces were carted off to farmhouses from grand establishments after more refined walnut or mahogany substitutes had been commissioned.

Walnut furniture

The age of walnut came in with the Restoration, and a strong Dutch

Fig. 8.6: Growth of walnut furniture 1968-1988

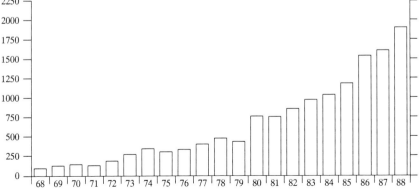

Source: Antique Collector's Club Antique Furniture Index

influence was evident in the introduction of marquetry. Macquoid saw this as a vigorous and original period 'practical in construction ... full of colour in the happy combination of upholstery and marqueterie' and found in its 'true decorative sentiment' the 'distinctly assertive English spirit'. Walnut pieces, dignified, light, warm and rich, have always been expensive, and walnut was the most fashionable antique style of the 1960s. As a result of this head start, walnut has not proved as good an investment as other areas over the past 20 years. But good walnut pieces will always hold their own, with Queen Anne, 'remembered for her cabriole legs', becoming very sought after, though rare. Phillips 1988 survey, which consistently puts furniture as its first market choice, marks early walnut as one of the best performers in the art market.

Mahogany furniture

Around 1720 mahogany started to supersede walnut as the most commonly used wood, a process more or less completed in 1730 when the French banned the export of walnut. Mahogany always conjures up a mood of graceful Georgian formality. Chippendale, whose hugely important *Directory (The Gentleman's and Cabinet Maker's Directory)* of 1754 influenced the designs of cabinet makers nationwide, assured that fashion was no longer dictated by technical feasibility but by the eye and imagination of the designer. In the 1750s, English furniture entered its most glorious age; the best mahogany pieces show exquisite workmanship and design, and fetch the highest prices of all English furniture.

Its ornament and rich decoration may not be to all tastes, or fit in all homes, but early mahogany has performed best over the last 20 years, and as furniture catches up with the fine arts, this sector is likely to experience a further boost – it is the closest to art, and the most removed from advanced carpentry, of all furniture. In its English grandeur, it is also the most beloved of American buyers, and some of the huge appreciation over the past two decades is due to the vast shipments of English furniture which

Fig. 8.7: Growth of mahogany furniture 1968-1988

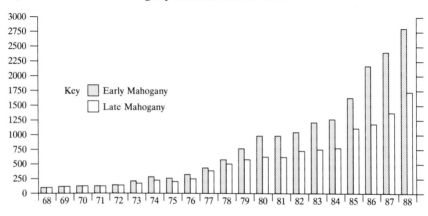

Source: Antique Collector's Club Antique Furniture Index

have crossed the Atlantic. If you can still afford it, it remains a marvellous buy, and is one of the best and safest investments in the art market. Phillips 1988 survey suggests 'fine eighteenth century and Regency' pieces as the best buy for 1988, with 'fine eighteenth century decorative' items having shown strongest demand in 1987.

Late mahogany had its heyday in the 1780s, and was influenced by the lighter, classical looks of Hepplewhite (*The Cabinet Makers and Upholsterers Guide*, 1788) and Sheraton (*The Cabinet Makers and Upholsterers Drawing Book*, 1791-94). It has performed much less well (see Figure 8.7), and there is no sign of the gap between early and late mahogany closing. The 1980s worship the decorative look, and the simpler lines of late mahogany are comparatively out of favour. Buy if you like it, though, for over the long term the wheel of fortune has never been known to stop spinning, but appreciation in the short term is unlikely to be as strong. These pieces do, however, fit better into some homes than the more elaborate earlier style.

Regency furniture

But the ornate look is in, and no sector has benefited more from it than Regency furniture. Ignored for much of this century, it came back into favour in the early 1980s, and is now much sought after for its almost effete daintiness and delicacy of line. It is epitomised in the satinwood furniture Macquoid characterised as 'so distinctly feminine in refinement, yet possessing a fascinating prettiness and brightness'. Rosewood was also common, but there are plenty of Regency mahogany and oak pieces to be found too, though always in the lighter, more fluid style.

Starting from a low base 20 years ago, Regency furniture has performed better (see Figures 8.8 and 8.11) than the ACC's overall Antique Furniture Index. It was given a boost in 1987 at the Great Tew house sale, when prices for Regency furniture in general and George Bullock in particular went through the roof. A pair of oak bookcases by Bullock, £64 when made for the house in 1817, fetched £82,000 against an estimate of £7-

Fig. 8.8: Growth of Regency furniture 1968-1988

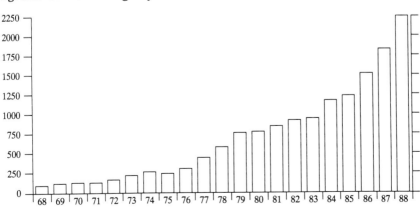

Source: Antique Collector's Club Antique Furniture Index

10,000; a Bullock cabinet was £110,000, and a very decorative sofa table, a quintessential Regency piece, made £38,500.

Part of the Bullock fever was due to the impeccable provenance associated with house sales, but Bullock, a slightly misty figure until Great Tew, has stayed in the limelight, and prices remain buoyant. The dark period in the bulk of this century, however, means that Regency prices still have a long way to go. Prices at Great Tew ranged from under £2,000 to over £100,000; Bullock chairs, chests and cabinets were fetching between £2,000 and £5,000, and less important side tables were between £1,000 and £3,000. That leaves much to play for in this market, with the lower levels still affordable to many collectors.

Fig. 8.9: Growth of Victorian furniture 1968-1988

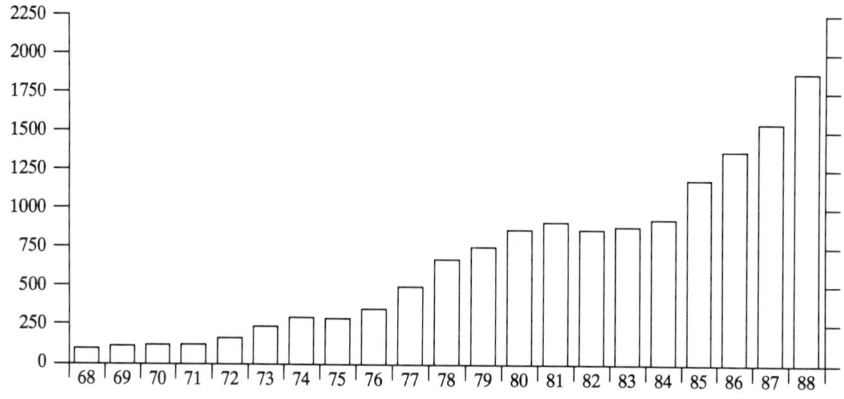

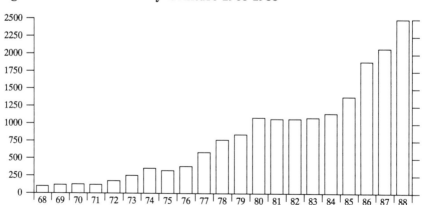

Source: Antique Collector's Club Antique Furniture Index

Fig. 8.10: Growth of Country furniture 1968-1988

Source: Antique Collector's Club Antique Furniture Index

Fig. 8.11: Antique Furniture Index by sector (1988)

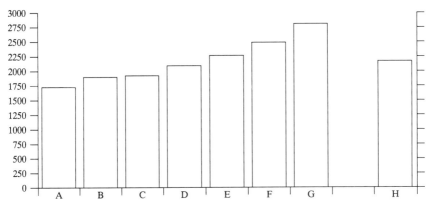

Source: Antique Collector's Club Antique Furniture Index

Key: A Late Mahogany; B Victorian; C Walnut; D Oak; E Regency; F Country; G Early Mahogany; H Aggregate

WHAT TO BUY

No matter what furniture you collect, or how much you pay for it, you will be entering a market awash with fakes, and with pieces which are not quite all they claim to be. But don't be put off; this is one of the hazards of the art market, and as long as you know what you are doing, or buy through a trusted dealer, you need not worry.

If you are buying from a dealer, safeguard yourself by demanding a description and date of the piece on your receipt – this should help clear up any misunderstandings which might later arise. A good dealer should offer a buy-back guarantee – both a sign that he is confident of the pieces he is selling, and a guarantee of liquidity should you suddenly need cash.

If you are buying at auction make sure, as in any sector, that you know what you are buying by attending the pre-sale viewing and examining carefully any piece you may be interested in. The checklist below offers guidelines on judging the aesthetic qualities of a piece, its authenticity and its practicality. All three are important if you have even half an eye on the investment potential of what you are buying; even if you don't, most fine antiques that you hope to live with for several years should be tested against these criteria. If you are satisfied, your piece should stand the test of time and market forces, for high quality workmanship and attractive designs always maintain high values. The analysis of two sales, one of important and one of more run-of-the-mill furniture, below, is an attempt to put these guidelines into practice.

Practical considerations

The cheapest piece of furniture at Christie's King Street sale in July 1988 was a Regency mahogany wine cooler which fetched £1,540. Standing on ormolu paw feet, adorned with ormolu lion masks and inlaid with rosewood key-pattern lines, it was a typically elegant and decorative piece. It fetched so little because it is perfectly useless.

Utility matters in furniture, and pieces that remain practical today are in greatest demand, their prices increasing as they become scarcer.

If you could furnish only one room with antiques, it would probably be a living room; usually the dining room, still the most formal room in most homes, and certainly not the bedroom. Prices reflect this, with formal dining room furniture the most sought after and bedroom furniture the least.

Since this preference has always operated, the most beautiful and decorative furniture has always been made for the living – and often the entertaining – rooms, which of course pushed up demand. Top of most shopping lists, therefore, is formal dining room furniture – a period dining table and a set of period chairs.

The latter particularly is becoming hard to find, and very expensive – the larger the set, the higher the price per chair, especially if two carvers are included. Very large sets – 12 or 14 matching chairs – are now very rare and expensive, and accordingly, the faking brigade has moved in. It's not worth their while producing a single faked chair, but it is worth it to manufacture a couple of identical chairs from an authentic model to upgrade a set of four to six or eight, or to add on a pair of carvers. With carvers, check that the seat width is slightly more generous than on the other chairs; with all sets, make sure the height of each is the same and – a giveaway, this one – that the weight of each chair is the same. If any of them feel lighter, they are probably of a different vintage, and may have come out of the warehouse a month or two ago.

Next in demand after formal dining room furniture are the accompaniments – sofa tables, posh and valuable when they were first made, sideboards and cabinets. With the exception of dining chairs, you will probably find furniture to put things on or in more useful than furniture to sit on, unless you like sitting straight upright in your living room all day. Sofas, chaise longues and daybeds are wonderfully decorative, but their spartan attitude to comfort has kept them relatively cheap, with many fine authentic pieces costing less than £10,000.

The size of modern homes has led to a premium being attached to small, manageable pieces, with the result that elegant long sideboards are left sitting in dealers' shops because living rooms are simply not big enough to house them. It sounds obvious, but make sure you don't take home something that is too grand, either in size or style, to fit – you will probably run into problems selling it on as well.

A market for grand lavish pieces, especially mahogany, has developed in the City, however, with firms keen to snap up massive breakfront bookcases, impressive high-backed chairs and great lumbering partners' desks. Good office furniture has become steadily more expensive over the past 20-30 years, although there is still a lot available.

As good English furniture increases in price, collectors are finding it harder to afford the large pieces. Investment buyers should compromise on size rather than quality – buy a superb small table rather than a second rate bookcase. As Plate 9 below shows, it is possible to buy top quality pieces, but apart from the cellarette, all the pieces which fetched under £4,000 at Christie's King Street sale in July 1988 were small tables. Small pieces like this have the advantage of fitting easily into any home, and if they are practical and decorative, they should always be a good investment.

Checklist

1. *The design* What collectors call the general sweep or 'line' of a piece, and its proportions. If these are wrong, the piece will be dumpy and ungracious – a chest whose drawer gradations are out of proportion, for example, or a top heavy tall boy or secretaire bookcase whose top half sits uneasily on its bottom half. Most of the pieces illustrated in the Christie's King Street list below are examples of excellent line and proportion – it is the most instantly striking and appealing point about good quality furniture.

2. *Decorative features* Less crucial, and more a matter of personal taste – plain to one person may mean over-ornate to another – but still an important factor in determining quality and price. Features to look for include interesting marquetry, crossbanding, carving, brass inlays, scrolling brackets, detailed cornices or mouldings. All contribute to the character of a piece. They help the price, especially for pieces which are in abundant supply, like card or tea tables.

3. *Colour, patination and grain* This is where aesthetic factors meet considerations about authenticity. An interesting grain always helps the price, while age produces a wonderful rich gloss – or patina – on wood, the result of the dusting and waxing of centuries. Over the years, wood also fades to a warm glowing colour, much sought after because it is very attractive and absolutely impossible to produce in a contemporary work-shop manufacturing fakes. Looking at the colour of a piece should help you work out its history. Large tables, for instance, may well have been used mostly in part, so it is to be expected that their leaves will be of varying shades. On the other hand, a secretaire bookcase cannot have been used in part – unless, that is, its parts do not come from the same source. If the grain, colour and patina of the two parts of such a piece do not match, it is likely to be a 'marriage', and should be avoided as not quite authentic.

4. *Authenticity* If the colour and patina of a piece look right, you should be favourably disposed towards it, but examine it very thoroughly for signs of age anyway. Try to see it in natural light, and from all sides – ask a dealer, or a porter at an auction preview, to move it away from a wall if necessary, and don't be afraid to appear utterly undignified as you inspect it – it's better than looking utterly foolish as you take home a fake that has cost you many thousands of pounds.

'It's sex', said one expert, as he was running his hand over a piece to 'test' for age at the preview of the Christie's King Street furniture sale featured below. A tactile sense really comes into its own here, for you can *feel* age – the layers of dirt and grime accumulated over centuries encrusted into the wood. Be suspicious of anything that feels too smooth and 'new'. This is an art that takes time to learn, but is a marvellous guide once you have mastered it.

Test for age *under* a piece of furniture – this is where it will have been lifted up, banged into and knocked about. Furniture is, after all, made to be used, and most pieces will have needed minor restoration or repair over their long lives. Substantial alterations will tell against a piece, but a little bit of glue here or there is a healthy sign – again, you can *feel* it if you turn a chair upside down, clamber underneath a table or pull out the drawers of a bureau to make sure they are a good fit. Look also for signs of use –

handmarks on the pedestals of a table (how else was it moved around?), scratches and dents on the surface of a bureau, worn patches on the arms of a chair. Try to recreate the history of the piece and what it would have been used for, and if the signs are not there, be on your guard.

Finally, even if it doesn't come naturally, cultivate something of a cynical temperament and start on the suspicious side by asking 'what would someone on the make have done to this piece to enhance its value?' This will usually bring you to the decorative features mentioned above; look extra hard at a brass frieze inlay, for example, which may have been added on late in the life of a piece.

5. *Condition*   Pieces in original condition are held at a premium, but such is the general wear and tear suffered by furniture that certain repairs and restorations are perfectly acceptable. Feet, which will have borne the brunt of the wear, are nice in their original state – again, feel for age, roughness and grime – but replacements are considered inevitable. Handles and escutcheons, most used and often first damaged, need not be original either. But check with all such replacements that the proportions fit and that the line of the piece is not weakened, maybe by bracket feet that are manifestly too large, or handles that are too small.

While certain signs of use are positively advantageous as a proof of authenticity, others are disastrous. Stains from wet glasses for example are not serious, and are a relatively easy job for a restorer. But the chief enemy of antique furniture these days is central heating, which dries out the atmosphere, creates rapid temperature changes and thus causes wood to expand and contract and eventually to warp and crack, reducing the value inestimably. For this reason, don't keep furniture close to the radiator and try to remedy the evil of a dried-out environment by using a humidifier or placing bowls of water around the room. If you can't give antique furniture a happy environment, it would be better not to buy it at all, for it will not hold its value in dried-out, over-heated rooms.

6. *Provenance*   Always important, this is relatively more so in a sector where pieces are unusually subject to restoration, and where little is signed. Be prepared to pay over the odds for good provenance, and try to go to the country house sales wherever possible. Here is the *crème de la crème* of authenticity – pieces which haven't moved from the house for which they were made. The accounts of grand houses often survive, providing a detailed inventory of most of their contents and their furniture makers. Chippendale always left accounts at the houses where he worked, but so did lesser figures. One reason for the leap-frogging prices for Bullock at the Great Tew sale was the provenance – Bullock had provided invoices for the important pieces which showed date, attribution and even the price when new.

7. *The catalogue*   Catalogues set out to make things clear, but they are a minefield for the unwary. With so little signed, it is especially important that buyers work out what is meant by phrases such as 'in the style of'. If pieces are not dated, that means they have been restored to the point where they are no longer regarded as truly authentic. Plate 14 below is a good example. The auctioneer does not *say* that he suspects this piece to be a reconstruction, but the informed buyer will know from looking at the style of the piece – apparently eighteenth century – and reading the catalogue entry, which does not include a date, that this is what is meant.

A DAY AT THE SALEROOM – CHRISTIE'S SALE OF IMPORTANT ENGLISH FURNITURE, 7 JULY 1988

Total sale percentage sold: 90 per cent.

Plates 1a and 1b   Two George I walnut stools with padded rectangular seats (lots 52 and 53)

Plate 1a: Estimate £2,500-£3,500   Fetched £4,620
Plate 1b: Estimate £2,500-£3,500   Fetched £24,200

Georgian walnut stools have never been in short supply, nor are they terribly glamorous items of furniture. But both the pieces are fine, authentic examples which made good prices – one nearly six times that of the other.

Both stand on attractive cabriole legs and are well upholstered – 1a in blue damask, 1b in floral needlework. The important difference is the decoration at the head of the legs – fairly typical scrolled brackets for 1a, highly unusual pierced and scrolling angle brackets for 1b.

Its staggering price of almost £25,000 – more than the much grander contemporary pieces in Plates 2 and 3 – shows the premium placed on rare and impressive decorative features. Robert Copley, one of Christie's furniture experts, said he had 'never seen a stool like it', and admitted to hoping that 'on a good day' it might have made £12,000, but not more. But note the conservative estimate he *actually* put on the piece; be prepared to pay well over the odds for the best examples of any type of furniture. Someone else will always be prepared to do so if you want to sell up.

Plates 2a and 2b   Two George I walnut open armchairs, with seats upholstered in needlework (lots 54 and 133)

Plate 2a: Estimate £6-8,000   Fetched £9,900
Plate 2b: Estimate £5-8,000   Fetched £14,300

To me, there is no doubt here that the person who paid the lower price took home the nicer chair. 2a, with its vase-shaped splat and shaped scroll-ended arms, is generously proportioned and immediately looks 'right', at ease with itself, one could almost say. By contrast, 2b appears convoluted, the shepherd's crook outscrolled arms a little disconcerting and the X-shaped cabriole legs positively clumsy.

Its carving is interesting – note the shell in the centre – but so is the carving in 2a, which has the advantage of lovely claw and ball feet. It only seems to have the edge in unusual needlework – parrots, foliage and humming birds rather than the more typical floral motifs – but no one is going to pay £5,000 for that.

The price difference comes down again to rarity – there simply aren't many X-shaped legged chairs like 2b around, while 2a, as decorative, authentic and well-made, is more common.

Also working in favour of 2b is provenance – it was the 'property of a lady', and thus preferable to pieces described under 'various (ie dealers') properties' – and historical reference, a plus point in proving authenticity

Plate 1a

Plate 1b

Plate 2a

Plate 2b

and importance. A very similar chair belongs in the Irwin Untermyer collection, and is illustrated in a volume describing the collection which Christie's catalogue draws to the attention of buyers.

Plate 3   A George I walnut bureau (lot 101)

Estimate £5-6,000   Fetched £9,350

For centuries, no self-respecting middle class home was without one of these, and as a result there are thousands around. But this is a particularly fine one, and it is no surprise to see it exceeding the estimate.

The colour here has faded to that warm, rich honey which positively glows with age – a collector's dream! Note too the beautiful pattern of the grain on the hinged top, as rich in detail as a painting, and the fine sweep of the piece – the pleasing proportions of the drawer gradations, and the shaped bracket feet.

The patina here leaves no real doubt, but further signs of age and wear are the scratches and dents on the sides and an ink stain in one of the oak-lined drawers.

Finally, the size of the piece – 3 foot wide, just over 3 foot high, a little under 2 foot deep – is just right for the modern home. If you had had £20,000 to spare in July 1988, this and the walnut chair in Plate 2a would have made a splendid start to a collection.

Plate 4   A George III mahogany commode (lot 32)

Estimate £7-10,000   Fetched £22,000

Like Plate 3, this is a model of its kind, the wood again honey-golden. First point is the lovely line and proportions: the bowed concave sided top and the concave cupboard doors flanking the drawers are very attractive; the fiddleback mahogany drawers are superb. Second is the detail – the rosewood crossbanding on the top, framed by ebony and boxwood lines, the inlaid fan oval, the herringbone rosewood borders on the drawers, the cupboard doors inlaid with ogee arches. It is at once abundant and restrained, and makes for a delightful piece.

Its provenance, the Fermor Hesketh collection which opened this sale, made it even more sought after.

Plate 3

Plate 4

Plate 5   A George II mahogany commode (lot 146)

Estimate £50-70,000   Fetched £407,000

If the last commode typified good 'late' mahogany, here is an example of 'early' mahogany at its magnificent best.

Georgian chests are among the most commonly collected pieces of antique furniture and come in three broad styles – straightfronted, bowfronted (as in Plate 4) and serpentine, as here. Serpentine chests are most valuable, and this piece, massively forceful in its deep rich mahogany colour, is in the very top range of the English furniture market. As American dealers fall over each other to have such pieces shipped across the Atlantic, their appearance at sales is getting rarer and rarer.

Serpentine commodes are favoured for their generous, sweeping line, which is one of the most instantly appealing points here. Detail and ornament, moreover, seem to drip from it – the edge of the serpentine top carved with cabochon and confronting C-scrolls, the graduated drawers edged with gadrooned beading and mounted with pierced ormolu rockwork swing handles. The frieze, carved with flowerheads and scrolls, adds drama, and the cabriole legs, carved with rockwork and foliate scrolls on scroll toes with shaped blocks, also look grand.

There is history behind this piece – Christie's catalogue devotes a page to telling it – and some controversy over its first owner. It follows a design by Chippendale dated 1753 in *The Director*, but it is unlikely to be by him. Christie's compares it to three other commodes 'attributable to the same, as yet unknown, cabinet-maker'; it shows how much research is still to be done in this field.

As top quality furniture starts to creep up towards the prices paid in the fine art sector – though there is still a long way to go – there is bound to be a knock-on effect in the less glamorous parts of the furniture sector.

Plate 6   A set of George II mahogany and parcel gilt side chairs in the manner of Robert Manwaring (lot 145)

Estimate £60-80,000   Fetched £176,000

Another example of the top range of English furniture, which still rarely exceeds £100,000.

One dealer examining these at the pre-sale viewing provocatively suggested that they might be fakes because they looked 'more period than period'. They would undoubtedly dominate most rooms in which they were placed, and they do epitomise the ornamental splendour of early mahogany – the back carved with acanthus and crested by a pagoda is an example of English furniture's 'Chinese Chippendale' phase.

No lily here is left ungilded – the shaped pierced interlaced back (compare the simplicity of the backs of the two walnut chairs, and add on several thousand pounds – each one in this set was nearly £30,000), the fronts of the seat rail covered with blind-fret pailing, the cabriole legs carved with cabochons, acanthus and rockwork and with scrolled toes.

As sets of chairs become rarer, collectors are willing to pay a premium for sets like this; they will always fetch more than six individual chairs of comparable quality.

Plate 5

Plate 6

Plate 7   An early George III mahogany breakfront bookcase attributed to
Thomas Chippendale (lot 132)

Estimate £40-60,000   Fetched £60,500

Although expensive, here is the age of mahogany back within reach of the
less than super-rich collector. It is, however, a marvellous example of the
bold, dramatic, solidly masculine style of that age. Breakfront bookcases
were prestigious in Chippendale's day as emblems of the wealth and social
status of their owners, and they are among the most sought-after pieces of
large English furniture.

Quality of decoration helps price – here the scrolling broken pediment
is carved with imbrication above a finely moulded dentilled cornice and the
pattern of the glazing bars is elegant and restrained.

The carcase here has been cut in the centre, and as a result the bookcase
was bought in when it appeared at auction in the US six months before this
sale. This inevitably prejudiced dealers, always reluctant to look at
anything once it has been rejected by the trade, and Christie's must have
hoped that buyers would have forgotten. In the event they were lucky, for
the bookcase reached the top of its estimate. Given the conservative
estimates in view of prices fetched by other pieces, however, it might have
been expected to go higher, and probably because this was its second run,
it sold as something of a bargain.

Plate 8   A pair of Regency brass inlaid rosewood lamp tables in the
manner of George Bullock (lot 89)

Estimate £15-20,000   Fetched £41,800

After Great Tew, Regency fever continues unabated. For me, the most
appealing point about this pair is that they have visual history written right
across them – you can interpret their life story just by looking. The
complex grain of the wood on each reads like a contour map reprinted, but
back to front, on both surfaces. This is a pretty good sign that they started
life together and one was not made in imitation of the first to enhance their
value as a pair.

Even better is the varied shade of wood on the top of the one illustrated
– glowing golden on one side, with a round dark patch towards the centre.
It is clear where the piece stood under the window to catch the sun, and
where the vase must have stood for years to leave one unfaded blotch. If
you find a piece like this, don't polish it until the difference in shade has all
but disappeared – so far no fakers have cottoned on to this sort of detail,
and it is marvellous guarantee of original condition.

Convincing colour is enough to sell a piece well. In addition, this pair
boasted elegant stylised brass inlays and lovely scroll feet with ormolu
paterae and anthemions. They are also a good practical size and a fine
example of the delicate Regency prettiness now very sought after.

As a pair, they fetched a lot more than twice the price of two comparable
single tables.

Plate 7

Plate 8

Plate 9   A Regency brass-inlaid rosewood card table (lot 27)

Estimate £3-5,000   Fetched £3,300

This was one of the few pieces which sold for under £5,000 at this sale, and is included here as a demonstration of the possibility – just – of acquiring high quality at reasonable prices.

New collectors are increasingly finding, however, that to be affordable a good piece will have to be small. Of the comparably priced furniture (excluding objects of art, mirrors, pictures etc) in this sale, all were small tables apart from the cellarette already mentioned.

Card tables were very popular in the eighteenth and early nineteenth centuries, so much depends on fine inlays or other decorative features. This one comes well up to scratch. The top is inlaid with lines and anthemions and a central honeysuckle medallion, heightened with ebony. Also attractive is the frieze edged with ebony and a brass-scrolled border, and the graceful scrolled X-pattern supports with gadrooned roundels.

The best card tables were made in pairs, but over long lifetimes many have been separated. If this had had a partner, the two together would have exceeded twice the price paid here.

Compensatory factors here, though, are the provenance – the Fermor Hesketh collection again – and historical reference (a very similar card table is illustrated in Joudain and Fastnedge's *Regency Furniture*, 1965). With this in mind, it is extraordinary that in a sale where estimates were so unceremoniously ignored, this was knocked down at the lower end of its estimate. If, as they say, there are bargains in every sale, this is one of them here.

Plate 10   A mahogany four-pedestal D-end dining table (lot 143)

Estimate £20-30,000   Bought in at £13,000

This is a typical formal mahogany dining table, made up of a central rectangular section and two rounded ends. As is often the case, these 'D-ends' have been used as a complete table, with the central leaves brought out only occasionally, and one more occasionally than the other. The varying shades of the wood demonstrate the history of the use quite clearly – the D-ends faded, one of the central sections starting to fade, and the other its deep original colour. A fine proof that it had been 'lived with' for many years, which is backed up by other age tests like handmarks on the pedestals and the odd scratch and dent here and there.

Unfortunately, none of this was enough to sell it. The reason lies in the catalogue entry, which gives no date or period – the piece is, as they say, 'out of period'; in fact it is late nineteenth century. Amid the eighteenth century splendour of this sale, it was despised, but it is among the most sought-after type of furniture in the market, and it is probable that at a less glamorous sale – 'fine', rather than 'important' English furniture, perhaps – it might have done better.

Plate 9

Plate 10

A DAY AT THE SALEROOM – CHRISTIE'S SOUTH KENSINGTON WEEKLY FURNITURE SALE, 20 JULY 1988

Total sale percentage sold: 92 per cent

Plate 11   A walnut and banded lowboy (lot 510)

Estimate £1-1,500   Fetched £1,980

The clue to this piece lies in the catalogue entry. There is no date or period, which is why it is here rather than at King Street. It is essentially an eighteenth century piece – it has very attractive line, lovely cabriole legs, a good walnut colour and an interesting grain – but the auctioneers suspect it has been reconstructed from other eighteenth century pieces. This was very commonly the case in the 1920s, when no great value was placed on the average, original antique. Craftsmen, with no intent to deceive, regularly hacked up large or damaged pieces of furniture to make small delicate ones like this. They created attractive pieces which are more authentic than a mere reproduction – hence the price – but will never be valued as much as an untouched original piece. That is fine as long as you know what you're buying; the worry would be to see this sold (for much more) as a Georgian piece.

Plate 12   A Regency mahogany extending D-end dining table (lot 340)

Estimate £2-3,000   Fetched £3,850

The larger the better with dining tables. This one has a rectangular fold-over top on a concertina action and, including three extra leaves, can seat up to 12. The thick grain of the mahogany is unmistakably authentic, the proportions are right, even if the piece is not the most elegant ever seen, and structurally it is in good repair. What lets it down is the condition of the top – a mess of scratches and stains which leaves the whole looking, in the words of one Christie's expert, 'pretty awful'. But he was the first to point out too that with just £150-200 worth of restoration, easily done at this level, the table could end up 'fantastic'. Structurally sound pieces whose surfaces have been knocked about a bit are an excellent investment for anyone willing to have a small amount of work done, and this was one of the best buys of the sale.

Plate 11

Plate 12

Plate 13   A late Regency mahogany bowfronted sideboard (lot 349)

Estimate £800-1,200   Fetched £2,750

It is easy to imagine Plate 14 (below) losing some of its central part and perhaps its brass rail and turning into something like Plate 13. Apart from any other details, the size of Plate 13 – just under 5 foot wide – makes it far more desirable, and as a result a lot of larger pieces have been cut down to make moderately sized sideboards. They will always be regarded as reconstructions.

Plate 13, however, is the genuine article – uniform in style, convincing in colour, inlaid with boxwood lines. Its problem is a massive crack running right along the width of the surface and probably the result of an overdose of central heating. This will be harder and more expensive to repair than Plate 12. With this in mind, the auctioneer placed a low estimate on the piece. It is sign of the strong demand for authentic Regency furniture that the price went so high.

Plate 14   A mahogany and satinwood banded sideboard (lot 507)

Estimate £1-1,500   Fetched £1,320

At the end of the catalogue description here the auctioneer ventures that the piece is 'early nineteenth century'. Yet he does not date it as he has done with Plate 13. The reason is that it is a mix – essentially Regency but unable to be dated as a period piece because it has clearly been tampered with.

The first giveaway is that its proportions look a little odd, but more serious are the flaws in the satinwood banding. Added on for extra, probably 'up to date', decoration in the days before authenticity was held at a premium, the banding has been diabolically executed – trailing off several centimetres apart around the sides, the lines simply do not match. Nor do the inlays of conch shells and flower filled urns, probably done at the same time, add elegance to this ungainly piece. It is unlikely that this will ever be anything but a slightly unhappy piece of furniture, and one which collectors would do well to steer clear of. Its flaws are so very apparent.

Plate 13

Plate 14

Plate 15   A rosewood and brass inlaid sofa table (lot 516)

Estimate £1,500-2,000   Fetched £3,960

Made to stand behind sofas in the Regency age of elegance, sofa tables have always been classy. This is a nice decorative example – note the stylised foliage, and the attractive down-curved legs, each ending in a lion's paw.

In good condition, a piece like this could make £6,000 and would sell at King Street. The condition of this one is described as 'distressed', which it certainly looks. A nasty split down the middle, together with a burn mark which has melted the glue under the veneer and curved the wood to expand into something like a bubble, will be very difficult to repair. Rosewood starts life almost black; over a couple of centuries it fades to a lovely light rich colour. For a restored piece to have a hope of being taken seriously, it is no good getting hold of new rosewood and crossing your fingers – the expensive 200 year old wood has to be used, and even then the piece will always be regarded as restored rather than untouched.

As with Plate 13, an attractive piece with potential is always a good buy. What is amazing is that this fetched more than Plate 9, in impeccable condition and from a good source, and also more than a Regency oak sofa table which sold for £3,850 in the King Street sale. It is possible that they were dwarfed by more important pieces, while this stood out at King Street for its inherent quality.

Plate 16   A Regency mahogany gentleman's toilet stand (lot 374)

Estimate £400-600   Fetched £605

Authentic, good condition, attractive – but absolutely useless today. Like the cellarette at King Street, it's hard to see these going up far or fast.

Plate 15

Plate 16

Plate 17   A Victorian mahogany partner's desk (lot 427)

Estimate £1,200-1,800   Fetched £1,320

Victorian desks are always in demand for city offices or grand houses. In relatively good condition, this one was a little too large for human comfort, but a partner's desk is always a good investment.

Plate 18   An Edwardian mahogany open armchair (lot 433)

Estimate £100-200   Fetched £385

Along with traditional eighteenth century and Regency pieces, Phillips Survey of Antiques at Auction 1987-88 placed 'the best of Edwardian' – 'gaining popularity year by year' – as the first market choices for 1988. Edwardian furniture makers are sometimes nostalgically described as 'the last of the cabinet makers'. Edwardian furniture is usually well made and its intrinsic quality makes it a good investment. At present it is still affordable, but there are signs that this could change.

The chair shown here was another of the best buys at the sale. The bone inlays are superbly done – notice the arabesques, also the arcanthus carved toprail and cabriole legs, the outscrolled arms and the lovely serpentine shape of the seat. A lovely piece and an excellent investment.

Plate 17

Plate 18

Plate 19 A Victorian yew and elmwood Windsor armchair, and two similar armchairs (lot 328)

Estimate £1,400-1,800   Fetched £1,650

Over the past few years, country furniture has done well (see Figure 8.10) and few country chairs now fetch less than £500. The amount of yew wood in country furniture is important – it always helps prices, and can be distinguished because it is very smooth.

These three are in different woods but make a harlequin set. A matching set should include at least four chairs (in the same wood) and, if of comparable quality to the ones shown here, would make about £1,000 per chair. Large sets of matching country chairs, which would normally be sold at King Street, are becoming very scarce. They are a good investment, and their high price obviously has a knock-on effect on the value of oddballs such as those here.

Plate 19

9 CERAMICS

I find it harder and harder every day to live
up to my blue china.

Oscar Wilde

Those little lawless azure-tinctured grotesques,
that under the notion of men and women, float about
uncircumscribed by any element, in that world before
perspective – a china teacup.

Charles Lamb, *Last Essays of Elia*

The sort of china Charles Lamb would have known was the Chinese export porcelain made in the East specifically for the European market. The Chinese have always capitalised on their thousand-year head start in porcelain making, and by the eighteenth century their ceramic wares, modified to take in apparently western-style painting, were flooding into Europe.

In 1708, a German alchemist hit upon the porcelain making process, and Meissen became the first European factory to produce rivals to the Chinese pieces. Meissen is still the most sought after of continental ceramics, but nothing produced in the West has ever excited collectors as much as the early classical Chinese pieces, of which the West had the first tantalising glimpses in the late nineteenth century.

Today, Chinese porcelain from the Ming, Qing and other periods is recognised as one of the greatest art forms of all time, and is one of the most internationally traded of all the art sectors. Hong Kong is the hub of the market, and Hong Kong Chinese and the Japanese, flashing around mighty Yen, are a strong presence, though a considerable American and European interest tends to make good any waning of oriental enthusiasm in times of a weak Hong Kong dollar. The collecting base is growing broader all the time, in sharp contrast to the market for continental porcelain, where interest is more or less national – the French collect Sèvres and Vincennes, the Germans and Swiss collect Meissen, the English collect Chelsea and Worcester. The low unit cost of most European ceramics discourages auction globe-trotting on the Impressionist scale, and hence European porcelain remains an area where the new buyer may set his sights on the very best and have some hope of achieving it. For the collector of Chinese ceramics, this looks increasingly less likely. A pear-shaped copper-red very decorative Ming vase shot through the £1m barrier to break the record for a piece of Chinese porcelain in Hong Kong in May 1988, fetching HK$17m (£1.16m). Six figure sums can be expected for top quality pieces.

CHINESE CERAMICS

Life is not always easy if you are a Ming bowl. The last 15 years have seen two trying periods – one of them disastrous but both in the end survivable. Porcelain, which the Chinese buried with their dead until the sixteenth century, was made to last, and the market too seems able to endure and go from strength to strength.

After the collapse in 1974, due in part to the effects of the Portuguese Revolution, which put China's oldest western contact out of action as far as buying porcelain was concerned, Chinese ceramics staged a dramatic comeback, achieving an annual growth of around 35 per cent on Sotheby's Art Index between 1975-80. The market has also borne up well in the 1980s under the strain of the uncertainty surrounding the future of Hong Kong, and as late as December 1986 it was, of the ten sectors which make up the Art Index, the market which had shown the most growth since 1975, notwithstanding a levelling-off of prices after 1984.

Over the long term, the market has always bounced back from temporary lulls, and it is unimaginable that Chinese porcelain should ever be downgraded as an art form. In recent years, very high sums were paid, especially for early Ming from the Edward T Chow collection, sold in the 1980-81 season, where prices were widely believed to have been unrealistically high. But when some pieces were resold as part of the collection of the Chinese shipping magnate T Y Chao in November 1986 and May 1987, many showed how big a profit could be made on a quick resale in spite of the high prices; in particular, a very rare fifteenth century blue and white moon flask (HK$7.15m at the late sale; previously HK$ 3.3m) and a very rare fifteenth century blue and yellow dish (HK$3.3m; previously HK$1.43m) showed growth rates of nearly 14 per cent per annum.

By the end of the 1986-87 season, the market rallied again, and in 1988 it rose a healthy 24 per cent, according to Sotheby's Chinese Ceramics index, although the more spectacular leaps among Impressionist and Modern paintings and furniture stole the limelight.

It remains a buoyant area with room for growth if you buy carefully. Many new Japanese and Taiwanese buyers are pushing up prices and important sales in Hong Kong in 1988 were just 1 per cent and 6 per cent unsold, and throughout the 1987-88 season there was a spate of record prices. In particular the earlier Tang, Song and Yuan dynasties are beginning to catch up with the flamboyantly expensive Ming and Qing Imperial wares. The blue and white porcelain from the Yuan dynasty (1266-1368) which immediately preceded Ming (1368-1644) and has been more or less ignored because there is so little of it, saw some exceptional prices. A record HK$7.48m (£536,970), fetched in Hong Kong for a Yuan dish at the end of 1987 was broken a few days later in New York where another example made $1.1m (£602,575), while in London another Yuan dish was £473,000. None of them would have exceeded £150,000 five years ago, and nor would the rare Yuan jar which made £605,000, twice its estimate, at Sotheby's later in the season.

The rarity of Yuan pieces is now coming into its own, while the continuing ascendancy of Ming and Qing is threatened by the possibility of over-supply. So many early pieces were buried along with their owners over the centuries, and they are so easy to excavate, that there is a real danger of saturation in the lower and middle ranges of the sector, as well as a real possibility of fakes, which are becoming increasingly sophisticated.

As a result, a two-tier market has been developing for some time, and collectors would be wise to stick to the top end, which should remain unscathed. High quality here includes impeccable condition; a chip will discourage many buyers, especially in Hong Kong, and a crack will put off even more as they will fear the piece may break in two at any moment. Some cracks are not visible to the naked eye, which, given the huge sums of money paid in this area, makes it all the more important for the new collector to buy through a dealer. For despite the spectacular prices paid, Chinese ceramics remains an area of largely academic and historic interest, demanding research and expertise if the collector is to buy sensibly.

CONTINENTAL CERAMICS

Last year a tiny teabowl under two inches high was brought to a valuation day at Tunbridge Wells organised by Sotheby's Sussex saleroom. Whisked off to London, it was the star of the show at a sale of European porcelain at Sotheby's in February 1988, where it sold for £19,800. Dated 1749, it turned out to be from the Vincennes porcelain works and displayed a colour reference code to test the various pigments used, invaluable for research into the factory.

For a piece of European porcelain, £20,000 is a very good price. The record for a piece of English porcelain is £102,000, paid for a saltglaze piece in 1986, and British items generally fall in the £300-15,000 range. The French Sèvres and the German Meissen are more valuable than their cruder English counterparts, whose styles were often merely derivative of the sophisticated designs which were fashionable abroad. All the markets have been boosted by intense American interest, but otherwise collectors tend to go local.

English ceramics

In the last five years, pieces from the English potteries have shot up in price, largely because of growing American interest in all forms of naive art, attaching a premium to earthy country styles from pre-porcelain days. Seventeenth century tankards, for example, have doubled in price since the market first took off at Sotheby's famous Lipski sale in 1981, when an exceptionally good and rare example made £6,800. In 1983 a similar London Delftware cylindrical tankard was £8,000 and another one in 1984 was £9,000. At Sotheby's in February 1988, a seventeenth century Southwark Delftware mug made £14,000.

Even more dramatic has been the rise of eighteenth century saltglaze bear jugs, which, long before the arrival of the teddy (see Chapter 13), celebrated the bear with clay chippings to simulate fur, a detachable head with a chain through the snout, and a collar. In 1981, saltglaze bears were around £250; one sold at Sotheby's in June 1988 for £7,000.

But the general trend towards the decorative and the easy to appreciate has largely tilted the balance in favour of nineteenth century pieces, with the ironic result that some nineteenth century reproductions are as desirable as their eighteenth century originals. In America especially, pretty nineteenth century English pieces fetched astonishing prices in the 1987-88 season. $121,000 (around £83,000) was paid for that most sought after style, a dessert service decorated with botanical motifs made by the Derby factory from 1795-1800, which in 1983 sold for $41,800, and $41,250 (around £28,000) was paid for a Worcester shell-decorated vase and cover from 1820 which was unsold in 1974 at $5,500.

Anyone looking for a bargain should hunt around for good eighteenth century pieces from the Derby, Bow and Chelsea factories. Worcester is always most sought after (there is more of it around, so it is easy to collect and buyers have more choice); Chelsea, which has had something of an overdose of hype in recent years, is becoming increasingly popular, while Bow, less sophisticated than either, is considered underpriced. Sooner or later it should start to catch up, and now is a good time to buy.

Botanical subjects, vegetable and animal forms and leaf-moulded pieces are already becoming popular, but some of the more classical styles have barely seen a price shift in the last five years, and could be in for a revival. A magnificent Derby vase and cover from 1760, for example, painted with scenes of musicians and exotic birds in a park, within gilt cartouches on a cobalt-blue background, seemed cheap at £550, though this was twice its estimate, at Sotheby's in June 1988. A month later a Royal Crown Derby vase and cover from 1903 fetched £2,640.

The later piece was just half the size of the earlier, and as collectors with academic interests are outnumbered by those with more of an eye for the purely ornate and decorative, this sort of practical question becomes increasingly relevant. Anything large or difficult to display – a large bowl, for example – scores minus points in the saleroom, while small cabinet pieces are held at a premium. This makes ceramic figures, which are in any case more interesting forms than conventional practical wares, especially popular, with sets obviously fetching a premium.

There are a great many good pieces of eighteenth and nineteenth century English porcelain available for under £2,000. Whether you go for the academic or the decorative appeal, it is vital to read up the history of the different factories and styles, for historical importance is what determines prices. A signed and dated piece which can be considered a yardstick for a certain type of ware will always command a premium, as will a style or design which is historically significant – a piece celebrating a coronation, for example.

As far as form and decoration go, rarity and aesthetic appeal are important in about equal measure. The most expensive piece at Sotheby's sale of nineteenth century English ceramics in June 1988 was an extremely rare set of Spode tulip cups and a stand from 1820, which made £13,200. The cups were modelled in the form of puce, iron-red and orange tulips with green stem handles, and many people would have considered them hideous. But sets like these come up so infrequently that there is always someone willing to pay over the odds. And tulip vases, which are more common, are riding high on the crest of the instant-impact wave of buying; several were sold at the Sotheby's sale, all estimated at under £1,200 and all fetching between £3,000 and £6,000.

A highlight of Christie's sale in June 1988 was a magnificent Derby dry-edge Chinoiserie group demonstrating the sense of smell. Chinoiserie decoration from the mid eighteenth century is very popular and this, showing a finely modelled lady in a conical hat and flowing coat holding a posy, a boy offering her further flowers, was a beautiful piece, and a superb example of the design of the period. It was also in very good condition, and far outstripped its estimate to fetch £20,900. By contrast, a companion piece which might have made £15,000 in good condition was a mere £3,300. A buyer new to the market would have been unlikely to have detected the replacements to the arms on the figures of the second piece, a bearded Oriental and a little boy demonstrating the sense of feeling. Unless you are very confident, this is a market to enter via a dealer.

European ceramics

It is unlikely that demand for English ceramics will spread substantially outside the English-speaking countries, for pieces from the great potteries of Meissen and Sèvres, as well as lesser known German and French potteries, are incomparably more refined and delicate.

To English taste, French eighteenth century porcelain is as alien and over-ornate as eighteenth century French furniture, and it is hard to imagine some of the ostentatious rose pompadour pieces feeling at home in an English sitting room. As an investment, early Sèvres was left behind in the 1960s and 1970s and is now catching up fast, helped by buying from American museums. However, it is an area, like French furniture, with plenty of pitfalls for the unwary, and even museum buyers feel on shaky ground, for the French porcelain market is awash with fakes and sadly

The importance of condition: the damaged Derby Chinoiserie group on the left made £3,300 at Christie's in June 1988; the one on the right, in excellent condition, was £20,900.

lacking in experts to distinguish them from the real thing. The Sèvres factory, moreover, passed through several rocky patches, and certain periods – especially the second half of the eighteenth century – are favoured by collectors over others. The result is a minefield for the new buyer, who, if he gets it right, should be assured of steady rises in a very fashionable area, but will have to take the risk of losing money, at least at first.

Meissen is a different and more cheerful story. The time to buy was just after the war, when German collectors couldn't afford it and no one else wanted it, and prices were derisory. Since its recovery in the 1960s, Meissen has dominated the European porcelain market. It was at once the first and the best, and it is unlikely that its position will change. American demand backs up strong German and Swiss interest, which while the Deutsche Mark and the Swiss Franc are buoyant ensures plenty of enthusiasm in London and New York.

Johann Bottger hit upon the recipe for making porcelain in 1708, and the most exciting work was done at the Meissen factory during the first half of the eighteenth century, although anything from the eighteenth century is much in demand.

Meissen pieces range from fine domestic ware to exquisitely modelled figures of animals and people, vases of flowers, candlesticks and leaf dishes. Price is determined by rarity, the quality of the decoration, which could be either simple or elaborate, the form, and the factory's mark, although this last has been forged for centuries. The best known Meissen marks are the crossed swords, usually in underglaze blue; others are various monograms including AR (Augustus Rex), which indicates a top quality piece made for Augustus of Saxony.

It is still possible to buy good Meissen pieces for under £2,000, which seems cheap for pieces of such demonstrably high quality. Meissen tea caddies, sugar bowls, milk jugs, coffee and tea cups and saucers, are all under £1,000, although unusual designs like the 'schneeballen' teacups and saucers, encrusted with applied flowers and turquoise leaves to look like snowballs, the interiors painted with Watteau figures and enclosed by a gilt cartouche and border, are more – they sold at Sotheby's in June 1988 for £3,850.

Figures are more obviously collectable, and here Meissen also catered for every taste. Prices range from a few hundred pounds to many thousands, and there are always collectors willing to pay over the odds for a complete set. Particularly sought after are pieces modelled by J J Kandler, who was the leading light at Meissen in the mid eighteenth century. Some of his moulds continued to be used well into the nineteenth century, and were imitated by others, but none have the vitality, originality and tender touch which Kandler achieved with his expressive delicately painted figures. A Meissen 'Crinoline' group of a seated lady wearing a black dress patterned with *indianische blumen* with a pug on her lap, taking tea offered by a negro servant and being paid court by a 'fop' in a crimson coat, kneeling to kiss her hand, look like something out of a Mozart opera and fetched £8,800 at Sotheby's in June 1988. Best loved of all are figures from the Italian Comedy series – Columbine, Pantaloon, Scaramouche and especially Harlequin. 'The Spanish Lovers', modelled as Columbine and Beltrame wearing Spanish theatrical costume, was £9,350 at the Sotheby's sale.

Popular figures, a Meissen figure of Hofnarr Fröhlich, the Court Jester, modelled by J J Cändler. It fetched £7,150 at Christie's in October 1988, the estimate was £1,500–£2,000.

Since the 1960s Meissen has had a stable body of collectors and its strength as a good, steady investment looks assured. Later areas of German ceramics have recently been rising faster, and in the last few years the spotlight has fallen on nineteenth century Berlin plaques, which have proved especially tempting to Japanese buyers. They are highly decorative pieces of painted porcelain showing instantly pleasing subjects, usually young women and children. Few now cost under £2,000, and attractive pairs are greatly in demand. Sotheby's sold a very good late nineteenth century pair, with two portraits of semi-naked girls sitting on velvet covered rocks, white satin robes draped round their waists, for £14,000 in June 1988; a similar pair was £7,000 in 1979.

If decorative pieces from the nineteenth century go on rising, there should over the long term be a readjustment to allow the eighteenth century to catch up. Continental ceramics has not been a sparkling performer in the art market in the last decade, and some substantial leaps between 1975 and 1980 (when Sotheby's Continental Ceramics Index rose by an average annual 26 per cent) gave way to a much quieter period in the early 1980s (see Figure 9.1). Since 1983, the Index has shown an average growth of 10 per cent per annum, but in the last couple of years the market has been more flamboyant again, registering in 1988 a rise of 27 per cent – more than for Chinese ceramics. Eternally fashionable periods like early Sèvres and Meissen figures should do well; the nineteenth century pieces do not have the same investment record, and it remains to be seen whether

Fig. 9.1: Continental ceramics -v- Chinese ceramics

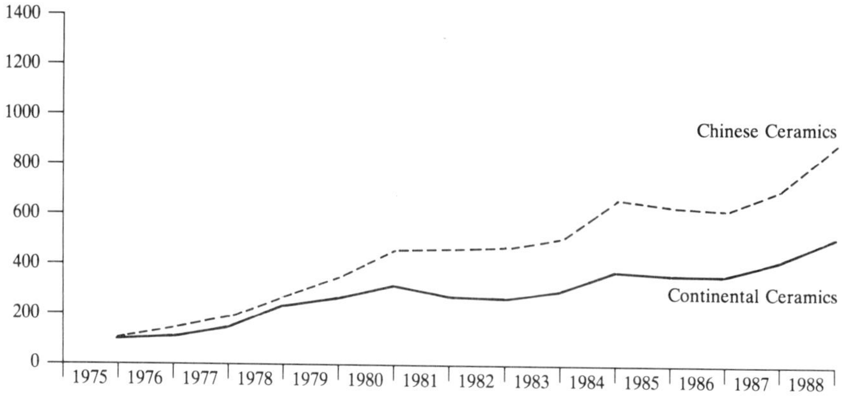

Source: Sotheby's Art Market Bulletin

items like the Berlin plaques turn out to be more than a temporary trend. But in the short term, the general love of the decorative should keep nineteenth century pieces buoyant.

STUDIO POTTERY

If you hoard old pottery, this could be a sector for you. A small bowl, bought in 1960 for £12, sold at Christie's in December 1985 for over £7,000, and plenty of pieces picked up during the 1960s for £10 or £20 now make three or four figure sums, astonishing their owners. Twentieth century ceramics, which in the early 1970s were considered an extension of crafty pursuits like weaving, have come in the 1980s to be recognised as an important area of the decorative arts.

In the last 10 years, prices have soared and fortunes have been made. But as a very young market, it is not an obvious choice for those interested in steady investment, and it is volatile, lacking much of a dealer presence to stabilise prices, full of private buyers bidding on whim in the saleroom – this is one area where you really can back your own taste without deferring to critical opinion, in a sense the antithesis of the activities of the investor, and the ideal market for the speculator. Bargains slip through, but collectors can also pay over the odds, and although prices continue to reach new peaks, it is too early to be sure that the market is invulnerable to artistic downgrading or external economic events. But the twentieth century decorative arts generally have seen an enormous growth in interest in the last decade, with the barrier of what is considered an 'antique' pushed further and further forward and then disregarded altogether as far as many collectors are concerned. Along with the surge in prices for twentieth century pictures, twentieth century furniture and other decorative arts are the biggest new collecting area. As the concept of a modernist aesthetic becomes better understood and researched, there should be more major reassessments in this area.

Traditional buyers stick to Bernard Leach, who started the first English pottery in St Ives in 1924, and his Japanese assistant Shoji Hamada. Japanese styles predominate in the glazes of their pots, which usually follow the traditional English vessel form.

Prices for Leach, as for most English potters, have had their ups and downs, but overall there has been a steady upward trend. Leach pilgrim plates were around £1,000 in 1983, £3,000 in 1985 and are now closer to £5,000. But average stoneware vases, slab bottles and bowls range from £200 to £1,000 and look certain to go higher. Prices even survived a number of fakes put on the market by a resourceful convict working from a Wolverhampton prison, and though demand for the more abstract forms of later potters sometimes leaves Leach looking dull, over the long term his work is a sound investment.

First of the 'seventies superstars', Leach has now been eclipsed by the biggest seller of them all, Hans Coper. The Coper phenomenon hit the art world in 1980 when Sotheby's, in its first sale of contemporary ceramics, sold a Coper vase for an astonishing £7,920 – then a record for a pot by a living artist.

After that, the market snowballed. Largely because of German and American interest, Coper is now established in a class of his own and is collected by museums and galleries the world over. American buyers are excited by his sculptural forms, asymmetrical shapes and patterns, and unusual manganese and buff glazes.

The market for Coper is large and international, and prices are outstripping those for all other ceramics. Coper regularly fetches £5-10,000 and more, even for small pots; a smallish pot made £19,800 at Christie's in November 1987. The huge, sometimes rather ungainly pieces, can go much higher, and the record for a Coper pot – and for any piece of studio pottery – is £38,000. Appreciation since 1975 has been startling – a characteristic spade form vase fetched over £100 in 1975, over £1,000 by 1983 and over £5,000 by 1986. Growth rates are likely to be steadier in the next decade, and although his heavy stoneware designs are not to everyone's taste, his reputation is established and he should keep well ahead.

Coper's name is usually linked with that of the Austrian ceramicist Lucie Rie, who came to London from Vienna just before the war, and brought with her an avant-garde style which looks un-English but which is very popular in the UK and America. Instantly recognisable by their sgraffito decoration, delicacy and pure geometric form, her pots are among the most sought after on the market and as late as the mid 1980s Rie herself was so astonished by the prices they fetched that, in her eighties, she was making trips to Christie's to find out what she should be asking for new work. Major pieces range between £1-2,500, though some fetch as much as £4,000, with smaller ones around £400. As supply diminishes, they are likely to appreciate further. Bonhams achieved a startling record of over £14,000 for a highly unusual Rie stoneware vase covered with a pitted glaze in November 1988. Other Rie pieces in the sale were way above estimate, especially those which had been shown in Rie's retrospective exhibition. Prices should be further boosted by the sale.

One effect of the '70s hype of these artists – Rie, in particular, was pushed by Fischer Fine Art, a large West End gallery, as well as by the

Crafts Council – is that not only exhibition pottery, but also domestic ware, is beginning to appear at the auction houses. And although domestic ware never sells as well as 'one off' pieces, simple stoneware coffee pots bought in the 1960s for under £10 now make over £300.

Around 30 per cent of currently selling Rie pieces are domestic. For many of the lesser known potters, who have traditionally relied on domestic sales, the proportion can be as high as 90 per cent. These bastions of the old school, oblivious to contemporary ceramics' new 'arts' image and fashionable customers, are embarrassed to charge much more than they did 20 years ago.

The workshops of potters like Owen Watson, an Englishman living in France, and Richard Battenham, in Blandford Forum, Dorset, who stick obsessively to the old-fashioned wood-fired kilns and ash glazes, can be the source not only of real bargains but of highly original pieces.

Looking at their work, it is hard to forget – as one does with Coper and Rie – that the modern ceramic traditon has its roots in the nineteenth century art and crafts movement, and the consciously modest style of William Morris & Co. This rustic style is now the domain of dyed-in-the-wool traditionalists such as Geoffrey Whiting, damning what he calls the 'dubious and wayward trend' in modern ceramics, and Michael Cardew and Alan Caiger-Smith, who over the past 50 years have revitalised the earthenware tradition.

Cardew, who died recently, was one of the most deliberately plebeian of potters, and followed primitive African forms learnt in Nigeria and from the African assistant, Ladi Kwali, whom he brought back with him. Fellow ceramicists regarded him as an exceptional artist, and his work is undoubtedly underrated – characteristic iron-brown oviform jugs dating from Cardew's 1925 Winchcombe pottery still fetch under £100. But interest is growing, and £2,808 has been paid for a slipware dish. Appreciation along the lines of Bernard Leach's work may take some time, but is likely in the long term.

Also likely to rise from their present price range of £100 to around £400 are Caiger-Smith's elegant, tin-glazed bowls, decorated in Islamic style with calligraphic motifs and rhombic shapes, and coloured in brilliant glazes of turquoise, cobalt-blue or deep pink. His work is highly decorative, among the best on the market, and must surely be massively undervalued.

Younger buyers, some of whom have turned to twentieth century ceramics as a reaction against the traditional collecting areas of their parents, have pushed up prices for more modern artists. They are particularly drawn to the colourful, geometric designs of Elizabeth Fritsch, whose works now fetch prices which put her in the same division as the Leach-Rie-Coper trio (she joined them on, of all things, the Post Office's celebration of ceramics on postage stamps in 1987, an extraordinary sign of the 'establishment' of this sector in little more than a decade). As abstract as Coper, she is lighter, brighter and more sensuous – pieces like a flattened ovoid vase painted in lavender, purple and orange bands, and a scallop-edged duotone spout pot, fetch £3-4,000.

Fritsch's extensive Crafts Council promotion has paid off – her work went up over 10 times between 1979 and 1981 – and has helped pave the way to recognition for a generation of younger potters. They make up what

The best of studio pottery: a stoneware vase by Hans Coper (£7,150 at Bonhams in November 1988), and . . .

a porcelain vase by Lucie Rie, with her typical sgraffito lines around the central body (£4,730 at the same sale).

is still a substantial buyers' market, and anyone who wants to start a collection will be able to pick up lively and innovative pieces at reasonable prices – for the moment.

For living artists not quite established in their field, selling through the saleroom, in any sector, can either be the making of them or a humiliation which can damage their careers. In this area, prices fetched at auction even for established artists sometimes fail to live up to those fetched at studio sales, but sometimes saleroom prices are much higher. Buyers should try out both.

Some young artists have had extraordinary successes in the saleroom. Magdalene Odundo, a young Nigerian potter, astounded Christie's in 1985 when a red clay vase she had made that year fetched £1,084. She is now a well-known and collectable name.

But craftshops are more likely bets for bargain hunters or casual browsers; try the Craftsman Potters Association in Soho, and the Crafts Council Shop in the Victoria and Albert Museum, in particular.

Names to look out for include Walter Keeler, whose stoneware vessels are easily recognisable by their rough, salt glaze, and Linda Gunn-Russell, who experiments with deliberately impractical shapes and non-functional forms, such as flattened teapots which look almost two-dimensional and are both funny and sophisticated. Also keep an eye open for the angular shapes and abstract decorations of Alison Britain, and the strong and irregular earthenware pots by Gordon Baldwin, both of which are to be found in the salerooms for under £1,000. Many excellent potters, however, don't appear at auction, and can be looked up at studio sales or through the Crafts Council.

Another newish name is Janice Tchalenko, whose flamboyant exhibition pieces found a natural market in New York in the mid 1980s. She is now also popular in the UK, and prices for her lovely colourful bowls, for example a clay 'tulip' bowl with bold red flowers on the outside and black ones inside, range from £400-600. Domestic pieces are cheaper.

At her pottery in Stoke, Tchalenko also produces decorative pieces for the chain store Next, as part of its home furnishings range. Ceramics in the high street is an altogether new phenomenon, and suggests that a growing breed of new collectors are not only being drawn from those who invest in decorative works, but also from those people who have never bought any sort of art before.

This makes it a very promising market, with everything still to play for. For both the traditionalist and the modern, prices at auction often scale well over their estimates – a fine large stoneware oviform vase by the traditionalist Katherine Pleydall-Bouverie, for instance, was estimated at £400-600 at Christie's in 1988 and made £1,870, and another made a record £3,250, while other work is available in the hundreds of pounds range. There are always new potters to discover, and gallery shops to promote them are constantly springing up. For the enterprising collector, this is a market to enter quickly. The main warning is to beware of any artist for whom a market seems to have been artificially 'created', for such markets can easily turn.

It is also worth noting that, furniture excepted, studio pottery was just the first and, so far, the most successful, of the British applied arts to make it to the saleroom. Twentieth century glass is now also included, and is doing well, and contemporary textiles may be the next to unroll onto the market place. Sales of twentieth century British decorative arts should give buyers diverse food for thought.

10 SILVER

It is a great man who uses
earthenware dishes as if they were
silver; but he is equally great who
uses silver as if it were
earthenware.

Seneca, *Letters*

INVESTMENT HISTORY

English silver, not an obvious choice for the speculator, is a traditionally safe investment. Long associated with silver coinage, it has been one of the most common alternatives to cash for centuries – one reason for the rarity of pre-1660 silver is that in times of political unrest, such as the Civil War, it was regularly melted down into coins to pay the troops.

Pieces of the highest artistic quality are today safe from the fluctuations of the silver bullion price, but the connection with silver coinage still plagues lower quality pieces, vulnerable because their actual silver content contributes in greater proportion to their total value. And as recently as the 1930s, the salerooms took bids for silver in shillings per ounce. The price per ounce for lower quality items is always close to melt value, while for the best pieces it is hundreds of times higher.

Historically, top pieces were specially commissioned by the very rich while the link with silver coinage has attracted what some dealers call the 'candlestick and coffee pot brigade' from the middle classes of the last four centuries. In 1969 this group came horribly unstuck when, after massive price rises over three years, the laws allowing tax relief on silver purchases suddenly changed, and the market crashed.

Top quality pieces began to recover in the early 1970s, but it was not until 1983 that a general revival got under way. Figure 10.1 demonstrates silver's poor performance since 1975 compared to porcelain and English furniture, but it only tells part of the story. The two most important features of the silver market are firstly the discrepancy between the levels of interest in English and continental silver, and secondly the huge gap between the appreciation rates for the top and the lower ranges. The two-tier market is more pronounced here than in many sectors.

As the figures in Chapter 2 show, continental silver has been by far the worst performer on the art market index; it has very limited, local appeal – Portuguese buy Portuguese silver, Scandinavians buy Scandinavian silver – and for anyone considering an investment, English silver is to be preferred. It has a large international following and is generally considered the best in the world. Americans, who feel the lack of much pre-1800 silver from their own country – and what little American silver there is is slow to move – are sometimes keen buyers, although this means that the market is held hostage to exchange rates rather more than some others.

Fig. 10.1: Sotheby's English Silver Index/FTA All-Share Index

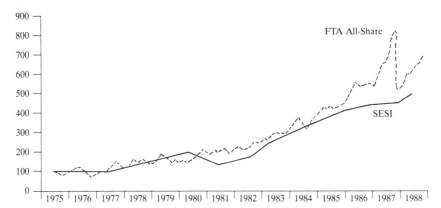

The sector whose performance silver most closely resembles is Old Masters, and the two share an exceptionally strong dealer presence which in the case of silver is heavily dominated by the London trade. This is not a sector where the salerooms have managed to tempt private buyers, and a small number of London dealers have kept the market steady and stable, with conservative estimates prevailing. Some work on profit margins as low as 8 per cent; others concentrate on the upper end of the market where turnover is slower and mark-ups higher.

At the top end of the market, rates of appreciation vary between 10 and 20 per cent a year, but they can go much higher for the very best. Further down, growth rates are slower, and at the bottom prices have been more or less stagnant since the 1970s. If you are looking at this market for investment alone, different dealers would advise a minimum investment of anything from £5-30,000, though the auction houses, understandably, would press the case for investment at much lower sums. If you are keen on silver and wish to spend under £2,000, you may not lose if you buy wisely, or you may choose to take the gamble that the lower end of the market, trailing for so long, will start to pick up. But there is no sign of this happening in the short term, and £2,000 spent on a watercolour or a piece of Regency furniture seems inarguably a better buy.

THE AGE RULE

At the top end of the market, there is ample evidence that silver is a good and safe investment. Silver collectors were provided with a tailor made example of investment buying in 1987, with the sale of material bought in the mid to late 1970s, when rampant inflation persuaded the British Rail Pension Fund to diversify into some alternative investments. Amid talk of the fate of retired engine drivers depending on market esteem for a Charles II candlestick or a pair of Regency wine coolers, almost £250,000 went into antique silver. The day of reckoning came in November 1987, when the collection was resold at Sotheby's, providing collectors, and maybe speculators, with a wide-ranging and representative marker of the fortunes of the silver market over the last decade.

The British Rail Pension Fund venture nestled comfortably at the upper end of the silver market, and the initial investment of almost £250,000 yielded a very respectable return of £1.3m, with the top seller, a pair of Queen Anne silver gilt salvers, fetching at £253,000 more than the entire collection had cost a decade earlier, and over eight times what the salvers had cost when the Fund bought them for £30,000 in 1978.

Fine early pieces like this are guaranteed to do well at auction – another pair of silver gilt salvers, dating from 1690 and engraved with the arms of the first Duke of Devonshire, were one of the star attractions in the collection of the Bolivian tin millionaire, Antenor Patino, which sold at Christie's in New York in October 1986. Silver gilt was his special love, and this exceptional pair, sold for £400 by Christie's in London in 1958, fetched $220,000. In just under 30 years, their value had increased 390 times.

Seventeenth century silver is much prized, so it came as no surprise that the fastest appreciating item from the British Rail collection was a pair of Charles II caskets made in 1673. The Fund bought them in 1976 for £7,700; 11 years later they fetched £82,500, a growth of over 1,100 per cent. Other early pieces included a pair of elaborately decorated Charles II ginger jars which made £209,000 as against £28,600 in 1979.

The old story that a collector who had invested time and love into his specialist sector would have done better is probably true, but what stood out most clearly from the Fund's purchases is the age rule. What the market wants is good, rare pieces from the seventeenth and first half of the eighteenth century, and the Fund's collection fetched consistently high prices in this area. The poorest performers were some items from the nineteenth century, which experienced a boom in the early 1970s but is now less popular. Massive centrepieces, for instance, were once beloved of Arab buyers, but they are difficult to accommodate in modern homes and have not appreciated well. The Macready Testimonial, by Benjamin Smith, bought by the Fund for £9,900 in 1976, fetched only £25,300 in 1987. The market for Victorian silver has all but dried up, and it is an area where investors should tread warily. A seventeenth century sideboard dish, for example, costs around 10 times as much as one from the nineteenth century, and the gap is widening. On the other hand, this does mean that Victorian silver is now comparatively cheap, and if there is another explosion of interest, anyone who buys in the present 'slump' should do well. The heavy, ornate styles are not to everyone's taste, however, and, as in all areas of the market, the rule is not to buy unless you can live with pieces like the Victorian 'novelty' salt cellar stands cast in the form of turretted medieval keeps (£880 at Sotheby's in 1988), or the dumpy, melon-shaped teapot by Hart and Roskell with its leafy lid, handle and spout in the form of gnarled tree trunks, and pert little leaves acting as feet (£682 at the same sale). There is no guarantee that because they are cheap today, they will be expensive tomorrow, or even in 10 years' time.

WHAT DOES QUALITY MEAN?

After age come a host of factors determining the price of an item: rarity, provenance, quality – sculptural form, engraving, the manner of any other decoration – condition, and, most importantly, the silversmith and his mark (see below). Mostly these come together, for the good original pieces were always specially commissioned for grand houses from the best craftsmen, and tend to be well-documented; selling off the family silver has never been undertaken lightly, and sales have been mostly recorded.

Best of all are pieces associated with royalty, which fetch a premium partly out of snobbery and partly because the silver market is obsessed with fakes (see below) and nothing is safer than a piece commissioned from a royal collection. Items marked 'royal' can usually be expected to exceed their estimates in the saleroom – a set of eight George II candlesticks by John Perry, the square bases engraved with the royal arms of 1756, fetched £35,200 at Sotheby's in February 1988, for example, when an equivalent non-royal pair would have been unlikely to exceed £20,000. In the same sale, a pair of George II Hanoverian pattern serving spoons made by Charles Jackson in 1727, engraved with the contemporary royal cypher, fetched £6,600 against an estimate of £1,250-1,750. Although non-royal spoons would not have approached this price, collectors should beware of trusting saleroom estimates, which in this sector are especially conservative – perhaps a hangover from the days when silver was in the doldrums.

In other ways, too, the vagaries of fashion have not been kind to silver, and many elegant pieces which showed their age were melted down to be remodelled according to the latest styles. One who ought to have shown history more respect was George III, who in 1808 sent various 'dated'

pieces to the melting pot in order to meet the cost of new silver coveted by his extravagant son the Prince Regent. The silversmiths singled out for the crime, Rundell Bridge and Rundell, saved the day by secretly selling off the most important pieces, and would no doubt have been gratified to see one of them, a pair of wall sconces made for William III in 1700, offered for £400,000 in March 1987 at the dealer Spinks, only the second pair of wall sconces ever sold by an expert who had been there for 30 years.

A sadder story is that of the Chandos Testimonial, a magnificent if monstrous Victorian silver-gilt candelabrum adorned with silver figures and animals, which could also be turned into a centrepiece by replacing its 13 foliage branches with a wheatsheaf crest. One of the most spectacular centrepieces ever made, it was sold for £820 at Christie's in 1954 and was destroyed immediately after the sale, save for its figures and animals. The nine figures, three farmers and six labourers in sentimental Victorian rustic tradition, turned up at Sotheby's in 1988, and made £11,000.

It is impossible to know how many pieces that would be cherished by collectors today have over the past few centuries gone the same way, but the supply of fine early pieces is certainly diminishing, and over the next couple of decades this should push up prices. Less common items are already held at a premium – a run-of-the-mill George III coffee pot should fetch between £1,000 and £2,000 as against perhaps £500 for the more frequently seen teapot of comparable quality. Comparable tea caddies, rarer than either, should make £3-4,000. Items so rare that they are impractical should be avoided, however.

Also commanding a rarity premium are certain forms or embellishments current for very short periods. One is the chinoiserie ornamentation found on silver between 1680 and 1689, which is fervently collected and appreciating well. A delightful example surfaced in 1987 – a monteith bowl racing trophy divided into 10 panels depicting the course of the race it celebrated, with the winner receiving the bowl in the final panel. It was awarded to Edward Chute of the Vyne in 1688; his family sold it through a dealer in 1987 for £250,000. Five years earlier a very similar chinoiserie bowl, also highly decorative, sold for £52,000 at auction.

The silversmith

Purists sometimes date the decline of silver craftsmanship from the death of Paul de Lamarie, widely regarded as the greatest silversmith of all time, in 1751, and refuse to buy anything but Queen Anne, George I and George II pieces. It comes down to personal taste, of course, but one can see their point, for set against the heavy urns and pots of the George III epoch the delicacy of the earlier style is incomparable. By the time of George III, moreover, the silversmith Matthew Boulton was *en route* to production-line silverware, and was selling to fellow silversmiths ready-cast additions such as handles and legs to finish off otherwise completed pieces.

The premium commanded by the best craftsmen is another extraordinary feature of the silver market. Way ahead here is Paul de Lamerie, whose work can fetch up to 20 times the price for comparable pieces by contemporaries, and nearly always fetches twice as much. He is followed by Paul Storr, whose grand, sculptural qualities typify the Regency

Glittering connections: an inkstand made in 1792 by Paul de Lamerie fetched £770,000 at Christie's in December 1988. Only one other piece of silver, also by de Lamerie, has equalled the price.

The more affordable range, a pair of George III wine coolers, £19,800 at Christie's in December 1988.

elegance which is especially in demand among collectors in the United States and Latin America.

De Lamerie lived half a century earlier and was the leading exponent of the rococo sensuality which graced some of the finest homes of the 1740s. A de Lamerie épergne holds the record as the most expensive single piece of silver sold at auction – it fetched £770,000 at Christie's in December 1986. This record was only equalled in December 1988 by an inkstand made in 1729 by de Lamerie for Sir Robert Walpole. No eyebrows are raised, though, when a de Lamerie piece makes over £100,000 – a kettle, stand and lamp from the Patino collection made $220,000 in 1986, for example, and a fine cake basket was offered by Spink in October 1987 for £125,000. And though cake baskets, like fruit stands, are currently popular because of their decorative appeal, a good George II example by a contemporary of de Lamerie such as Edward Wakelin would be unlikely to exceed £30,000. And at Sotheby's in February 1988, a magnificent pair of wine coolers, with royal connections, on which the maker's mark of Paul de Lamerie was overstruck by that of Paul Crespin, fetched £462,000.

What de Lamerie has over his contemporaries is illustrated by two pieces in Sotheby's July 1988 sale, both George II coffee pots almost identical in weight and height and very similar in form. Both had elegant tapering bodies, finely sculpted leaf-wrapped spouts, and domed lids headed by cone finials. One, made by Gurney and Cooke in 1749, fetched £2,750. The other, made by de Lamarie five years earlier, had the sort of decoration that shoots a piece into another price league. Engraved with armorials and a crest, chased flowers and rocaille, it was even adorned with scrolls below the finial, and was a delicate, restrained example of a top Georgian coffee pot. It fetched £22,000, almost 10 times as much as the plainer piece, and it is easy to see that the prestige of the name was not the primary reason.

De Lamerie has driven all before him and because his top pieces are so exceptional, more average work has been carried along with it. Some dealers are beginning to fear that the market for his pieces is becoming saturated. With the decline of the dollar, Paul Storr pieces are spending longer than usual in dealers' shops, but the market for de Lamerie is large and international, and a falling off looks unlikely for some time. Nonetheless, the shrewd investor should look around for the work of contemporary makers, especially among the early eighteenth century Huguenot craftsmen, for names that might be tomorrow's giants. The trouble is that many excellent makers such as Nicholas Sprimont and Philip Garden just did not produce enough to be collectable or even recognisable. But there is plenty of research to be done in the silver market, and an abundance of signed pieces makes life easier.

Hallmarks

Hallmarks on silverware offer at once a protection for the buyer and a minefield of temptations to the forger, for clear makers' marks and dates go a long way in establishing high prices, and potential profits here are so enormous that the potential punishment – a jail sentence, since interfering with hallmarks is illegal – does not always deter. The following list of hallmarks tells you what to look for, but the art of the forger can often overcome years of expertise. If you have any doubts about a piece, you can have it checked by the Assay Office at Goldsmiths Hall, the ultimate authority not only for marking all new silver but also for detecting fakes. This service is free.

In examining pieces, buyers should look for four essential hallmarks:

1. *The leopard's head* This is the sign that a piece is 'sterling' silver. As pure silver is too soft to be worked into objects, it has always been alloyed with a harder metal. The proportion of pure silver in the alloy was set at 92.5 per cent by Edward I in 1300, and this definition of sterling silver has remained unchanged except for a brief period (1697-1720) when the proportion was 95.8 per cent. On silver from this period, a lion's head in profile is substituted for the leopard's head.

2. *The maker's mark* This usually takes the form of the initials of the silversmith. Many silversmiths employed large numbers of assistants, and their mark simply means that the piece is from their workshop and had passed their 'quality control'. In contrast to most of the fine and decorative arts, there is no way of distinguishing between the work of a master smith and his assistants.

3. *The date letter* Since 1478, a 20-year cycle has been used, following the alphabet but omitting i and v-z. Each cycle has a different style of letter and surround.

4. *The 'lion passant'* The exact form of this has evolved over the centuries. He was introduced in full frontal view in 1544, but in 1822 he was redesigned in profile as a 'lion passant'. On silver from 1697-1720 he is replaced by the figure of a Britannia standard.

Other marks to look for are those of some provincial assay offices, and from 1784-1890, the mark of the monarch's head, indicating that duty had been paid on a piece. One curious result of this is that a piece from 1890 tends to be marginally more valued than a similar one from 1891, as collectors of Victorian silver like the mark of the Queen.

Paying duty was the bane of a silversmith's life, and 'duty dodging' was his way of diminishing the cost by transposing the hallmarks from a small piece on which duty had been paid to a larger piece on which it hadn't. Very respectable silversmiths indulged in this practice, but until recently it was illegal to sell 'duty dodgers' unless they were re-hallmarked. In deference to the quality of some of these pieces, the law was changed and antique duty dodgers (those over 100 years old) can now be sold legally.

Also sold legally, but greatly to be avoided, are pieces which have been 'embellished' by subsequent generations. Eighteenth century mugs or tankards often became nineteenth century jugs, while the eighteenth century épergne was sometimes divided and resold as several sweetmeat baskets. Goblets have also turned up as sweetmeat baskets, and sugar basins as teapots. In most of these cases – and there are numerous others – something about the proportions will look inherently suspicious, the hallmarks will be odd, or signs of repair, like rough soldering where a later piece has been attached, will give the game away, but problems of authenticity partly explain why many buyers prefer to leave the risks to dealers. It is almost never worth buying a piece that is repaired or worn.

One advantage of collecting silver is that once you have bought a piece in good condition, it is not especially easy to damage and unlikely to smash.

The only risk comes from over-cleaning; all silver needs is to be washed in warm soapy water, rinsed and dried with a soft cloth. If you can't face regular polishing, stick to silver-gilt pieces, which need less care.

SMALL PIECES

In its forecast of saleroom trends for 1988, published at the beginning of the year, Phillips placed silver in fourth place as the 'market choice for 1988'. Items considered most underpriced were early spoons and vinaigrettes, and it could be in small pieces that new collectors might begin. A selection of items such as Stilton scoops and grape scissors would make an interesting collection, and many such pieces can be picked up very cheaply. Vinaigrettes and snuffboxes have had chequered careers recently, rising to unexpected heights in 1985, but falling away since. They mostly fall into the £250-350 range. Wine-related pieces are also modestly priced, and have been doing better. Corkscrews and coasters form a substantial body of this sector; wine labels can start as cheaply as £40 for a single item, rising to over £2,000 for a George III set by a well-known maker.

At all levels of the silver market, usefulness, especially at the dinner table, ensures popularity, which is partly why the 'coffee pots and candlesticks' market has stayed alive. There is much here at under £2,000, but no guarantee that it will move fast or high. Silver cutlery may be appropriate here. In general, cheap, matched sets by big names like Paul Storr can cost up to £50,000, and should be a safe investment. For at the lower levels, antique silver shares with antique furniture that curious relationship to equivalent modern reproductions – much cheaper to buy, at the lower end, it is much more valuable once you have bought it. And though this lower range may not appreciate, everyone has to buy cutlery, and pieces from the saleroom will certainly be worth more than what instantly becomes mere secondhand tableware from the local department store.

MODERN SILVER

If your research takes you forward rather than back in time, you might want to gamble on modern silver, which is just beginning to establish a presence in the saleroom. All the twentieth century decorative arts are undergoing a boom at the moment, and look set to go much higher. Concentrate on fine design and well-known makers, but be prepared to pay over the odds. A five piece octagonal tea and coffee set made by Aspreys in the 1970s fetched £5,060 (estimate £2-3,000) at Sotheby's in 1988. Silver sales, sales of twentieth century decorative arts, and markets and antique fairs, are good places to look. Some dealers sneer at modern pieces, so the private buyers may face less competition. For Georgian silver, though, a dealer is recommended in this trade-heavy market, unless you are very sure of yourself.

11 BOOKS

> A book's a book, although there's nothing in't.
> Byron, *English Bards and Scotch Reviewers*

The language of the book collector sounds like a secret code to the mere book lover. Take some of the catalogue entries from Sotheby's major sale in June 1988: 'printed on vellum, large printer's device on title, woodcuts . . . every page within a border, initials supplied in gold on blue or terracotta panels, eighteenth century red morocco, gilt border, spine gilt in compartments, blue endpapers . . .' is part of the description of a sixteenth century Book of Hours that fetched £3,300. 'First edition, half-title, drophead title with ornamental headpiece, contemporary ownership inscription, occasionally slightly discoloured or spotted, uncut, original marbled wrappers, slightly rubbed, small portions of the spine torn away' identifies a first edition of Cantillon's *Essai sur la nature de commerce en général*, which made £8,800; a second edition, printed a year later, made £2,200. And William Hooker's *Exotic Flora*, which made £1,760, includes '233 hand-coloured engraved plates, some double-page or folding, some slightly trimmed affecting captions, slight soiling, tear in fold of plate 173, repair to last leaf of text in volume III, half-title in volume II only . . . .'.

These titles represent three of the strongest areas of book collecting – early printed books, economics and botany. Their buyers, if they were at all typical of the book collecting breed, will have been fuelled by a double passion: the love of a particular area of learning and the love of books as fine objects. Contemporary bindings, hand-coloured illustrations, the type of printing, the presence of an apparently insignificant initial blank page or half-title, are all important when a book is valued for more than its contents. A book collector instantly recognises signs of quality and desirability – uncut edges, for example – and also poor condition – leaves worn or frayed at the edges, missing pages – in the same way as a silver collector makes a beeline for the marks that confirm the history and authenticity of a piece. For the book lover to become a successful book collector, he has to key into a whole new way of viewing what the Duke of Gloucester once accused Edward Gibbon of writing – 'another damned thick square book'.

BOOKS AS AN INVESTMENT

'Damned thick square books' have been a flourishing collectors' market for centuries, and represent one of the most stable of alternative investments. With the exception of twentieth century first editions, which hit rock bottom in 1931 (when they were a much 'newer' market than they are now), rare books survived the 1929 stock market crash virtually unscathed, and apart from a few dips in the demand for middle and lower range books, the market has remained buoyant since 1987's Black Monday too.

There is a tradition going back even to the time when books were rare luxuries that acquiring books is an unworldly pastime; one remembers Chaucer's Clerke of Oxenford who would rather have 'at his beddes heed/ twenty bokes, clad in blak or reed/Of Aristotle and his philosophye/than robes riche, or fithele, or gay sautrye.' There is still something of that mood among collectors today, and a few flamboyantly ignore the investment element – one collector of modern firsts, for example, throws away the dust jackets which can make a tenfold difference to the price because he finds reading a book in its jacket inconvenient.

As in any market, the official line from the Antiquarian Booksellers Association (ABA) is to discourage book collecting purely for investment purposes, but over the past decade prices have risen so fast that private collectors have been forced to regard an enjoyable hobby in a more serious light, and the ABA admitted in a 1981 newsletter that 'of course the true collector still buys a book because he wants it, but it is probable that both he and his bookseller are more aware of its price and its potential future price than they would have been even 10 years ago'.

The price of a book is determined by its rarity, its historical interest, its condition and its subject matter. Fashion for collecting areas comes in fits and starts, but the best books in all categories always hold their own, and it is these that have seen the greatest appreciation.

The importance of condition

As prices rise, condition becomes increasingly important in all areas of the rare book market. Ideally, a book should be as close as possible to its condition when first published, no matter whether an incunabulum (a book published in the early days of printing, before 1501) or a modern book, have its original binding, and be absolutely complete – the absence of even a blank leaf at the beginning is a disaster – and with no markings other than by the author; a former owner's name is detrimental to prices.

Foxing – reddish-brown spots – comes with age and some light foxing must be expected. Browning is more pervasive and ugly and is usually the result of exposure to damp; it will seriously reduce the value of a book. It is important to keep books away from areas which may flood (ie not on a shelf directly underneath the bathroom) and also out of direct sunlight and not near a radiator; frequent temperature changes will cause them to expand and contract, which can be ruinous.

Some dealers use three broad standards to define condition – good (to describe a reasonable secondhand copy with no serious defects), nice (above average) and fine ('particularly fresh, clean and sound', according to Bertram Rota's catalogue). A nice copy of a title can fetch up to twice the price of a good one, and a fine copy three times as much. Beware 'reading' or 'working' copies – their condition is too poor for them to be viable investments.

The prospects for the market

In most sectors of the book market, with too many people chasing too little stock, prices look set to rise. The only cloud on the horizon is that institutional buying, by libraries and universities, once a mainstay of this market and the delight of dealers from whom they bought almost in bulk, has been down over the past 10 years because of cuts in education budgets, and is likely to diminish further. Endowment funds of American universities particularly tend to be tied into the stock markets, and some have been substantially weakened. But this decline should only accelerate an existing trend, and during the last decade dealers have been busy cultivating new private buyers, who have now matured (they hope) into seasoned rare book lovers. And for the collector, one advantage of books finding a new home in a private collection is that they may well surface again; once a rare book disappears into a university library, it goes, like a painting bought by a museum, more or less out of circulation.

With rare books becoming rarer, there has been a decrease in the number of sales at the leading auction houses in the last 10 to 15 years. But there are still several major sales a year at Sotheby's, Christie's and Phillips, with monthly general sales of lower quality works supplementing these. In June important specialist sales are held to coincide with the Antiquarian Booksellers Association fair in London. The specialist book auction house of Bloomsbury also holds between eight and 10 auctions a year.

How to purchase

If you are building up a collection, your best bet is to scour the salerooms, tell their experts of your interests, and to get in touch with the specialist dealers in your field, putting your name on as many dealers' mailing lists as possible. Saleroom catalogues are always an interesting market indicator, and most dealers issue several catalogues a year, though as little as 10 per cent of their stock may appear in the catalogue. Many books are sold between their acquisition by the dealer and the printing of his next catalogue, and several are swallowed up by 'wants lists', by which a customer gives a list of books especially wanted, which the dealer will then look out for. Nevertheless, catalogues contain many excellent items and the prices are a useful guide to the value of your own collection. Some entries are restricted to author, title, and date of edition; others will give extensive details of condition, any illustrations or plates, and the size – folio (fol.), quarto (4to) or octavo (8vo). With good cataloguing by reliable dealers, it is possible to buy safely by post; a good dealer will take back any book that has been inaccurately described or is discovered to be defective.

Handbooks (see Bibliography) give information on specialist areas covered by dealers. As in any field, there is the odd shark, but the Antiquarian Booksellers Association has fairly stringent entry requirements (nominations by four existing members of several years standing, evidence of satisfactory trading and accounts, no record of complaints), and its 250 members should be reliable.

Along with its annual fair in London, the ABA also organises one other fair of international interest each year, which takes place either in Bath, Cambridge or Edinburgh. The Provincial Book Fair Association is easier to join, and some provincial book fairs resemble penny bazaars where the unwitting can lose heavily, though if you are very quick you may spot a bargain. Unless you are extraordinarily lucky, browsing in secondhand bookshops won't make you a fortune, but buying the best copies you can afford from the salerooms, if you feel confident enough, or from dealers, should be safe and lucrative.

THE HISTORY OF IDEAS

'Learning hath gained most by those books by which the printers have lost', lamented the seventeenth century historian Thomas Fuller, but he would have been gratified to see a few centuries on, in the antiquarian book market at least, a huge following for scientific and medical literature, books on botany and natural history, economic and philosophical treatises, and historical and literary texts.

Every field of learning has its book collector, and for collectors and investors alike, the wisest way of amassing a collection is to concentrate on a subject that interests you, for recent sales have demonstrated that what the market most values are books from good specialist private collections. The specialist areas covered in this chapter are a mere handful from the numerous collecting possibilities, and collectors may already have specialist areas of their own in mind, or may be drawn to those in dealers' or salerooms' catalogues. Scholarly tastes, a love of books as historical objects, as decorative objects, or simply a love of literature, can inspire a collection, and libraries can be formed round the widest of subjects – continental literature, for example, or children's books, which is one of the strongest fields – or the narrowest, such as angling or cookery books.

Botany and natural history

Sotheby's sale of colour plate books from the library of Robert de Belder in 1987 proves the case for specialisation. A distinguished horticulturalist, Robert de Belder conceived his library, according to Sotheby's, as an historical adjunct to the development of the botanical garden, and the sale included around 400 of the finest botanical books available. It was a massive international affair in which telephone bidders battled it out with London and foreign dealers, and the total fetched £5.9m, almost twice the upper estimate.

The top seller was Besler's *Hortus Eystettensis* of 1613, which in 1981 had been bought for £90,300. In the intervening six years it went up nearly seven times in price to fetch £605,000, breaking the auction record for a botanical book. It was one of the very few copies to retain its brilliant contemporary colouring, and an example of how buying the best you can afford, even if it seems overpriced at the time, usually pays off.

Among other high prices at the sale were a large paper copy of L'Heritier de Brutelle, *Stirpes novae* (1784-91), with coloured illustrations (£107,800; £46,200 in 1979), and Prevost's *Collection des fleurs et des fruits* from 1805 with 48 coloured plates (£154,000; £28,600 in 1979). The most popular botanical book ever, Thornton's *The Temple of Flora* (1799-1807) made £187,000 – £100,000 more than its previous record. A copy with late issues of the plates sold in 1976 for just £2,200, showing the importance of original condition, as well as the sudden rise of the colour plate book after a slump from the late 1970s until 1984.

Like botany, natural history books have an obvious and direct appeal, and are also buoyant. Probably the most famous colour plate book of all is

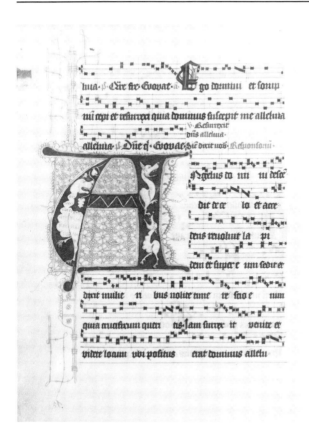

The upper end of the market in antiquarian books: a page from a Latin antiphonal, 1430, m/s on vellum, bound in contemporary pig skin. (£33,000 at Christie's in December 1988).

John James Audubon's *Birds of America* (1827-38). The record for the very rare complete book is $1.7m, but book collectors are not accustomed to paying those sorts of prices, and a copy was bought in in 1987 at £520,000. More reasonably, much is available, even in sales of important and valuable printed books, at around £2,000, and prices of around £200 are common at general sales.

Science and medicine

Scientific and medical books are valued by collectors for their historical importance rather than their decorative subject matter, and seminal works fetch the highest prices. Even here, though, condition matters very much. One of the most revolutionary medical texts, for example, is Vesalius' *De Humani Corporis Fabrica* (1543). An exceptional first edition has made £44,000; in 1986 one in very good condition made £27,500, while in 1987 a less fine, but still good, copy of the first edition was £18,700.

By the nature of their subject, early medical books have a limited appeal, and first editions of some early classics can still be found in good condition for surprisingly low prices. In 1987 Sotheby's sold Estienne's *De Dissectione Partium Corporis Humani* (1545), the first work to include illustrations of the nervous system, for £7,150, and classic works on the kidney (Malphighi's *De Viscerum Structura* of 1666) and the ear (Valsalva's

De Aure Humana of 1704) for £2,750 and £2,420 respectively. Even more cheaply came, in much less good condition, medical works in the general sale – a first edition of Boulton's 1713 *A System of Rational and Practical Chirurgery* was £165 in 1988, and someone with a sense of humour perhaps bought a later edition of a seventeenth century work, *The English Midwife Enlarged* for £49. This is an area which offers plenty of scope for the new collector. Prices have shown a steady though not especially exciting rise.

Economics and philosophy

Economics and philosophy both have their following as collecting fields, the former particulary popular among Japanese buyers, and both are showing strong rises in price due to the paucity of good original works on the market. English writers in demand include Hume (*Treatise of Human Nature* was £6,050 in 1987), Locke (*Essay on Human Understanding* made £6,240) and Adam Smith (£8,360 for *An Inquiry into the Nature and Causes of the Wealth of Nations*).

When rare well-known works do appear, they command outstanding prices and regularly outstrip estimates – the second edition of *The Communist Manifesto*, of which only seven copies are known and none are in the British Library, the Bibliothèque Nationale or the Library of Congress, made £30,800 in 1988 – but less famous early classics which are also scarce remain affordable. A second edition of Malthus' *Principles of Political Economy* was just £858 in 1988, and it will probably always be overshadowed by his more important work on population; while Ricardo's rare and influential *On the Principles of Political Economy and Taxation* made £958. Given the scarcity of good books in this area, fine works in nice condition should appreciate well.

TRAVEL LITERATURE

Colour plate books are now buoyant, and this makes travel literature, a massive sector taking in atlases and maps, an interesting area with plenty to offer the new buyer.

Travel books have always been popular, and there are a great many of them around in sales of both general and important books. As topographical literature derives much of its appeal from illustrations and maps, fresh bright plates and general good condition are the most important features, and can add huge premiums to prices. Sebastian Munster's *Cosmographia*, a magnificent work printed in Basle in 1628 containing lavish double-page woodcut maps, seldom fetches more than £2,000 at auction but Sotheby's sold an exceptionally good copy in 1988, including the often-missing engraved title, for £4,620.

Prices start at under £100, although this is unlikely to get you anything very lavish, but in the £100-500 range there is an enormous choice, and this price puts collectors within reach of some fine eighteenth century titles. The salerooms often lot up cheaper works together, and it is possible to come away with several volumes, not necessarily first editions, for under £200.

At the upper end of the market, top prices are fetched by exceptionally fine copies of rare and important works, especially early texts which were the product of unusual and rather daring voyages. Very sought after among English aquatint views is Chamberlain's 1822 *Views of Rio de Janeiro* (£48,400 in 1987), while Karl Bodmer's *Travels in the Interior of North America*, with 81 partly hand-coloured aquatints, made £121,000. It was the result of a journey made through the west of America just before the mass migration of settlers irrevocably changed the life and culture of the American Indian, and was thus a unique record.

Maps

Cousins of the travel book, and appearing in the same sales, are maps and atlases. Portolan maps, charts of the sea made by Italian navigators, are the rarest and command enormous prices. In December 1987 Christie's sold a Portolan atlas, produced in Venice in 1544, for £660,000, an auction record for an atlas. That, however, was exceptional, and a lot of historically important maps still seem cheap, and even the £55,000 paid at Sotheby's in 1987 for the *Rudimentum Novitiorum* of 1475 did not seem excessive for a rare copy of the earliest work to contain proper maps.

Like topographical paintings, the popularity of a map depends on the wealth of the present inhabitants of the area it depicts. Early maps of America, not surprisingly, are in huge demand, while maps of remote country areas of France sell for around £50, even if they are the work of the highly skilled sixteenth and seventeenth century cartographers. This is the bottom end of the market, and many a beautiful map passes through the salerooms for under £100. Their investment performance has not been encouraging – as well as oversupply, in part the fault of dealers who break up atlases they cannot sell complete into individual maps, early maps have particular problems of authenticity in relation to the colourists who were employed to hand colour them at extra charge – but their highly decorative appeal suggests that they are an area to watch.

Architecture and design

Architecture and design is a topography-related newish area which the new buyer might consider. Prices have surged ahead recently, with, for example, Kips' *Britannia Illustrata* (1707), a much sought after record of English house and garden design, making £3,960 in June 1987 at Sotheby's and £7,150 in the autumn. But this is so young a market that there is not much of a track record, so it is one for the speculator rather than the steady investor.

INCUNABULA AND EARLY PRINTED BOOKS

Such is the power of the printed word, and the mystique surrounding the *early* printed word, that there will always be collectors willing to pay a premium for a book simply because it is old. The downside of collecting fifteenth (incunabula) and sixteenth century books is that you have little choice of content; the bonus is that there are still books available at under £1,000, which seems extraordinary.

Age, fine condition and contemporary bindings are of paramount importance here, and determine the price of the early bibles, books of hours and scholastic treatises that make up this market. Price ranges are so vast that any list is really a case of 'comparing apples and pears': they range in price from, in 1987 and 1988, £176 for a Dutch bible printed in Antwerp in 1566 or £528 for the Gospels printed in Basle in 1519, to $5m for half a Gutenburg bible. But at the top end, appreciation is rapid: in 1988 the dealer Maggs paid £238,000 at auction for a seventeenth century Oxford University Press bible which had cost just £560 in 1945.

Historical importance and rarity play their part. The only known copy of the official issue of the Edict of Worms, *Der Romanischen Kaiserliche Maiestät Edict wider Martin Luthers Bücher*, a cornerstone in the history of the Reformation, and, as the first printed ban on specific works, a landmark in the history of book censorship, made £55,000 in 1988. Poor old Henry VIII's efforts at altering the course of history were obviously considered a lot less important, and a rare work printed for his eyes alone by Cardinal Pole fetched a mere £1,980 in the same sale. In 1987 Henry VIII's own copy, with the Royal Library pressmark, of Theodorus II's *Codex* (Basle 1528) in a contemporary London binding was £2,860. As the supply of works from the fifteenth and sixteenth centuries inevitably diminishes, especially the best bindings, such works should be a good investment, although it is not for nothing that anyone trying to read them in the British Library has to observe special rules and restrict themselves to special reading rooms. These are the most difficult books to store and maintain, and they suffer greatly from changes in temperature and atmosphere.

ENGLISH LITERATURE AND MODERN FIRSTS

This is at once one of the most accessible markets and the one which puts the essence of book collecting on the line. Those who shy away from the scholarly are immediately drawn to it, yet most of the books here, and especially the well-known top sellers which are endlessly reprinted, are available for a fraction of the price in paperback. You have to be devoted to the importance of the first edition, its original condition and its place and history in the market to be successful in this sector, which at present is still more a domain for the collector than for the investor.

One important attribute for the collector is a good memory for worthwhile and rare books. Behind many of the most prized first editions from all centuries lies a story. If you possess an 1865 copy of *Alice in Wonderland*, for example, you are sitting on one of the few copies of the first edition not withdrawn by its illustrator, Tenniel, who was dissatisfied with the way the illustrations had turned out. One of the rarest modern firsts is Anthony Powell's *What's Become of Waring*, so scarce that a joke question among collectors is 'what's become of *What's Become of Waring*?'. Published in 1939, it sold only 1,000 copies before the warehouse in which stocks were kept was destroyed by the Blitz. It is now highly desirable and over the past few years the price of an average copy has doubled from £125 to around £250; with a jacket, it costs nearer £2,000. And if the Blitz put *What's Become of Waring* on the book collector's map, the Great Fire of London is responsible for the premium prices now paid for Shakespeare's Third Folio. Published in 1665, few had sold by the time of the Great Fire in 1666, and most perished in the warehouse.

Occasionally, charred copies turn up. Much rarer than the earlier Second Folio, which sells for around £50,000 and would otherwise be more expensive, a Third Folio fetches closer to £80,000.

Every collector of literature wants fine early editions of Shakespeare and Chaucer, but these are extremely scarce and very expensive. Good first editions from the sixteenth and seventeenth centuries are rare and expensive, and even the eighteenth century does not offer collectors of literature a vast range of work. Maybe because the best is so seldom available, prices here are slow to move, and the market is unpredictable; maybe the laws of supply and demand have a bearing, and the second-best is good enough. But this is not an obvious area for the new buyer.

Nineteenth century literature is a steadier market, with enough interesting books available to stimulate collectors but supply limited by the short print runs common before the twentieth century. Before 1900, a print run of 1,000 copies would have been considered lavish; Fielding's *Amelia* had an exceptionally large print run of 5,000 – copies are available at around £100-200 – but for obscure authors like 'Ellis Bell' a print run of 300 was average; *Wuthering Heights* is now one of the most sought after of all first editions. Literary reputation and rarity are responsible in about equal measure.

Classic novelists like Thackeray, Trollope, Dickens, Jane Austen, and from the eighteenth century, Fielding – *Pamela* is considered to be the first novel in English – and Defoe should always remain popular, and prices are by no means exorbitant, with first editions still to be found in the £100s, though exceptional examples may be several thousand pounds. Buyers may be attracted to this area because condition, though important, is relatively less so for nineteenth and twentieth century works because the quality of the paper, compared to that of earlier centuries, is anyway inferior, and so expectations are reduced.

Modern firsts

Twentieth century first editions – 'modern firsts' – are the obvious choice for the literary punter, who has one advantage over even the publisher: time is on his side for, under no pressure to make a quick profit, he can back his judgement and then bide his time until posterity proves him right. This is an ideal market for the new collector because it requires less specialist knowledge and much less cash to start with than most other fields.

Most modern first editions have a long way to go before managing even three or four figure sums. Good modern literature, though, is bound to go from strength to strength; the problem is deciding what is good, for critical reassessments can play havoc with values in this vibrant, changeable market. This makes works from the first part of the twentieth century obviously more stable, for steady prices over decades are clearly more reliable than spectacular leaps. William Faulkner's *Absalom, Absalom* (1936), for example, was already changing hands for £40 at a charity sale in aid of the Republicans in the Spanish Civil War; by 1963 it sold for £6,000 at auction – a rise of 5,000 per cent – and it would be worth twice that today. By contrast, D M Thomas's novel *The White Hotel*, a bestseller when first published in 1981 at £9.95, was fetching £300 in 1983, but by 1987 it was difficult to sell for £25.

One way of minimising such risks is simply to buy favourite authors at publishers' prices as they appear in the bookshops. Antiquarian book-sellers are often prepared to order new books for you, and occasionally a new copy of a work finds its way into a catalogue at the retail price – usually there is a reason, which might hint at potential investment value. George V Higgins' thriller *Outlaws* (1987), for example, appeared in the 1987 catalogue of the leading London dealer in modern firsts, Bertram Rota, at the retail price of £10.95, with a note that it preceded the American edition, for which textual changes were made. Most such purchases will become mere secondhand copies worth rather less than you paid for them, but a few should start to rise in value.

The early works of most well-established living writers – the household names of fiction – sell at a modest premium on publishers' prices. A Bertram Rota catalogue in 1987, for instance, included Iris Murdoch (£40 for *The Bell*), John Braine (£40 for *Room at the Top*), Anthony Powell (£35 for *Casanova's Chinese Restaurant*), Richard Adams (£30 for the first American edition of *Watership Down*), and poets Seamus Heaney and Ted Hughes, whose work is steadily increasing in price.

Once a living writer's reputation looks like being established beyond doubt, prices can go much higher; the first edition of Graham Greene's *The Power and the Glory* made £308 at auction in 1988, and a presentation copy – always held at a premium – of the first edition of *Stamboul Train* was £1,100.

These sorts of prices are more often fetched by the dead – Lawrence's *Twilight in Italy* was £385 in 1988, and a signed limited edition of *Women in Love* made £1,210. A very good seller is the rare first edition of *Ulysses* – £2,750 in 1988.

Salerooms also sell less expensive modern firsts, and these tend to be lotted up in job lots and can be cheaper than prices in an average second hand bookshop. At one of Sotheby's monthly general booksales in 1988, a collection of 101 volumes, mostly first editions, by Huxley, Hartley, Shaw, the Sitwells, Somerset Maugham and others, fetched £143, while a collection of 99 volumes of modern poets including Spender, Walter de la Mare and Housman was £110. Such bulk buying is not foolproof, however, and buyers should look carefully at the condition to spot missing pages and other defects.

Lesser known writers, for example the American surrealist Robert Coover, are just beginning to be collected, and come cheap – £15 for his *Pricksongs and Descants* in 1987 – while the new names in poetry are James Fenton and Andrew Motion, whose first volume of poetry was only published in the 1970s but is already selling at a premium. Tipsters are suggesting Peter Ackroyd as the next highly collectable novelist, but the popularity of his clever but artificial historical novels could be a passing phase. Other up-and-coming names include Bruce Chatwin and Ian McEwan.

But the joy of this business is backing your own horse, bearing in mind also that a host of other factors, only indirectly (if at all) related to the quality of the text or the reputation of its author, come into play to influence prices. Literary merit is certainly not everything; one theory runs that nostalgia money is a big factor: as with pop memorabilia, popular works or those loved in childhood become more expensive when their former fans reach the height of their spending powers. This would explain the rapid rise and fall of G A Henty in book collecting circles, and may be a reason to be wary of prices in the £100 range now being asked for first editions of P G Wodehouse.

Scarcity is a better tried and tested factor. Broadly, an author's early work tends to be rarer and therefore worth more. In most cases, the author was less well known early in his career, so print runs were smaller and fewer people bothered to preserve their copies, which, moreover, have had more time to get lost or damaged. For the modern first collector, the first volume of a set is almost always the bugbear to track down. The first of A A Milne's *Pooh Quartet*, *When We Were Very Young* (1924), is worth many times as much as all the other volumes – it sold for £440 in 1987. The same is true of Ian Fleming's *Casino Royale*, which had a print run of only 1,000 in 1955, in relation to the other James Bond books. The rule is not universal however; early works by Kipling, for instance, are not at all scarce as he achieved fame quickly, and are therefore no more valuable than his later books.

Meanly, first editions, especially if they are inscribed, by authors who died young are generally more valuable (the authors had less time to publish or to sign). Nostalgia, or necrophily, often leads to a rise in price immediately after an author has died, but when the obituaries and eulogies stop flowing, prices can sink again, reviving with later, steadier critical acclaim or a place on a university syllabus. Longevity, conversely, does not help – prices for Samuel Beckett, aged over 80, have been static for years.

An autograph by the author makes a book less common, and should push up the price, though here again there are no hard and fast rules. Some writers – often those achieving great fame or popularity in their lifetime – were very liberal with their signatures; inscribed novels by H E Bates, who indulged in frequent signing sessions at Hatchards bookshop, are less valuable than those by Graham Greene, who is not so generous. A simple signature or a signature with the words 'inscribed for X', as T S Eliot used to write when asked to sign, is always worth less than a more personal incription, and there is nothing to say the signed limited editions now being offered by publishers of works by their best known authors – £50 for a signed edition of J G Ballard's *The Day of Creation*, as against £10.95 normal retail price, from Gollancz in 1987, for example – will hold their value. Some presentation copies, however, are hugely valuable. John Fowles' *The Collector*, the novel with which he made his name in 1963, is worth £300 in mint condition with the original dust jacket, but a copy inscribed to the artist Fred Uhlman, 'with my compliments – and hopes that the "lecture" on art are not too implausible – John Fowles January 1964', pushes the price up to £450.

One extraordinary and famous point about modern firsts is that with a dust jacket a book can cost up to 30 times as much as it would without one, making the jacket, ludicrously, more expensive than the book itself. The increase, of course, depends on the rarity of the jacket, but for some books it is striking. A dust jacket for Kenneth Graham's *The Wind in the Willows*, a rare and popular collectors' item, would quadruple an average first edition price of between £350 and £500. A jacketless *Brighton Rock*, by

Graham Greene, is available for around £100; with a jacket, the price rockets to between £2,000 and £3,000. As for *The Adventures of Sherlock Holmes*, only one copy in a dust jacket has ever come on the market, and the American dealer Mark Himes asked $10,000 for it.

MANUSCRIPTS

At Sotheby's sale of English literature and history books in December 1987, lot 46, a collection of 126 volumes by or relating to John Buchan, many first editions and some signed, fetched £660, an average of just over £30 a volume. Lot 47 was the typescript of Buchan's last novel, *Sick Heart River*, with extensive autograph revisions, and fetched £4,400.

This goes to show that while a book collector of modest means can hope to own, in editions of varying value, works of great literary or historic interest, prices for equivalent manuscripts tend to soar beyond the average collector's reach. Because there is only ever one of them in existence, even a modern manuscript can cost a fortune – Sotheby's sold an admittedly exceptional one, the 1912 manuscript of Einstein's theory of relativity, for £633,244, double its estimate, in New York in December 1987, while in 1988 the manuscript of Kafka's *The Trial* made £1.1m, a record for a twentieth century literary work. But for anyone who can afford them, manuscripts are a very buoyant alternative investment.

The much publicised PEN sale of manuscripts in 1987, in which living writers donated manuscripts and other material to raise money for PEN's Writers in Prison Fund, was a good marker of modern literary reputations, and collectors of modern firsts as well as of manuscripts will have picked up some hints. Top seller was the working papers of some Seamus Heaney poems (£2,640); next came drafts of Roald Dahl's screen version of *You Only Live Twice*, the James Bond story by Ian Fleming (£2,640). Ayckbourn's typescript for *A Small Family Business* was £385, Anita Brookner's autograph manuscript of part of *A Friend from England*, with astonishingly few corrections, was £770, and Margaret Drabble's working papers for *Realms of Gold* fetched £1,100, suggesting that buyers should snap up any new novels that appear by either writer. A Graham Greene signed first edition was £330, and a typed draft of P D James' thriller *A Taste for Death* was £1,320. As at all charity auctions, the PEN sale prices may have been unrepresentatively high, and collectors should be able to find cheaper material elsewhere.

AUTOGRAPHS AND LETTERS

But if you hanker after the written as well as the printed word, collecting autographs and letters can be an affordable and lucrative alternative – a mere letter from Einstein would set you back £750, and if you had bought it 10 years ago, you would have made a tenfold profit, for then it cost just £75. Prices have risen considerably recently, but interesting items can still be found for as little as £20.

What determines the price of a document is its age, its historical importance and the status of its signatory. Royal and literary personages seem to have captured collectors' imaginations more than politicians – for example, a document signed by Elizabeth I, along with Mary Queen of

Scots the most popular of autographs, was £5,500 in 1987 (up from £1,500 in 1976) and worth double a letter from Cromwell to his cousin Anne, which sold in 1986 for £2,500. And while Byron's signature has increased in value six times over the last decade, to around £3,000, Winston Churchill has gone up from £120 to £750. As a general rule, letters in the hand of the dead are worth more than those by the living, for the supply is finite, but at the lower end of the market both historical and contemporary items can be found for between £30 and £40 – the price, for instance, of letters signed by both Edward Heath and Gladstone. Literary autographs are also available at this end of the market; a cheque signed by Tennyson would cost around £65, although a letter would be more.

Groups of papers and letters are of course more expensive. Three hundred and twenty pages of working drafts and correspondence relating to the Secret Treaty of Dover, Charles II's plan of 1670 to take Britain back to the Church of Rome, fetched £313,500 in 1987, while, more frivolously, a group of papers concerning Conan Doyle's involvement in the famous Cottingley Fairies hoax made £7,700. With single letters by famous names, sensational material will shoot up the price of a letter – one by Dickens was unearthed in 1987 in which the novelist recommended 'conveniences of *all kinds* at Margate (do you take me?) and I know where they live . . .'. It fetched £3,960. A collection of papers relating to the black entertainer Josephine Baker also sold for an astonishing £7,480, which just goes to show that there is always someone prepared to spend a lot of money on their hobby-horse. Investors should beware of a price like this, which depends on the whim of a few rich collectors; manuscripts with a solid historical or literary interests, the sort that would attract university libraries if they could afford them, are a safer bet, and less vulnerable to shifting reputations or popularity.

If you like trying your hand at talent spotting, you may consider collecting or even soliciting for free the signatures of the potentially famous! A more realistic form of cheap speculation is to scour the junk shops and secondhand bookshops for items like signed theatre programmes; such printed ephemera are also collectors' pieces in their own right. Even here, though, it pays to know who signed a little (for example Rudolf Valentino) and who signed a lot (for example Laurel and Hardy), and to assess prices accordingly. Christie's South Kensington hold specialist sales of this nostalgia area, which includes signed photographs by film stars and the royals (£150-£250 for Queen Elizabeth II; twice as much for Queen Victoria), and cheaper autograph letters. Here letters by several different hands – say, by eight different artists – are often combined into one lot and sold at around £100. Only one of these might be valuable in 10 years' time, but if prices continue to appreciate as they have done, it will be worth buying the whole lot for the investment potential of a single item. While no one would wish to waste their time 'forging' a rare book, forged autographs can be a problem. Often the age of the paper used gives the game away; if in doubt, dealers and saleroom experts should be able to advise.

One area which the salerooms consider underpriced are continental manuscripts and letters, and this could be an area to investigate, as the only reason for the discrepancy between these and homegrown material is that fewer English-speaking buyers have so far caught on. Letters by Claude

Monet sold in 1987 for between £605 and £990, which does not seem exorbitant, and it seems likely that had Jorge Luis Borges been English his 13 love letters would have gone higher than £6,500.

12 SCIENTIFIC INSTRUMENTS

Knowest thou the ordinances of heaven?
Canst thou set the dominion thereof in the earth?
Job XXXVIII: 31-33

Not everyone who collects scientific instruments understands how they work, but most would admit to some kind of metaphysical pleasure from the possession of a few landmarks in the history of knowledge. This is what spurs on most collectors; to the eternal chagrin of the experts, the intrinsic beauty of scientific instruments simply as fine objects has never been fully appreciated. As decorative as clocks, and possessing much the same attributes – beauty, sculptural qualities, age, the craftsmanship of master makers using the finest materials – they have never come anywhere near in price. Buyers remain a specialist band – 25 members started off the Scientific Instrument Society in 1983; now it numbers 450 – but if collectors of fine objects, especially of eighteenth century brass, ever realise what they are missing, prices could soar. At present, the stigma of utility means that fine, authentic pieces, although getting more expensive, are available at what still look, comparatively, like bargain prices.

But it has not always been so. In the eighteenth century, the rich and the royal developed something of a craze for the scientific instrument. George I appointed John Rowley 'Master of Mechanics', and some of the most beautiful instruments ever made were first used by royalty. Like the best silver pieces, the best instruments have impeccable provenances because they were always the preserve of the wealthy. But although they fetched kingly sums in their day, scientific instruments, unlike silver, were never recognised as collectors' pieces, and over the centuries interest declined. By the early nineteenth century, it had become anathema for something useful also to be beautiful, and as scientific instruments became more functional, makers ceased to bother about the fine engravings, the ivory and ebony fittings, that gave the instruments such decorative appeal. Harriet Wynter, one of the leading dealers, dates this sad decline around the end of the eighteenth century, and deals only in pieces up to 1830. Purely functional pieces from the nineteenth century have to be very rare or historically important to sell well.

INVESTMENT HISTORY

The nineteenth century attitude is more or less what plagues the market now. Museum buying, for example, is held up because technical institutions cannot stretch to decorative works of high quality while art museums would not consider buying technical objects.

Until the middle of this century, museum curators were often donated or left scientific instruments that they simply did not understand and never exhibited. Prices were derisory – 30 shillings (£1.50) for a pocket globe in the 1950s which would now fetch £1,500; £65 at Sotheby's in 1963 for a large planetarium which in 1988 made £4,180. Many were given away free, and the salerooms never held specialist sales; pieces were tacked on to the end of sales of clocks and barometers. In 1971, Harriet Wynter was the first dealer to exhibit at Grosvenor House showing only scientific instruments, and her customers would have been shocked at the idea of paying over £1,000. The £100,000 mark was finally passed at Sotheby's at the end of 1987, but much is still to be collected at under £1,000.

After some frenetic rises in the early 1980s, prices in some areas are levelling off, and there is scope for taking advantage of the temporary lull. In other areas, demand stays strong. As scientific instrument collectors are on the increase, so are the prices they are willing to pay, and buyers should be confident of continuing appreciation. At the top end of the market, where magnificent eighteenth century pieces would shine in the most gleaming collection of brass objects, there is a chance of a dramatic increase if the market ever widens to include collectors of more general decorative objects. The advent of the interior decorator has already broadened the collecting base to some extent, although they are catering for clients unlikely to want more than one example of any item.

Some scientific instruments are always going to be more accessible to the imagination than others, and prices reflect this. Sheer metaphysical appeal should keep a globe several thousand pounds ahead of a sextant, and though the absence of an astrolabe in a collection may torment a buyer, few will pine for a cupping and bleeding set.

GLOBES

Perhaps it is the boardroom Napoleons who fancy spinning a literal world at their fingertips that have pushed up prices for globes. Certainly most people can relate to a globe, and this area has seen very rapid appreciation in the first part of the 1980s.

The first globes were celestial spheres, and terrestrial counterparts only began to be produced in the sixteenth century. Most sought after today are the pairs of globes from the seventeenth and eighteenth centuries without which no self-respecting library of the time was complete. A good pair might cost around £20,000; in 1983 the going rate was £5,000, which today barely gets you a much less decorative, single globe from the nineteenth century. Pocket globes, increasingly favoured for their small size, are also bounding ahead; £500 in 1985, £1,500 is usual in 1988. They were all the rage in the eighteenth century, when leisured gentlemen pored over them in coffee houses as they discussed Captain Cook's latest trip.

Globes of any size costing less than £1,000 should be viewed suspiciously; if damaged, they are among the most difficult of all scientific instruments to repair. Even specialist paper restorers cannot cope with them, for as one dealer commented, 'if the paper has gone, how can you repair a bit of air?' But no scientific instrument was intended solely for decorative value, and some wear and tear, and therefore restoration, is inevitable. As early globes get rarer, even those in only moderately good condition can command high prices; one such pair made £8,800 at auction in 1988. Some dealers may recommend their own restorer, but it is worth bearing in mind that repairs to globes need to be especially sensitively done, and are expensive.

At auction globes come under the prosaic generic heading 'demonstrational apparatus', and their cousins in this category are also performing strongly. Best known are the armillary sphere, showing the universe according to Ptolemy, and the orrery, a model of the Copernican heliocentric system. A planetarium showing the relative motions of the sun and the planets was developed by George I's John Rowley for an earlier patron, the Earl of Cork and Orrery, in 1710. Early orreries in brass, silver and ivory have always been expensive; around £2,000 in the 1970s, a fine one can now make up to £35,000, and even a nineteenth century example, if it is in good condition, in its original box and with the maker's label, should fetch around £13,000. For most instruments, a trade label can add on a premium of around 20 per cent.

As the number of quality pieces from the seventeenth and eighteenth centuries coming on to the market declines, prices at auction are far outstripping estimates; one example in 1988 was a rare brass armillary sphere from the mid eighteenth century which Sotheby's had estimated at £6-10,000; it fetched £16,500.

INSTRUMENTS OF TIME

Dum licet, utere (while it is allowed, use it), is inscribed on a sundial in northern Italy, and it sums up something of the appeal of a dial or an astrolabe. If a globe reminds man of his cosmic insignificance, a dial bears witness to his mortality.

Sundials

An instrument which has marked the passing hours for centuries is bound to inspire a degree of metaphysical awe, and for many collectors a love of early time-measuring instruments is part of a wider astronomical and philosophical questioning. But these instruments also provide tangible evidence of how other periods and cultures recorded time, and, unlike globes, they don't damage easily. In fact, appropriately enough, they age well, developing a warm golden patina which serves to set off their fine engravings and calligraphic details to better advantage than ever. A variety of styles and geometrically imaginative devices make early dials a collector's paradise, and it is usual for them to fetch the highest prices at a scientific instrument sale.

But then they were always the preserve of the rich, who spared no expense in commissioning them. George I, for instance, used to make his stately progress home to Hanover accompanied by an ornate portable dial which told him the correct time at each town he passed through. One of the first dials to show the minutes (in Arabic numerals) as well as the hours (in Roman figures) was a royal example, one of George I's silver and gilt brass ring dials, engraved with the heads of fantastic beasts and a mask of putti on both faces, which sold at Sotheby's in 1987 for £68,200.

Another well-connected example, this time with imperial associations, was an eighteenth century French brass equinoctial crescent dial by

Baradelle, which was among the treasures taken by Napoleon's Chief of Police 'Comte Real' when he emigrated to America after the fall of the Empire. The dial was kept in the 'Cup and Saucer House' built by the optimistic count to harbour Napoleon should he escape from St Helena. It survived when the house was burnt down, and sold at Christie's South Kensington for £14,300 in 1988.

The end for these spectacular instruments came not with the development of the clock or watch but with the adoption of national, and later universal, time. The great age of dialling began in the sixteenth century and remained strong right through the eighteenth. The earliest collectable instruments are sundials made in Augsburg and Nuremburg at the start of the sixteenth century, and it is the rare early examples which are most sought after.

The most expensive scientific instrument ever sold at auction is a very rare gilt brass and silver combined astronomical compendium and bookbinding, made by Erasmus Habermel in Prague in 1597 and combining astronomical tables with a silver compass. It exceeded its £40-60,000 estimate to make £181,500 at Sotheby's in 1987, more than twice the previous record.

But prices over £10,000, even for rare and beautiful dials, remain exceptional, and there is real scope for the collector here. At the same sale a Reimann gilt brass and ivory diptych dial made in Nuremburg in 1606, adorned with cherub masks, zodiac signs and figures of courtiers, and listing the latitudes of 60 European towns, was estimated at £5-8,000, and saleroom experts were astonished when it made £57,200.

The most representative sale of dials in recent years took place at Christie's South Kensington in 1988 when Seth Atwood sold off some of the duplicates from his huge collection at the Time Museum in Rockford, Illinois. Atwood started his collection in 1934, and the huge variety of sixteenth and seventeenth century dials, as well as the number of unusual one-offs that he has been able to amass in 50 years shows how young a collecting area this is – especially as the Christie's sale offered only the *surplus* of the collection. By scientific instrument standards, prices were buoyant, but for authentic decorative pieces from the sixteenth, seventeenth or eighteenth centuries, they seemed cheap. A 'cheap' buy, of course, does not necessarily mean a good investment, because an item may always simply stay cheap, but as one of a diminishing number of high quality yet affordable collecting areas, dials have a lot to recommend them, and they could begin to attract more widespread interest, and, inevitably, higher prices.

Rare dials from the sixteenth century aroused most interest. Though unsigned, a sixteenth century Italian pocket dial in the form of a circular watch case, engraved with allegorical female figures perhaps representing spring and autumn, made £8,800; a German example from 1559 by Christoph Schissler was £5,280 and a sixteenth century oval gilt copper and silvered compass dial compendium made by Hans Ducher in Nuremburg in 1593 seemed a bargain at £3,960.

From the seventeenth and eighteenth centuries, Charles Bloud of Dieppe's ivory dials seem cheap – one was £2,200 at the Christie's sale, and Sotheby's sold one in 1988 for £715. A fine and rare equinoctial ring dial by Benjamin Scott, a pupil of Master of Mechanicks John Rowley, who later emigrated to St Petersburg, made £3,960, and another English piece, a silver equinoctial dial by John Marke who sold mathematical instruments in silver, ivory or wood 'at the sign of the Golden Ball in the Strand neare Somersett House', in the seventeenth century, was £3,520, three times its high estimate. A sundial by Anthony Snewins, one of the best Dutch makers – he worked in that hotbed of artistic activity, Delft, between 1645 and 1680 – fetched £13,200; sundials are much rarer than the little pocket dials that the nobility carried around with them.

Some of the most delightful of these are the brass book-form dials whose outer faces clasp together like fine sixteenth and seventeenth century books to enclose a dial. A seventeenth century example by Leonhardt Miller, with half-length portraits of the Virgin and another saintly figure engraved on the 'covers' made £1,650. A fine collection could be made around the theme of unusual dial formats – the Atwood sale included a seventeenth century pill box by Christian Boilling of Dresden incorporating a perpetual calendar with sun and moon dials (£3,520), an eighteenth century perpetual calendar snuff-box (£1,430), an eighteenth century dial miniature, half a portrait and half a dial ((£1,760) and a magnificent nineteenth century lacquered wood Chinese incense timekeeper in the form of a river paddle steamer decorated with butterflies and flowers. Astrolabes apart, oriental instruments have not taken off in the west, and this was estimated at £500-800; so obvious was its quality and originality, however, that it fetched £4,950.

Other oriental dials were cheap, however – a Japanese one was £187, a Chinese boxwood example £418, a Korean one £352 and a Sanskrit walking stick dial £462. Most were estimated at around £100 and for new collectors this could be another affordable area which may be about to see some rises.

At all levels, however, the market for dials is discriminating, so make sure that whatever you buy is in good condition, signed unless it is very early or very unusual, of great decorative appeal and where appropriate contains detailed original engraving. Although supply is fairly abundant – there simply aren't many collectors, and dials were made to survive the ravages of the centuries, as well as to record them – it is hard to imagine the best instruments not taking off, and this may be the last chance to buy at what the next decade will see as bargain prices.

Astrolabes

At the other extreme are astrolabes – much rarer and very valuable. Long a source of wonder and mystery, the astrolabe is an astronomical model illustrating the celestial sphere in relation to the earth. By simulating the movement of the stars around the celestial pole, mechanical solutions to astrological and astronomical puzzles can be found.

Astrolabes do not put in frequent appearances at auction, and because they are so popular they are especially vulnerable to the art of the forger. Islamic astrolabes continue to be produced (for tourists) today; even in the eighteenth century, however, they were so popular that contemporary engravers used to make non-functioning examples for decorative use; these can also be passed off as genuine. Astrolabes are probably the most complex of all scientific instruments, and unless you are very experienced

Still plenty of scope for buyers of scientific instruments: an Italian brass astrolabe made £17,500, a very high price for this sector, at Christie's South Kensington in April 1988 . . .

but, more typically at the same sale, a late 17th / early 18th century brass equinoctal compass dial was £3,080.

or have done a great amount of research, it would be unwise to buy in this sector without the help of a dealer.

The most stunning part – and the most stunning prices – of the Christie's Time Museum sale in 1988 were the 16 astrolabes. With an astrolabe, the earlier the better, and the top lot was an Italian example from the 1570s which made £71,500, way out of the normal scientific instrument price league. The prices for the less rare eighteenth and nineteenth century examples were more modest: among eastern astrolabes a couple of Persian examples made £8,800 and £11,000, Maghribi instruments used by the *muwaqqit* of the mosque to call the faithful to pray at the correct hour ranged from £4-6,000, an unsigned European astrolabe of indeterminate age managed nearly £5,000 and someone paid £275 for a twentieth century English paper, wood and pasteboard astrolabe made as a teaching instrument along sixteenth century German lines.

Age triumphed again for the most extraordinary instrument of the sale, a thirteenth century Andalusian astrolabe made in Seville and 'modernised' or completed in the sixteenth century by a Flemish maker. It fetched £30,800 and expert Anthony Turner's assessment of its attractions epitomises the historical appeal, the evocation of 'ideas and culture long since disappeared' that motivates collectors in almost any scientific instrument sale. The instrument, says Turner, 'marries in total harmony the work of master craftsmen from very different, often opposed cultures. At the same time it symbolically encapsulates the whole phenomenon of the movement of knowledge from Islam to Europe in the High middle ages. It is an elegant and touching witness to a crucial historical development'.

NAVIGATIONAL AND SURVEYING INSTRUMENTS

After a series of leaps in the early 1980s, prices in these specialised sectors are levelling off. Navigational instruments have been popular among retired seafarers and collectors of marine paintings, but prices for most sextants have reached a plateau at around £300, and the market has become somewhat indigestible at present. With the exception of early or rare pieces – for instance, an early English berge miniature sextant, which made £1,980 at Sotheby's in 1988 – navigational instruments seldom rise above £1,000. The outlook for the next few years at least is not exciting.

The story is the same for other specialised sectors such as surveying instruments. Most surveying instruments are from the nineteenth century; they have curiosity value rather than decorative appeal, and are therefore less sought after. But even a very early piece at Sotheby's in 1988, a rare pair of dividers with brass covers and a brass handle, dated 1531, fetched just £3,180 – surely cheap for such a slice of history. And in the same sale a pocket surveying quadrant dated 1616 in its original carved fruitwood case made just £1,100.

Most common are the nineteenth century brass theodolites, which have settled down in the £350-700 range and look unlikely to break out of it. As usual, exceptional items are worth seeking out, and should continue to rise. In 1987 Sotheby's sold an Everest-type theodolite by Troughton and Simms – the best known makers – for £2,420; the piece was inscribed IKB 1848 and had been owned and used by Isambard Kingdom Brunel. Rarity was also responsible for the £6,820 paid in the same sale for a superbly engraved Italian brass graphometer from the seventeenth century, and for the £16,500 paid at Christie's South Kensington in December 1985 for a miniature 'cannon barrel' theodolite made by J Sisson in the eighteenth century.

MEDICAL INSTRUMENTS

The market for medical instruments is also comparatively flat after sharp rises at the beginning of the 1980s. This is a rather macabre area, dominated by some fairly gruesome pieces from the nineteenth century which would do well in a fairground horror chamber. Prices for some items have actually fallen – L N Fowler ceramic phrenology heads from the nineteenth century, for instance, fetched around £1,000 in 1984. In October 1985 Christie's South Kensington sold one for £450, and in November 1987 two offered at Sotheby's made little more, at £462 (for one with a small chip) and £572.

It is difficult to imagine enough collectors getting interested in, say, a nineteenth century amputation set (£380 at Christie's in South Kensington in July 1988) or a nineteenth century brass tortoiseshell hearing aid (£140), for prices to be pushed up, especially when, as has happened in the last couple of years, American collectors are not buying.

OPTICAL INSTRUMENTS

Optical instruments are a science developed almost entirely in modern times, and hence offer much scope to the new collector. A collection can be comprehensive, well documented and, in an area dominated by pieces from the nineteenth century, not too expensive.

Fortunately, the use of brass was widespread in microscopes and telescopes until around 1900, and good examples appear regularly in the salerooms. This is another area to have experienced a lull in the mid 1980s, but this is likely to be temporary, because microscopes and telescopes are obviously collectable; instantly attractive, they come in a wide range of shapes and forms and there are a lot of them around. This is an excellent market to enter now, before prices move ahead to another plateau.

Ornate early examples will remain way ahead of the rest, and these are rare and expensive. For microscopes, the best known makers from the eighteenth century are John Marshall, Edmund Culpeper and W & S Jones, and prices for their pieces can soar. Christie's South Kensingtom sold a rare brass screw-based microscope signed Culpeper for £6,500 in July 1988; along with it went a range of accessories, all in fine materials – lenses, ivory slides, an ivory compound tube, objectives, stored in their original green fishskin case, which must have helped the price. Sometimes accessories like a collection of specimen slides are sold alone, and their original mahogany, oak or pine cases enhance the value.

Sotheby's April 1988 sale included a superb selection of eighteenth century microscopes which met with a mixed response. A Culpeper instrument made £7,700, an eighteenth century German one was £3,300 and star of the show was a rare and ornate John Marshall microscope with gilt borders and scrolling motifs, brass engravings, a vellum covering and ivory handles. It fetched £24,200.

A couple of lacquered brass compound binocular microscopes were £440 and £495.

This is an exceptional price for a microscope, but shows the importance of ornament and fine material in the early instruments. Nineteenth century microscopes turn up more frequently; unsigned, they can be found for under £200, and even signed £3-500 is a common price. Andrew Ross was one of the best nineteenth century makers; a microscope made by him in the 1860s fetched £605 at Sotheby's in 1988. Others to look out for include Elliott Brothers, R & J Beck, and J Swift & Son. Microscopes from the 1920s and 1930s are just beginning to be collected. At under £100, they are a lot less decorative (by this time brass was seldom used) and too cheap to appear in the salerooms, but they could become popular if the supply of brass examples diminishes. Markets like Bermondsey are good hunting grounds.

Microscopes had a strong boost in the early 1980s when interior decorators *en masse* discovered that they could be turned into lamps, and this pushed up prices at the lower end of the market. At the same time, telescopes were sought after for much the same reason as globes: they added intellectual elegance to a room, and some Manhattan apartments began to be considered incomplete without both. These trends are tailing off, but the interior decorator has left his mark, and telescopes and microscopes are a few hundred pounds more expensive.

With the fine materials used in telescopes – brass, horn, ivory, ebony and vellum – it is no surprise to find highly skilled makers. The two most sought after telescope makers are the eighteenth century giants, James

Short, 'Optician solely for Reflecting Telescopes', and William Hershel, a musician who experimented with telescopes as a hobby and discovered the planet Uranus in 1781. Though their work is rare, prices remain affordable; a Short brass telescope on a stand, in its original case, fetched £1,980 at Sotheby's in 1988.

Other eighteenth century telescopes are still available at under £1,000, while those from the nineteenth century can still be found for a few hundred. Here the London firm of Dollond was most prolific, and buyers should beware of disreputable imitators who got away with marking their pieces *Dolland*, and look for fine materials, good condition and makers' marks.

Speculators might also like to take a look at some of the optical toys hovering on the fringes of the scientific instrument market. Frivolous objects at, perhaps, frivolous prices, but the profits from a craze in kaleidoscopes and their relations – anything from the anamorphoscope (a device for showing clear images of distorted originals) to a zoetrope (a moving image device) – funded many a serious research project in the nineteenth century. At present prices can be under £100 and seldom exceed £300. But other toys, as well as scientific instruments, have taken off unexpectedly from here, and if nothing else these objects are an amusing appendage to any collection, as well as a curious footnote in the history of science.

13 TOYS

What do you suppose Lord Sebastian wanted? A hair brush
for his teddy bear; it had to have very stiff bristles,
not, Lord Sebastian said, to brush him with, but to
threaten him with a spanking when he was sulking. He
bought a very nice one with an ivory back and he's
having 'Aloysius' engraved on it – that's the bear's
name.

Evelyn Waugh, *Brideshead Revisited*

TEDDY BEARS

What are the limits of teddy affection? *Are* there any limits? The auction
houses clearly hope not, for as devoted collectors pay ever higher prices for
easy-to-please, loyal companions, they can rejoice at the discovery of a
market which has stayed buoyant right through the 1980s.

Publicity following each record price is not quite what it was, and fewer
battered old bears are being sent off to the salerooms as a result, but the
figures still tell a reassuring story. In 1980, the odd teddy bear changed
hands for around £100. In 1983, Bunny Campione of Sotheby's included
several in a general sale of toys and dolls, and one sold for £360. Two years
later, two top quality old bears at Sotheby's fetched £1,870 and £2,090, and
the first exclusive sale of bears at Christie's South Kensington in December
1985 attracted collectors from all over the world.

In 1986 the market looked as if it had reached its peak when a silver
plush bear made £5,200 at Sotheby's – he had been acquired for 18s 9d in
1904, and his mint condition was a result of his 'unloved' state ever since –
he had not even been given a name, but is now known as Chester, after the
Sotheby's saleroom that made his fortune. In June 1987, however, his
record was broken three times in a single Sotheby's sale, to be held finally
by a white plush muzzled bear, dating from 1913, who fetched his owner a
cool £8,800. By then, the *average* price for a bear at Sotheby's was £1,263.

In 1986, Bunny Campione warned anyone hoping to make a profit from
an old bear to strike at once, for such a gimmicky market needs only one
sale to turn sour, a couple of American dealers to stay at home, for a
downward spiral to set in. In 1988, it seems sensible to reiterate this advice
– surely, one thinks, prices cannot go any *higher* – but there is no
evidence of diminishing fervour among the arctophiles.

They have, however, become more discerning, and since 1983 the
cheaper bears have been sifted out. Interest now concentrates on pre-1930
bears, and as bears only came in with Teddy Roosevelt in 1902 – the
legend is that they were named after him when, out hunting, a desperate-
faced cub dissuaded him from killing its mother – this makes for an
exhaustible supply. Earlier bears, which stood on all fours, lacked the

anthropomorphic appeal of their descendants, and never really caught on; though extremely rare, they still fetch less today.

Bears are supposed to be creatures of Very Little Brain, and so it is appropriate that as an investment market they are among the simplest. Only one manufacturer – the German firm of Steiff – really matters, and they conveniently sewed silver buttons into the left ear of all their bears. Age and affection have tended to lose a lot of these, but the fur and features of these long-limbed, clumsy-looking Steiff bears make them instantly recognisable to collectors.

Condition is also straightforward. Ears (intact) and fur (soft and unworn) are important if a bear is to make a top price; chipped eyes, broken growlers and restitched paws are less vital. Even damaged bears with worn plush, however, can fetch over £1,000. Size and colour also determine prices – bigger is better, and white is the most popular colour, black the least.

But it is hard to be scientific about a market which depends so palpably on sentiment, for even dealers – who are all also collectors – will buy a bear simply because they like it. Most dealers, and most teddy fanatics, are American, and with London the great clearing house for bears, the question of whether sentiment can override a falling dollar is interesting. On the other hand, in the fantasy land of the Californian who has welcomed 3,000 teddies into his home, or of the American woman at Christie's first exclusive teddy sale who bought 30 miniature bears, carried them out in separate bags in case they quarrelled, and planned to book each one an individual seat on the flight home, currency exchange rates may play little part.

The salerooms, of course, play up the sentiment for all its worth. Sotheby's often includes a bear's name in the catalogue entry. Christie's South Kensington's July 1987 sale included in the description of a fairly ordinary golden plush teddy its 'provenance': 'This bear went with its owner every night to an air raid shelter during World War II in Cologne', while in its Christmas 1986 sale a 1909 Steiff increased his value by being offered along with a photograph of himself with his original owner.

But even if sentiment does not continue at fever pitch, and the bubble bursts, Steiffs are well made, characterful and, getting rarer, are certain to remain market leaders. The top ones should fetch at least four figures at auction; many others should continue, as they do now, to sell for several hundred pounds.

Collectors looking for bargains might turn their attention to more modern Steiff bears from the 1950s, which are cheaper, or to some of the other soft toys from the Steiff factory, for instance the cheerful felt clowns. Later English-made bears, such as those made by Merrythought in the 1930s, are also beginning to attract interest, and 1920s and 1930s teddies are among the recommendations for 1988 in Phillips survey *Antiques at Auction*. These often cost as little as £40; at auction they tend to be sold in job lots of, say, five bears for around £130. Individual English bears seldom fetch more than £100, though Sotheby's sold one for £420 in June 1987. Other English names to watch are Chad Valley and Farnell. If you are buying these with an eye on appreciation, buy a top quality example even if it does cost more, because if this market takes off condition is likely to be as crucial a factor as it is with the Steiffs.

A much-loved Steiff plush teddy, £1,210 at Christie's South Kensington, December 1988.

DOLLS

Few would buy a bear purely for investment – the hardhearted can have a better, or certainly a safer, time elsewhere, and teddy bears are rather the quintessential 'fun' market gone mad. Dolls probably have as much affection lavished on them, but their collectors are a more sober breed, and this is a firmer, more established market where investors can look confidently towards steady, if less spectacular appreciation. A couple of dips apart, the doll market has been thriving since the 1960s. It is strongest in America, where prices at doll fairs and conventions are higher than in England, but it has a healthy following throughout Europe and Japan. As it becomes a better known and researched sector, more collectors are feeling brave enough to enter the fray, pushing up demand and prices.

Consistent high-fliers in the saleroom have been nineteenth and early twentieth century French bébés and German character dolls, and the obsession among collectors here with series, size and mould numbers, as well as an emphasis on peak condition, acts as something of a protection for the investor – you may sacrifice sentiment to the pedantic examination of the numbers and initials that mark your doll, but at least you are putting your money into more than a pretty face, or a convincing snout.

Condition for dolls is paramount. A crack at the back of a porcelain or china doll can halve its price, while damage to the front reduces the value inestimably. Maintaining the quality of fabric dolls needs even more care, for although they do not break, they are particularly susceptible to their environment and can be ruined by extremes of heat or moisture. They are also vulnerable to moths, and so should always be kept in the open.

The doll market, therefore, is considerably more complicated than that for bears. A handful of makers – the French Bru and Jumeau, and the German Kammer & Reinhardt, Simon & Halbig and Gebrüder Halbig – have come to dominate, but there are thousands of others, and plenty of scope for collectors willing to spend anything from £50 a go to over £5,000.

The French and German bisque-headed dolls usually date from 1870 to 1910. Most cost several hundred pounds but they are appreciating well and the finest now fetch several thousand: four figure sums for many good quality dolls with original clothing; five figure sums for the very rarest. Top quality dolls still outdo top quality bears.

For doll collectors, a good memory can pay enormous dividends. Most of the bisque-headed dolls have a series, mould and size number at the back of the neck and broadly speaking, the rarer the number the more valuable the doll. Failing to recognise a series number, though it happens rarely among saleroom experts, can result in a price discrepancy of thousands of pounds, and the occasional bargain for the canny collector.

Serious collectors tend to opt either for one type of doll, or for successive numbers in a certain series. In May 1986 a record-breaking doll from the very rare Kammer & Reinhardt 100 series fetched £24,200 at Sotheby's. A slightly more common example from the same series made £4,500 a few months later.

But organised collecting has its limits, and even here the luck of the auction comes into play – a serious collector may already have a very rare mould number, leaving a less obsessive bidder to pick up a rare doll for £2,000 instead of the expected £4,000. Cultural differences also have an effect. Generally, English and German buyers bid for both the expressive German character dolls and the pretty French ones, while French buyers are more insular, and tend to stick to their bébés.

Here, faces really do make fortunes, and exceptionally beautiful French dolls with dimples, pierced ears and fixed paperweight eyes – Jumeau workers in the 1890s made the large, appealing eyes in a special factory, and had to undergo a five year apprenticeship – regularly fetch over £3,500. Others, according to size, mould and condition, range from £200 to £2,000.

A good Bru bisque-headed doll, for example, fetched £1,600 at Phillips in December 1987; in the same sale a blue-eyed stunner made by the lesser-known French manufacturer Pettit Dumontier sold for £6,000. Curiously, blue-eyed dolls do better than brown-eyed, and pouting, or closed mouths, are preferable to open ones; odd features, like eyes looking slightly to the side or winking, can appeal to collectors for rarity value. German baby-faced 'googly-eyed' dolls, often dressed in amusing clothes, are very sought after and start at around £2,000.

Original clothing is a feature in the price for all dolls. French dolls, appropriately, have the edge in fashion-consciousness, but clothing for all nineteenth and early twentieth century dolls was sumptuous, and an original dress with matching bonnet and shoes will place its owner at a premium in the saleroom. Sold separately, a doll's dress at £200 is common, and can exceed the price paid for many dolls.

Bargains, though, are still to be found in less fashionable sectors of the doll market, where appreciation since the 1970s has been slow and in some cases static. Interest in Japanese dolls has declined to the point where Sotheby's no longer sell them, though they remain popular among Japanese buyers. At present a fine composition-headed Gosho Ningo, with enamel eyes and a cloth and papier mâché body in its original silk crêpe kimono is unlikely to cost more than £100. Christie's South Kensington sometimes sell them in lots of two or more; £170 for two is an average price. This seems cheap for such appealing faces and finely made bodies and clothes, and they might return to general favour. Now would be a good time to buy.

Since the mid 1980s, there have been signs that some of the less fashionable areas of the doll market are catching up. Early English wooden dolls have always lagged behind the French and German character dolls, but an exception in 1987 was a very rare and elegant William and Mary wooden doll dating from 1690. It was the oldest doll ever sold at auction, and by a long way the most expensive; it fetched £67,100 at Sotheby's. However, crudely carved early wooden dolls are generally considered undervalued, and are an area to watch. Elaborate original clothing should boost the price. Foreign examples sometimes appear at sales of tribal art, currently in the doldrums, and the source of possible bargains.

In wax, the important names are Montanari and Pierotti, both Italians living in Victorian England. Wax dolls are refined, delicate creatures that unfortunately tend to crack given the slightest changes of atmosphere or temperature. Early wax over composition dolls and waxed papier mâché dolls dating from around 1840 are very often sold cracked; poured wax dolls, in which the wax was poured into a mould and hardened, and hair inserted by a hot needle in the scalp, have survived better; dating from the 1880s, they were more expensive and it seems that their fragility discouraged them from actually being played with. As a result, they sometimes appear in mint condition with their original clothes; in the £100s a few years ago, these now fetch over £1,000 and are especially popular if they have retained a makers' mark or the stamp of a shop. Lesser examples start at around £80 and must be a bargain.

Also undervalued are twentieth century cloth dolls in stockinette, velvet or felt by makers such as the German Kathe Kruse, the English Norah Wellings or Madame Scavini, who worked for the Italian firm Lenci. Lenci dolls, with their slightly pouting mouths and elaborate clothes, are marked by the firm's name in the sole of the foot, and turn up regularly at auction. Starting at under £100, they are cheaper than a good condition Kathe Kruse doll, which should fetch around £400. Prices are beginning to creep up, but there is a lot of scope here.

In a new development, Olivia Bristol at Christie's South Kensington included some unusual Chad Valley cloth dolls in a sale in October 1986. Snow White and the Seven Dwarfs, with pointed cloth faces, fixed blue glass eyes and velvet limbs, fetched £308, but a painted felt portrait doll of Princess Elizabeth in 1938, estimated at £400-800, failed to sell. Nevertheless, as an increasing number of modern toys do well in the salerooms – a Father Christmas drawn by a clockwork reindeer, made in the American zone of Germany just after the war, fetched £770 at Christie's Christmas 1986 sale – Chad Valley dolls, and especially original 'character' ones, are an area to watch. Bunny Campione of Sotheby's also foresees fragile celluloid dolls, abundant in Germany and very cheap, as a sector likely to take off soon, while Anna Marratt at Phillips believes fine dolls' house dolls, costing around £50-60, are undervalued.

VEHICLES AND SOLDIERS

However sexlessly we are now supposed to bring up our children, the toy collecting habits of their parents remain immutably gender based. For every middle-aged woman who hordes antique dolls, there are several hundred men who get obsessive about model trains and Dinky cars, tinplate submarines and lead soldiers. Steiff or Jumeau, though they cared a great deal about quality, never imagined that they were producing collector's pieces; toy soldier manufacturers like the patriotically named William Britain, on the other hand, cottoned on quickly to the collecting potential of a range of miniature regiments, and even though their eye was on the regular profits from pocket money rather than saleroom activity, they penetrated to the heart of the collecting mentality.

Britain launched his first army of hollow-cast lead soldiers, the Life Guards, in 1893, and like all subsequent sets, they were attractively packaged in boxes that have been collector's items in their own right. With each of the thousands of sets given a series number, lead soldier fervour passed from the schoolboy to the collector as soon as the use of lead ceased in 1966. Since the 1970s, when a box cost around £50, prices have risen steadily; figures in the £100s remain common, but the rarer sets now fetch many thousands. Phillips, acknowledged as the world centre, has consistently placed lead soldiers as one of the most healthily appreciating sectors in their annual analysis of saleroom trends. With a strong market for even the later examples – a 1940 set of the Royal Horse Artillery in khaki uniforms and steel helmets, not colourful enough to be a big seller in its day and therefore rare now, fetched £7,200 in 1985 – and no fear of supply drying up, these well made toys are among the safest collectables. Zoo and farm animals, produced between the wars when sales of Britain's soldiers suffered from a less enthusiastic attitude to things military, have also ridden high on the lead soldiers boom, as have gardening sets, which sometimes match prices paid for the rarer soldiers.

Notwithstanding some encroachments on the market by German firms – notably the imaginative Dresden-based Heyde – whose English packaging shows a gloriously garish, stereotyped view of the British army defending its empire, Britain's soldiers were always the best sellers, and around 75 per cent of collectors specialise in British models. The Germans, though, have their own golden age of miniatures, and tin plated vehicles from turn-of-the-century Germany have been collected for years. Rival giants were Bing, self-styled 'greatest toy factory in the world', and Marklin, but a host of other contemporary German manufacturers appear in the salerooms. Demand is high and appreciation steady, but so widespread was the manufacture of these little tin cars and boats that there is always a chance of a bargain among the valuable models stored away unknowingly as junk for years. This is a market to enter at any level; the best Bing and Marklins fetch over £1,000, but all are exceptionally detailed in construction and paint work, and comfortably able to withstand the passing years, increasing their value as they do so. Boats – which tended to end up at the bottom of

A Bru Jeune bébé doll, fashionable in her day, made £6,050 at Christie's South Kensington, September 1988.

the pond – are the rarest, and prices can be steep; a fine Marklin model of HMS Barfleur, dating from 1924, sold for £20,900 at Christie's in 1987.

Marklin and Bing also dominated the model train market until the 1920s, when the English Hamby began to assert itself. In a generally buoyant and very diverse sector, Hamby sets are among the fastest rising. But the quality and detail of scaled models, whether powered by steam, electricity or clockwork, is so fine that almost any trains, including contemporary models, by reputable makers should appreciate. Sets from the 1950s can be as valuable as earlier ones, and there is also a strong market in accessories – a Marklin station for a mountain railway including a ticket office, seating area and descent gate, for example, made £280 at Phillips in 1987.

The British vehicle really came into its own in the 1930s, and Dinky cars have been collected ever since. And just as a sense of history, the excitement of being in at the beginning of a new age of transport, breathes life into the pre-1914 Bing and Marklin toys, so it is a period flavour, together with the sheer scope of the market, that makes Dinky irresistable – hence the premium placed on those carrying advertisements, and on the earliest models. The pre-war vehicles are obsessively sought after, and though production and sales were enormous, the toys were so cheap that few buyers bothered to preserve them, and most were thrown away. As a result, the rarest items can fetch several thousand pounds, and as supply gets scarcer, they should climb higher. As with all diecast models, condition is especially important, and Phillips go so far as to warn customers in their catalogue that 'items described as fatigued are subject to disintegration'. Haircracks are the beginning of metal fatigue, and though sometimes only observable through a microscope, can enormously reduce the price.

Speculators might note the dated quality that makes diecast toys so appealing, and look to the Japanese toys from the 1950s and 1960s which sung the praises of a dawning space age. Japanese manufacturers were as original as the Germans at the beginning of the century, and many of their battery-operated spacecraft had innovative light and sound effects. Robots are already catching on in the salerooms, and Phillips has reported tin robots from the 1960s in especially high demand. But prices for most Japanese toys are low – £18 for a battery-operated Planet Explorer, £28 for a Nomura Bartender, at Phillips in December 1987, for example. These may soon be as coveted as Dinky.

THE FUTURE FOR THE MARKET

Like teddy bears and Dinky before them, other sectors of the toy market, such as early board games, currently very cheap and seldom appearing in the saleroom, may also take off one day, although there is no evidence of rising prices at present. But it is difficult to see how the dream ticket of the miniature can fail – well-crafted items which become instantly obsolete (when a production line finished) and yet form part of a wider market where strong supply, at varying levels, can only spur collectors on. Condition is important – rust is acceptable, broken parts or decaying paintwork are not – and poor maintenance, especially of lead soldiers, which must be kept dry and out of sunlight, can ruin the toys, but they are not fragile and are easy to display, rearrange and play with. And as collectors increase in number and sophistication, so does documentation and literature, and, inevitably, prices.

14 WINE

It is only the first bottle that is expensive.
French proverb

If they were ever anthologised, a volume of Mrs Thatcher's favourite fairy stories would surely include the tale of the dustman-wine collector. Intrigued by the labels on the empty wine bottles he picked up on his rounds, he eventually collected enough of them to exchange for a full bottle; now retired, he is the owner of an extraordinarily interesting and valuable wine cellar. Not surprisingly, it is located in Paris, where the dustbins are no doubt crammed with more and better wine labels than in London or anywhere else.

Maybe the French dustman was apocryphal, but it is certainly true that there is plenty of scope for the entrepreneurial investor in this area, and that a minimal capital outlay is required to start up – at Christie's in King Street the average price for a two-case lot is £300-350, and down the road at the South Kensington offshoot prices start at £2 or £3 a bottle.

THE CASE FOR INVESTMENT

Wine, like works of art, is a non-income bearing investment where financial gain comes from capital appreciation alone. Also like works of art, wine is in limited supply; moreover, worldwide demand, partly as a result of the move away from spirits, is on the increase.

The *appellation contrôlée* system operating in the key growing area, Bordeaux, permits an annual production of around 2,250 bottles of wine per acre, give or take a few according to the quality each year. But as soon as each new vintage is allocated to purchasers and shipped, supply starts to decline as more and more bottles are drunk. The premium attached to those that remain is enhanced because for wine, quality goes hand in hand with age.

Clarets from the top vineyards used to take 20 to 30 years to mature; modern methods of vinification have reduced this to around 10 to 15. Young wines begin to put in an appearance at auction aged about five, when prices still have some way to go. Once mature, wines keep for years and even centuries – eighteenth century vintages sometimes surface at auction, and the most expensive wine ever sold was a 1787 Lafite engraved with the initials of Thomas Jefferson. It fetched £105,000 at Christie's in 1985, aged almost 200.

Buying young

Time is a crucial factor in the investment returns for wine. Over the years, the value of wine is pushed up by a double factor – there is less of it, *and* it tastes better. The first rule for the investor, then, is to buy young. For the investor-drinker, it does not take a genius to work out that a quick route to profitable sybaritism is to buy each year twice as much young wine as you imagine you can (possibly) drink, sell half of it after about five years, and reinvest the proceeds in new young wine. The only snag is that if you don't have a wine cellar, you will have to pay a wine merchant to store the wine for you. Wine is highly susceptible to heat, light and sudden changes of temperature, and does not take kindly to living in a box under the stairs or the corner of the garage.

Buying through a wine merchant is the private investor's way into the *en primeur* market, which offers the chances of highest appreciation. The wines are bought the year after they have been made, at the best available price closest to the 'opening price', while they are still in their casks in Bordeaux. They will never be cheaper, yet the risks of buying 'in the dark' are minimal because the experts can tell, by hallmarks such as an intense depth of tannin, which ensures a happy longevity, the quality of the wine long before it comes within sight of the bottle.

PASSING THE CLARET TEST

The catch is that not all wines are worth keeping. If you are a claret – and most wines bought for investment are – no one is going to be interested in you unless you came from the right place at the right time.

The constant in that equation is the place, which the Bordelais settled once and for all in 1856 when the great wines of the Médoc (*le roi des vins, le vin des rois*), the most important in Bordeaux, were categorised into *crûs classés*, with the top 60 ranked by chateau as *grands crûs classés* and further distinguished into five groups known as *premiers crûs* (first growths), *deuxièmes crûs* etc.

Traditionally, investors have homed in on the top 60 chateaux, and the premiers crûs, and especially the magic name of Château Lafite-Rothschild, have become something of a password for prestige and elegant living. A long-standing grudge borne by another branch of the Rothschild family was finally removed when the rival Château Mouton Rothschild was elevated to first growth status in 1973.

But being a first growth claret from the Médoc isn't everything, and although these wines have usually proved good investments, there are some from the other growths which have performed just as well or better, with lower opening prices (see below).

Some red Bordeaux suitable for investment

First growths
Ch Lafite
Ch Latour
Ch Margaux
Ch Mouton Rothschild
Ch Haut-Brion

Other growths
Ch Beycheville

Ch Brane Cantenac
Ch Cos d'Estournel
Ch Ducru Beaucaillou
Ch Gruaud Larose
Ch La Lagune
Ch Leoville Lascases
Ch Montrose
Ch Pichon Longueville Lalande

From outside the Médoc
Ch Ausone (St Emilion first growth)
Ch Cheval Blanc (St Emilion first growth)
Ch Certan de May (Pomerol)
Domaine de Chevalier (Graves)
Ch Figeac (St Emilion)
Ch Lafleur (Pomerol)
Ch La Mission Haut-Brion
Ch Pavie (St Emilion)
Ch Pétrus (Pomerol)

The other regions in Bordeaux – Graves, St Emilion and its tiny
neighbour Pomerol – are also worth looking at, especially the Pomerols.
A very small production at most of the Pomerol estates, combined with a
tremendous international following acquired in recent years, makes these
wines some of the very best investments around. Château Pétrus put
Pomerol on the connoisseur's map, but other châteaux have been pushed
since by the wine merchants, always on the look out for a good but little
known wine whose reputation can do with a boost. In particular John
Armit, who set up John Armit Wine Investments to cater for private
buyers wanting to invest at least £5,000 in young wines, has helped make
Ch Certan de May and Ch Lafleur popular.

Château Lafleur is the answer to those who lament that 'they don't make
them like this anymore', for the 1980s vintages are widely thought to
resemble those made in the heady 1940s. As with many of the best things in
life, quality is high because quantity is low; the aging old vines (around 50
years old) produce very little but what there is has a marvellously
concentrated flavour, almost like essence of wine.

A question of timing

'It sometimes happens,' reports the *Encyclopaedia of Wine and Spirits*,
'that a good vintage is glorified by the appearance of a comet. One such
year was 1630, but 1811, more famous, is the vintage usually referred to as
the comet year'.

This must have gladdened the hearts of Christie's, which sold a bottle of
1811 Lafite in June for £20,000. They thought it might have been the best
vintage of all time, but unable to quote tasting notes, fell back on Maurice
Healey's *Stay me with Flagons* which enthuses about Lafite 'drinking
gracefully at 115 years of age' in the 1920s, and on a classic, Warner Allen's
A History of Wine which obscurely tries to help by ranking the 1811 Lafite
with the Opimian vintage of 121 BC.

The great variable in the investment equation is the quality of each new vintage, and it is this that causes the experts to murmur '1947' or '1961' in tones of awe and wonder. A case of 1947 Ch Cheval Blanc at Christie's June 1988 sale made £2,500 (£380 ten years ago); the good but less glorious 1949 was £1,550 and the unexceptional 1950 was £230, even less than the still immature 1983, which made £260.

In the last decade, modern vinification techniques have closed the gap between the very worst and the very best vintages – computers cannot actually go out and change the weather in Bordeaux, but they have removed any scope for human error and they now determine when mere mortals start picking and control temperatures throughout the wine-making process. In addition, châteaux owners have been coerced into greater rigour in selecting what is good enough to be bottled under their prestigious labels – the most serious ones discarded 25-35 per cent of their 1985 harvest – and out-and-out disasters like 1963 and 1965 look unlikely.

In a way, this makes it harder to get the investment right. On the other hand, although the overall plateau is high, the peaks still stand out, and 1970 and 1982 have both been billed, along with 1961, as 'the vintage of the century'.

1961 was a small vintage of exceptionally high quality which is now rare and very expensive. A single bottle of Ch Latour 1961 was £477 at Christie's 'finest and rarest' sale in June 1988; by comparison a whole case of the 1962 was £650. And as the 1970 vintage gets rarer, prices here are starting to soar: a case of Ch Lafite which was £70-90 in 1975, is now closer to £800.

In recent years the wine trade could hardly believe its luck when 1981, 1982 and 1983 all turned out to be superb vintages, according to one wine merchant 'perhaps the best series ever'. Cyclone Hortense put a stop to any collective hubris that might be taking root by striking just after the 1984 harvest began, and 1984 is not a vintage to keep.

On the other hand, 1982 has proved to be an outstanding performer, as is shown in Figure 14.1, which gives the investment record of the three vintages bought by John Armit Wine Investments. They operate on the assumption that the optimum compound interest is realised between four and six years after the purchase in the summer after the harvest. If you

Fig 14.1: Investment record of Bordeaux vintages 1981/1982/1983

	Cost of investment*	Value of original investment in 1987	Compound increase per annum
	£	£	%
1981 vintage (bought in 1982)	9,210	29,120	25.9
1982 vintage (bought in 1983)	13,285	42,335	33.6
1983 vintage (bought in 1984)	14,535	28,365	25.0
* Based on opening price available			

Source: John Armit Wines

Fig 14.2: Investment record of top Bordeaux vintages 1966-1979

	Value of original £10,000 investment in 1987 £	Compound increase per annum %
1966 vintage (bought in 1967)		
First growths	365,370	19.7
Other growths	516,025	21.8
1970 vintage (bought in 1971)		
First growths	170,860	19.4
Other growths	299,060	23.6
1975 vintage (bought in 1976)		
First growths	82,940	21.2
Other growths	88,275	21.9
1978 vintage (bought in 1979)		
First growths	50,670	22.5
Other growths	50,350	22.4
1979 vintage (bought in 1980)		
First growths	35,410	19.8
Other growths	42,610	23.0

Source: John Armit Wines

want a longer-term investment, however, the performances of the best vintages of the last 20 years, illustrated in Figure 14.2, are reassuring.

For anyone looking to buy in the secondary market, it is worth noting that back in 1986 these returns were even more glowing – the 1982 vintage (bought in 1983) had almost trebled in price in three years, and averaged an annual return of over 40 per cent. Since then, both the recent vintages and the best from the 1960s and 1970s have shown little more than level-pegging prices at auction, and 1988 could be the time to pick up a bargain before the next boom.

In particular, a declining dollar has left a yawning gap in demand for the much-hyped 1982s, which were sometimes cheaper than in 1985, when they were barely out of their casks. Among first growths Château Lafite reached £680 in 1985 and only £550 in the 1987-88 season; Château Margaux, £580 in 1985, managed just £480 in 1988 and Château Mouton-Rothschild saw an undramatic rise from a top of £715 to £750.

If the 1988 vintage is as disappointing as the 1987, the 1982s, and also the 1983s, could be back on course for another price surge. So rapid is the growth of fine wine in its early years that if you bought the 1982s *en primeur* you would still have got a good run for your money; those who lost out were the first eager buyers at auction in 1985.

Quirks in the market

A knack of advance trend spotting, which can be invaluable to speculators in other alternative investments, is not really possible in the wine business, since much is known about the vintage as soon as it is produced and most investors buying *en primeur* will trust their wine merchant rather than flit to and from Bordeaux in the crucial time after the harvest.

Some vintages, though, do turn below or above early hopes – 1973, for example, showed some promise but turned out dull, while 1979 proved better than expected. Moreover, a vintage that is declared exceptional, like 1961 or 1982, is not necessarily so in all parts of Bordeaux. In the Margaux commune of the Médoc, for instance, some châteaux produced better wine in 1983 than in 1982, and prices reflect this: Château Palmer 1983, for example, was £320 at Christie's in July 1988 while the 1982 was £260.

Other possible winners are good vintages which are eclipsed by the outstanding ones which preceded them. The 1979 vintage will not keep as well as the better 1978, but is excellent for medium-term drinking and very good value: at Christie's fine claret sale in July, a case of 1979 Château Lafite was £320 against £550 for the 1978 vintage, and a case of Château Mouton-Rothschild was £250 against £420 for 1978. The poor old 1983s, which had the misfortune to follow the glorious 1982, are even more over-shadowed.

Finally, investors should be aware of some idiosyncracies in the secondary market. Wine is thought to mature better in magnums, and small quantities of the larger bottles fetch higher prices at auction, so buyers of young wine should include some magnums (six per case) and double magnums (three per case), for a small additional charge, in their 'portfolio'.

When bidding in the saleroom, check in the catalogue to see whether the auctioneer offers 'options to buy parcels'. This allows the buyer of the first lot of any wine the option to take further kits of similar bottle size at the same price.

Wines sold at auction are either sold 'duty paid but available in bond', or 'duty and VAT paid', which is the best way for private investors to buy at auction. 'In bond' means stored in bonded warehouses free of duty, which is good for overseas buyers who can subtract the excise duty.

NON-CLARETS

Most wines bought for investment are clarets; very little burgundy is sold at auction, and only about 10 per cent of all wine in the salerooms is white. Of the whites, Château d'Yquem, a Sauternes which was ranked alone as a *premier grand crû*, is the most sought after and expensive – Christie's sold a bottle of the famous 1847 vintage, according to Michael Broadbent 'perhaps the most magnificent wine ever tasted', for £6,600 in 1988. The Yquem producers are intensely jealous of their reputation, and in a less than perfect year bottle the wine under a different label, so there is never a worry about quality.

PORT

Around 15 per cent of wine at auction is port. The eighteenth century academic Richard Bentley used to say of claret that 'it would be port if it could', and his contemporary Dr Johnson boasted of being a 'three bottle a day man'. The English love affair with port goes back centuries, and some of the major English shippers have enjoyed thriving business uninterrupted for centuries.

Most port is intended for early drinking, but in exceptional years some shippers 'declare a vintage', leaving wine from the best vineyards to mature in wood and bottling it a couple of years later as vintage port. It takes 10 to 25 years to reach its peak, supply is limited, vintages and producers are well known and the result is a wine that looks tailor-made for investment.

Rates of growth are good and as the appeal of port slowly spreads beyond British shores to America, prospects look promising. The best vintages in recent years have been 1945, 1955, 1963 and 1977, all 'widely declared' – declared by many rather than just a few shippers, though one of the largest producers, Cockburn, did not declare 1977. The top shippers vary in style; the major ones include the three die-hards Croft, Taylor and Warre, and Cockburn, as well as Dow, Ferreira, Fonseca, Graham, Quinto do Noval, Rebello Valente and Sandeman.

While claret goes up steadily in price, the movement for port surges ahead as a series of plateaux and peaks, and is easy both to watch and to anticipate. Prices rise when port first makes its appearance at auction, then level off and sit still until the previous great vintage thins out, continuing to go up in steps as the older vintages become rarer.

The 1977 vintage, for example, started off at around £120 a case, then rose to £200 and has stayed there ever since, waiting for the 1963s and the 1970s, another good year, to be drunk up. But the 1977s are a strong tannic breed which look set to age well, and prices have some way to go yet.

Between 1985 and 1988, all port, like claret, saw a levelling off in demand, but the stepping stones to pricelessness of Taylor's great 1963 vintage show what a good long-term investment port can be. A case was £15 in 1971, around £40-60 from 1973 to 1977, and rose to £100-150 in the years up to 1982. In the peak year of 1985 a case reached £520; in 1988 top prices were around £550, with a minimum of around £400. But as the connoisseur's dream, Taylor's 1945 vintage, now sells for £100 a bottle, and the 1963 vintage is on the road to replace it as the drink for the 1990s, the investment outlook is strong.

'The good ship temperance sails slowly for the port' used to be a confident chant among Victorian teetotallers. They knew not what they said, but for those looking for a sure and steady market, the words have some truth now. Whatever happens internationally, UK demand persists and port looks a good bet.

15 MOTOR CARS

Mr Wooster being one of those easy-going young gentlemen
who will drive a car but never take the trouble to study
its mechanism, I felt justified in becoming technical.
'I think it's the differential gear, sir. Either that
or the exhaust.'

P G Wodehouse, *Carry on Jeeves*

The motives for the automobile enthusiast are not hard to fathom. First
there is the romance – the pleasure of whizzing round the countryside,
Bertie Wooster style, in a vehicle whose gleaming coachwork and fine
leather upholstery induces you to believe for a few hours that you have all
the time, leisure and luxury in the world. Then, if you long for the days
when fixing the car was a matter of spanner and screwdriver, there is the
mechanical simplicity, the joy of tinkering on a winter evening with a
vehicle whose every part you understand. And not to be underestimated is
the prospect of a good day out at club meetings, a must for anyone on the
look out for spare parts or a good restorer, but also a popular social
occasion.

AUTOMOBILES AS AN INVESTMENT

Automobiles are at the fun end of the alternative investment spectrum,
and yet they form one of its most stable sectors, with the investor-collector
feeding happily off the boundless passion of the enthusiast. But this is a
market well geared up to the investor. Truly international, it is dominated
by no one nation because the top dozen marques originate in various
countries. At the lower end of the market, British collectors stick to good
old British marques, where the strong body of interest has never been
shaken, and is consolidated by the growing number, and size, of owner-
clubs. And both top and bottom rungs of the automobile market have
been flourishing for decades, are awash with experts and sophisticated
collectors, and share a strong body of literature and an excellent annual
price guide, *Coy's Complete Collectors' and Investors' Car Value Guide*.

There is no point in buying an old car unless you want to run or cherish
it, because these cumbersome beasts demand a lot of loving attention and
careful upkeep. One of the downsides of ownership is the expense of
maintenance; even if you don't drive them, old cars must be stored in a
warm place which has been dehumidified to prevent rust, and they must be
checked, and preferably driven, at regular intervals to ensure good
working order. A number of storage companies exist to perform this
service, and if you cannot be sure of maintaining your cars yourself, they
are well worth the expense, for the value of a neglected car sinks rapidly.

But if you are attracted to old automobiles, and can keep them in good
condition, the financial advantages are considerable. The first is an

excellent record of appreciation of at least 15 per cent a year for most marques, and of 25-30 per cent for some marques in some years. Such is the enthusiasm of collectors that there is almost always someone willing to pay slightly more than you have done, and selling at a 10 or 20 per cent profit the day after you have bought a car at auction is not unknown. This is one of the few sectors where the market does not care how recently it has seen an item, and it is possible and common to sell on at a profit after a couple of years, rather than wait the decade or so that is advised in most of the art market sectors.

More collectors are being drawn to old vehicles every year, pushing up demand, while supply of the older models is diminishing. For with the exception of the very expensive, £1m plus cars, which live in museums or in their owner's special posh garages rather like sculptures, having achieved 'work-of-art' status, cars do not last forever, and if you use them they will eventually wear out. Spare parts can do wonders, but they are not cheap – a Bugatti engine in bits sold for £32,000 at auction in December 1986 and the 'mechanical remains' of a Hispano Suiza H6B, estimated at £2-3,000, were sold at Christie's in 1988 for £12,650. It can be more economical to purchase another car than to pay for the fabrication of a new part. Diminishing supply should keep the market buoyant, but beware of the potential expense should you need spare parts.

But on the plus side, old cars can be used while they are appreciating in value, sometimes saving the owner the expense of buying a new car, which can only go *down* in value; they are easy to transport (facilitating sales on an international level), difficult to steal profitably (most are fully documented and their locations recorded by the marque's owners' club), and quick to convert into cash at a price you can take a good guess at – as with prints, roughly accurate estimates are one of the advantages of owning something unusual but not unique. And for enterprising owners, one further advantage is the possibility of hiring out the car to film companies or PR or advertising agencies, or even hiring oneself out along with it for weddings or publicity stunts.

CHOOSING YOUR CAR – THE RANGE OF THE MARKET

Motor cars can be categorised precisely. Veterans were built before 1919, though only those predating 1 January 1905 qualify for the annual London-Brighton run, which celebrates the abolition in 1896 of the law requiring a man waving a red flag to precede an automobile. 'Vintage' cars were built between 1919 and 1939, and 'classic' cars any time after than. 'Post-vintage' is sometimes used to describe the breed produced from 1939-1950, and with an increasing number of later cars dating even from the 1980s appearing at auction, it is a useful way of breaking up the mammoth field of 'classics'.

The exotics

Age helps a car's price, but is not the most important factor. The broad rule is that cars which cost most when new fetch the highest prices now. That creates a top league of high fliers – Bugatti, Rolls Royce and perhaps Bentley – followed by a second rung of internationally sought after marques which include Hispana Suiza, Ferrari, Porsche, Isotta Franchini, Mercedes, Alfa Romeo, Jaguar and oddballs like Duisenberg.

These are the 'exotics', and buyers are intoxicated by the magic of the name, as well as by the character and history. What they call in the trade 'body style', dashing coachwork, famous ownership and a racing history all push up prices here.

Sporting prowess accounts for the wild escalation in prices in the mid 1980s of fashionable marques like Jaguar, Ferrari and Alfa Romeo. Jaguar SS100s, for example, rose from around £35,000 in 1986 to over £50,000 in 1988. A stunning example of the importance of historical pedigree came when Coys of Kensington sold an LNW 100, the most famous of the breed, which had belonged to Ian Appleyard, shown in the catalogue posing with the car in Monte Carlo, for £165,000 in 1988. The previous auction record for an SS100 was £67,000. The £75,000 paid in the same sale for another SS100 shows the sort of premium collectors are prepared to pay for an illustrious name.

The owner of the Appleyard car bought it in 1983 for £24,000, and could hardly have expected it to go up more than six times in five years. Other sporting marques at the first of Coys 1988 sales demonstrated that collectors can look to healthy appreciation in even shorter periods.

Ferraris have probably shown the most frenzied appreciation of all in the 1980s, and a 1971 Ferrari Daytona, bought in Monaco in May 1987 for £90,000, sold in February 1988 for £122,000. A Mercedes 300 SL roadster, £45,000 at Christie's in April 1987, resold at the Coys sale for £59,000.

As for Alfa Romeo, the most sought after sports car is the 8C 2300 which, when it was introduced in 1931, inspired Mussolini with the idea of gaining national prestige on the race tracks. In 1979 an Alfa Romeo 8C 2300 short chassis sports car fetched £28,000 at Christie's; by 1988 they were closer to £300,000. Coys established a record in July 1988 when an 8C 2300 supercharged works team car which Chinetti and Varent drove in the 1933 Le Mans fetched £380,000.

Figures 15.1-15.5 show the rise in average prices for some of the most sought after models of all time among Bugatti, Rolls Royce, Bentley, Mercedes and Hispano Suiza. Appreciation, given the odd dip or two which investors in any market should be prepared to ride out, is rapid at the top, and there is always a knock-on effect from 'stunner' prices like the record £5.5m paid for a Bugatti Royale in 1987 (over £1m more than was paid in 1986, when one sold for £4.4m), to lesser models. Mercedes saw a huge price increase in 1984, and as the table shows, less exciting cars roughly echoed patterns at the top. Any of the pre-1979 models are now very collectable. As with all the exotics, and indeed with all cars, very early models command a premium because they are so very difficult to find. Veterans, unsurprisingly, are becoming very rare. In 1988, for example, Christie's sold a 1904 Mercedes side entrance phaeton, which had an impeccably documented provenance and had completed the 1978 London to Brighton run after a period of display at the National Motor Museum, for £264,000.

Figures 15.1-15.5 also show the spiralling effect of a one-off high price; when Bentley's 1930 Speed Six Blue Train fetched £246,000 at Sotheby's in December 1984, vintage Bentleys were assured a continuing rise – vintage prices, though nowhere near the 1984 level, have been considerably higher

Fig. 15.1: Vintage Bentley 1919-1931 (£,000)

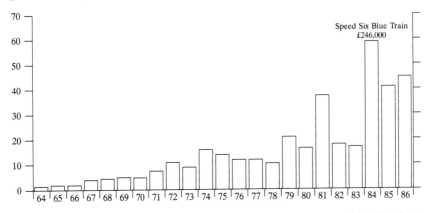

Source: Coys Complete Collectors' and Investors' Car Value Guide

Fig. 15.2: Bugatti Type 35 (£,000)

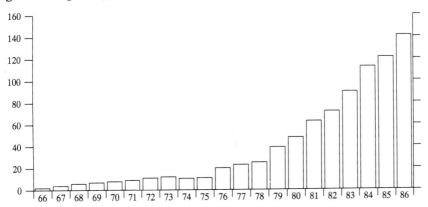

Source: Coys Complete Collectors' and Investors' Car Value Guide

Fig. 15.3: Mercedes SS & SL (£,000)

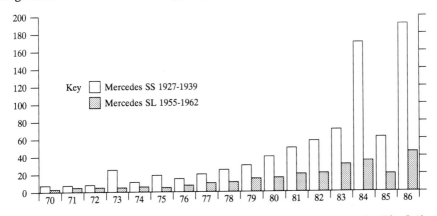

Source: Coys Complete Collectors' and Investors' Car Value Guide

Fig. 15.4: Rolls Royce Silver Ghost 1910-1924 (£,000)

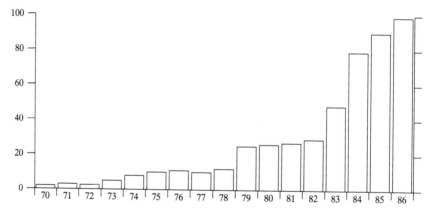

Source: Coys Complete Collectors' and Investors' Car Value Guide

Fig. 15.5: Hispano Suiza H6 (£,000)

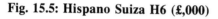

Source: Coys Complete Collectors' and Investors' Car Value Guide

ever since than at any time before. This is worth bearing in mind when looking at rates of appreciation for Rolls Royce Silver Ghosts, which in 1987 shot up around 25 per cent on 1986 prices. Rare pre-1909 Silver Ghosts have fetched £150,000, and good pre-1914 examples of the automobile voted 'the best car in the world' by *Pall Mall* magazine in 1911, could expect to reach £100,000. A superb 1912 Silver Ghost fetched £121,000 at Christie's in 1988; if you had been content with a later model, a 1919 Silver Ghost tourer was £29,700 at the same sale. And so sought after is the Ghost series that a 1923 Rolls Royce Silver Ghost chassis, in poor condition but 'the basis for a major rebuild', fetched £14,300 (estimate £2-3,000). For the dedicated collector looking to pick up an exotic on the cheap, going for a restoration job is an excellent investment, but be prepared to do a lot of work.

Choosing winners at the exotics level is beyond the reach of most of us, but such a flourishing market ensures that more moderately priced models stay on the boil. For more modest collectors, desirability means not the

The extremes of the car market: £112,000 for a 1937 Bentley tourer, in excellent condition at Coys, July 1988.

name 'Bugatti' but character and style, hard to judge in the abstract, but immediately apparent to the aficionado. Basic guidelines are that a tourer (open roof) fetches almost twice as much as an otherwise identical saloon (closed roof), and that unusual coachwork, an attractive bodyshell and fine upholstery will all help the price. And a car which has seen a lot of love and care will reflect the attention lavished on it when it comes to be sold on: a magnificent 1937 Derby Bentley with coachwork by Vanden Plas, for example, sold at Coys for a record £112,000 in July 1988, which sounds a lot until you read that the car had undergone a three year restoration costing £70,000. The result, according to Coys, was 'one of the finest Derby Bentleys in existence' and the market obviously agreed.

In comparison to those for the fine arts, auction catalogues drool unashamedly over such best-selling attributes. Take, for example, a more modest 1955 Bentley Continental, which Phillips were selling in December 1987. 'This most excellent car', enthuses the auctioneer, '... finished in Dawn Blue, the imaginative Park Ward styling suits the S1 series chassis superbly and provides a sporty yet roomy accommodation ... the light blue upholstery and carpets are in fine condition and the wood trim facia and door caps make for a very pleasing effect all round'.

Well, now you know what to look for! 'This most sought after British classic' was estimated at £15-20,000; in the event a collector from Geneva came to England specially for the sale and paid £21,000 for it. Ten years earlier, the same car was fetching around £2,000 in the salerooms.

The Bentley Continental appears frequently enough at auction, but is always snapped up. Rarity is no guarantee of high prices in this market. A car may be rare because it is very old, like the International Motorcar Company's 1901 Charette, which Phillips sold for £13,000 in 1988, or because it was so expensive (and intentionally exclusive) when new that only a few were produced – like the six Bugatti Royales or the 39 Ferrari GTOs. In both cases, rarity should boost prices and such cars should appreciate better than the average. On the other hand, a car that is currently in short supply because it was considered inferior, and therefore sold badly when new, is unlikely to appeal now – even a famous disaster, Ford's 1950s middle range car Edsel, which was billed as the car of everyone's dreams and turned into the greatest motoring failure of the century, 'a modern American anti-success', as one critic called it, failed to sell when offered at auction in 1988.

The universal cars

But there is a thriving trade in what were the cars of many people's dreams, those Austins, Morrises and Humbers, run-of-the-mill marques which are much in demand in the national market. Within all marques, there is a huge range in price, and an interesting or unusual example of a homely marque can do as well or better than a more glamorous cousin. At a Phillips sale in 1988, for example, a swish silver Porsche from 1952 made, at £6,000, the same as a modest little 'Top Hat' Ford saloon, which, however, dated from 1920 and had been beautifully restored. A 1909 Ford Model T roadster with all original period features, known as the 'Tin Lizzie', the car which put the world on wheels, was £9,750 at Coys in 1988, but is not exactly a practical alternative to a Ford Escort. On the other hand, 'an evocative piece of excellent '30s Americanism', a 1930 Chevrolet coupé, could offer its owner a chance of practical motoring. 'Tough enough to survive the appalling back country roads, yet elegant and powerful enough to be seen in about town', was what first sold the 'cast iron car', which fetched £65,750 in July 1988.

The sturdy British look is irresistable at auction, and investors can look to an average annual capital growth of around 15 per cent on such vintage wonders as a 1929 Morris Cowley saloon, in original maroon and black, which fetched £4,300 at Phillips in 1988, or an Austin Seven 'Chummy'. 'Perhaps the most charming and desirable of the early Austin Sevens, the Chummy has an enthusiastic following which is only rivalled by more austentatious marques', quipped Phillips 1987 catalogue. The 1927 tourer fetched £4,400; by comparison, Sotheby's sold a couple of Chummies in 1967 for £200 and £340, and another one, a tourer from 1929, for £1,700 in 1979. Christie's in 1988 sold another typical 'nostalgia' vehicle from the Austin 7 series, 'Britain's answer to the universal car', a 1936 Ruby two-door saloon, for £6,160. Restored in the workshops of the National Motor Museum, its original condition had been carefully preserved and it still had mica type spark plugs and correct pattern 400 x 17 tyres.

'BARN DISCOVERIES'

One method of affording vintage vehicles is to compromise on condition,

This Mulliner-backed Daimler, a barn discovery, went for a mere £800 at Phillips, March 1988.

and the most romantic way to do so is to buy a 'barn discovery'. Long abandoned and written off by their owners as rubbish, these are vehicles discovered, often in a barn, in fairly rough state, sometimes good enough to be driven to the site of a sale, sometimes not. After decades of hibernation, they are rusty, their tyres may be down, and component parts like indicators or head lamps may be missing. The engine will probably be a little unsure of itself, but the car will be cheap – sometimes as little as 10 per cent of the price of an equivalent vehicle in good condition. A 1934 Mulliner-bodied Daimler, complete although in need of total restoration, a barn discovery in Phillips March 1988 sale, went to a new home for £800, and some can cost even less. The cheaper end make an affordable and lucrative hobby for the enthusiast, for with time, care and some funds, they can be restored to their former glory, and valued accordingly. At the other extreme, a barn discovery from a garage behind a butcher's shop in Walsall, a 1936 Mercedes Benz 500K Special Roadster, which had been laid up since 1956, its bodywork corroded, its seats devoured by mice and its bonnet detached from its hinge, fetched £1.595m at Christie's in July 1988.

CONDITION

That goes to show what rarity and prestige can compensate for, but in general condition is important. At Coys sale in February 1988, a Derby

Bentley Park Ward sports saloon was considered cheap at £9,000, but a very similar car in poor condition and in need of restoration was £5,500. Beware particularly of rust and of fakes, though few people bother to make fakes of any but the top, £100,000 plus, sporting models. Vintage and classic car buyers are fortunate in being protected by the efforts at documentation, and the expertise, of marques' owner clubs. There are over 50 of these in the UK, with membership costs ranging from £5 to £30 a year. They are listed in *Coys Car Value Guide*.

Two guarantees of original and fine condition are exceptionally low mileage rates and very few owners. Phillips March 1988 sale contained a magnificent example of the latter, a handsome olive green Bentley tourer which came off the production line in 1926 and had been owned by the same family since 1927. Original accessories such as Smiths head and side lights were in place, and the original inner and outer wheel discs and the beaded edge tyres, generally discarded as obsolete in the 1930s and 1940s, had survived intact. The car fetched £46,000.

THE NEW INVESTMENTS

As vintage cars get rarer, they are becoming blue-chip investments. Where else can the investor turn? Classics from the 1950s and 1960s are a good bet; those considered modest in their day have a long way to go, for like the Austin Chummy, they have ample nostalgia value. Mini Minors have seen an upsurge of interest in the late 1980s, and in 1988 a one-owner ('a careful lady') Wedgwood blue example from 1959 in original condition made £1,000 at Phillips, while a Morris Mini Cooper fetched £6,050 at Christie's. Nothing could be more evocative of 1960s America, for example, than a big-finned 1960s white Cadillac with contemporary duotone interior which Coys sold in 1988. It looked almost like a piece of pop art which has rolled down from the canvas or off the movie screen to fetch a macho £11,750 before zooming off to impress somewhere else. Even cars from the 1980s are doing well – a 1981 De Lorean 'with the necessary credentials for a future classic' outstripped the price of many a present classic to sell for £13,500 in 1987.

For the speculator, auction houses are quick in this sector to point out 'future classics' or 'fast appreciating' models. This means that the act tends to be half way over before you can get in on it, but it does ensure buoyant markets at these levels. One other school of thought is to capitalise on the oddball, offbeat manufacturers about whom little is known. Such marques offer the opportunity for personal historical research, which is made possible by the National Motor Museum, and there is always the chance that the manufacturer you have picked becomes widely popular.

The hunting ground for vintage and classic cars is wide, and includes the personal columns of newspapers, local Post Office advertisements and the pages of *Exchange and Mart*. One lesser-known place to look for bargains is among the uncatalogued entries at a car auction. It is one of the quirks of this sector that even catalogues of the leading London auction houses do not list all the lots that are to be sold – they are among the hardest sales to organise, and there are always late arrivals. Cars which do not make it into the catalogue often sell more cheaply if they are auctioned without the public warning of a catalogue appearance, and thus in the possible absence of their most fervent devotees.

Good quality cars, however, need not be expensive and should always hold their own as a good long-term investment. Associated markets include motor cycles and automobilia – motoring mascots and badges, vehicle lamps, books – and both these are buoyant.

16 ANGELS

A good many inconveniences attend playgoing in any large city, but the greatest of them is usually the play itself.
Kenneth Tynan, *New York Herald Tribune*

In New York people don't go to the theatre – they go to see hits.
attributed to Louis Jourdan

As alternative investments go, only horse racing is giddier than backing theatrical productions. There is at best a one in four chance that you do not lose money – and losing here can mean not simply failing to make a profit, but watching every penny you invested sink without trace. And yet the top theatre producers are regularly turning away as much investment as they accept. Why do people do it?

There are two reasons. One is the not insubstantial profit that can be made if you strike lucky. The other is that this is a *fun* sector, not a home for your life savings but a nice little outlet for a bit of surplus money with which you feel like taking an enjoyable gamble. It is not every asset, after all, that *literally* performs overnight, and that guarantees that you can be there on the first night.

To get involved at all, you have to enjoy the theatre – preferably straight down the line commercial theatre and, even better, musicals, though some high-brow plays do well in the box office too. Like anything else you put your money on, you then have to have confidence in the product. The trouble with a play or a musical is that you are gambling on not one but a whole nexus of unknowns – the people involved, technical feasibility, audience appeal, a suitable venue.

But minimum investments are low at £500 or £1,000, and given that this brings perks like first night parties – or, more drearily, getting to see the accounts for a show – you can afford to sit back and enjoy the unpredictability. And the surprises can be considerable. Back in 1981, for example, a producer tried to find the funding for a musical version, directed by a Shakespearian theatre director new to the West End, of some T S Eliot poems. The show sounded esoteric to say the least, and even the music of Andrew Lloyd Webber failed to provide investors with the reassurance of a big name, because he was working for the first time without Tim Rice.

Cats cost almost £500,000 and, unusually in commercial theatre, the previews started before the show was fully capitalised – not a good sign. But seven years on, investors are still making 200 per cent a year on their initial outlay. The money comes partly from packed London houses, but also from America, where at any one time there are likely to be four different versions of *Cats* performing. The touring Bus and Truck Company takes an impromptu version of *Cats* around the United States, and can alone make up to US$900,000 a week. When considering backing a production, one important factor is whether it would be logistically and commercially possible to transfer it to the United States. The musical in America is almost a national art form, and shows usually do staggeringly well once they get there.

HOW TO JOIN THE RANKS OF THE ANGELS

If you are thinking of becoming an angel, the first element to consider, however, is the producer and his record, if any, of successes and failures. *Cats* was produced by Cameron Mackintosh, one of the best known and most successful producers in the world – along with *Cats*, are record breakers like *Les Misérables* ('The Glums' opened in America with advance bookings of US$12m), and *Follies*. Modestly, Cameron Mackintosh admits that anyone who had backed him over a five year period would be 'very much in the black'. But even he has had his failures, and if, for example, you had chosen to back only *Blondel*, a musical rendering of the life of a medieval minstrel by Tim Rice which received enormous hype and looked set for a long and happy run, you would have lost everything you put in – the show lost all its £300,000 investment. Other Cameron Mackintosh flops in recent years have included *The Boyfriend* and *Cafe Puccini*.

It is not easy, even in retrospect, to identify why these failed while *Cats*, *Les Mis* and *Follies* succeeded. But sticking to a trusted producer should mean that at least winners and losers even out. Producers, too, like to turn to the same backers again and again. In the 1950s, a producer would sit down to dinner with his lawyer or doctor or accountant and cobble together the backing for his latest idea. Escalating costs have rendered that method obsolete, but regular backers are still held at a premium. Cameron Mackintosh keeps an 'A' list of investors who have supported him through thick and thin and always offers them first refusal to invest in a new show. If he needs to look further afield, he turns to a 'B' and finally a 'C' list. And another established and flourishing producer, Michael Codron – *Hapgood* was a major success in 1988 – raises capital for his shows from the same 20 investors, in equal shares, every time; if one drops out, the next is waiting to take his place.

Getting on the 'A' list of investors of a well-tried producer is the surest method of making money as an angel, but it takes time. For new investors, getting in now with a potential 'big' producer could be the start of a long and fruitful relationship. One way is to write to a producer whose work you admire – producers are always named in theatre programmes, though they tend to go unnoticed by the non-punters in the audience. An easier way, and one which guarantees a response, is to write to the Society of West End Theatres (SWET), who will add your name to its list of would-be investors and circulate it to producer members. Within about a month, you will start receiving proposals on theatrical ventures.

PICKING A WINNER

But how do you judge them? That will be the make or break decision, and the following checklist highlights important points to look for in a proposal. In the end, it is probably the first – your personal impression of what the show will be like – that will swing you one way or the other, but when you are shooting in the dark, weighing up the facts can save you from financial disaster.

1. *Your personal response to the show*   Would you enjoy going to see it yourself? If so, it is likely that other people would too.
2. *Its commercial appeal*   Would it make good family entertainment? Does it have, as it were, coach party or tourist appeal? British farce (for example *Run for your Wife*, with over 2,000 performances at the Criterion Theatre) or classic thrillers (*The Business of Murder*, in its eighth year at the Mayfair, or, famously, *The Mousetrap,* in year 36 at St Martin's) are just what the doctor ordered; such plays always have a better than average chance of pulling in the crowds. If you had backed Michael White's production of *Sleuth*, for example, you would have got your money back 40 times over.

But do not dismiss more sombre stuff, for serious plays are currently undergoing something of a commercial revival – Hugh Whitemore's *Breaking the Code*, for instance, produced by Michael Reddington and Triumph Productions and starring Derek Jacobi as Alan Turing, the mathematical genius who cracked the Enigma Code but was hounded by the establishment for his homosexuality, had a long and successful run at the Haymarket Theatre in 1987. *Educating Rita*, the work of producer Derek Glynne, is another example of a serious play which achieved massive commercial success.

3. *A play or a musical?*   This depends partly on your funds and taste, but also on how long you are prepared to wait for your money. Higher running costs for musicals – *Phantom of the Opera* cost £2m to stage, *Follies* was £1.6m – inevitably take longer to recoup, even if they do play in bigger theatres. So although it is usually clear early on whether a musical is a hit, it can be years before you see your share of the profits, and what is a certain winner for a play is no guarantee for a musical. *Little Shop of Horrors*, for instance, ran for two years and still lost one third of its money.

Plays are cheaper overall, though even a play low on scenery and special effects cannot get away with less than £100,000 now. But if they are going to make money, plays must do so sooner; they have much shorter runs, and some are only intended to have very short runs – crucial actors may be available for only a limited period, or the venue could be restricted. In such cases, look realistically at the break-even rates of the proposal – there is less time to make up for over-optimistic forecasts later on.

4. *Big names*   If you have heard of the director, or some of the cast, or if the producer has a list of credits to his name, you will be more inclined to trust him. Moreover, a well-known actor, who has the pick of available parts, is hardly likely to agree to a project which sounds like a flop. But that is not a flawless rule, and the most extraordinary people do appear in the most extraordinary plays.

5. *The contract*   Outside the United States, where such agreements are governed by law, contracts for angels vary widely. Traditionally, the investor gets 60 per cent of the profits after his capital has been repaid, with 40 per cent going to the producer. But there are no hard and fast rules, and every contract is slightly different. For example, Tim Rice's hugely successful *Chess*, produced by his Three Knights Company in association

with Robert Fox, includes a profit share element for the crew. But with takings of £60,000 a week (it cost £4.5m to stage), this should hardly detract from the substantial gains being made by its backers.

6. *The extras* These can be crucial to your winning or losing money, and it is as well to be clear about them at the contract stage. Producers sometimes throw in a number of additional incentives, and especially worth looking out for are proposals which offer profits from any foreign, and particularly Broadway, transfers, as well as TV and film rights.

7. *The technical details* Examine carefully any factors likely to enhance the risk of an already risky business. Be wary of high ticket prices, or a high audience break-even point; if profitability depends on full capacity in a large theatre, rather than 50 per cent or lower attendance at a smaller venue, the prospects for profit diminish.

8. *The venue* Look at the suitability of the venue from both an aesthetic and a geographical point of view. A full-scale chorus line may sound terrific until you find that all the producer can dredge up to stage it on is a converted warehouse; if this is so, how much confidence can you have in the rest of his schemes?

Public prejudices about a venue, though, are not much of a worry, as they are usually overcome if the show is good enough. Her Majesty's Theatre in the Haymarket had not seen a successful production for 15 years (since *Fiddler on the Roof*), but it is now impossible to get a ticket for *Phantom of the Opera* there.

THE ONLY GUARANTEE IS THE THRILL

As West End costs soar – ticket prices, which have more than doubled since 1980, are just the tip of the iceberg here – the small investor who buys a 'unit' (say, £1,000) in a production is becoming increasingly the bedrock of commercial theatre funding. There is no shortage of productions looking to eat up your money, but all producers warn you that you might never see it again. There are no guarantees in this business, but a lot of thrills along the way, and a highly successful performing asset if you have the luck to back a winner.

17 FORESTRY

> He that plants trees loves others beside himself.
> English proverb.

THE CASE FOR FORESTRY

The Chancellor's axe fell on tax concessions to the forestry investor in the 1988 budget, and foresters are still reeling from the blow. Tax relief via Schedule D assessments, which allowed costs of planting and managing a wood to be set against tax paid on other earnings, has been replaced by a system of grants. Anyone locked into a forestry scheme before March 1988 continues to get tax relief until 1993, but at the new rate of 40 per cent.

That new rate is the crunch of the issue. In the heady days of 98 and 83 per cent income tax, forestry was not only a good investment for anyone paying the higher rates; it was – after leasing and industrial building allowances were phased out – the *automatic* third port of call after the tax refuges of the mortgage and the pension fund, and moreover, the only one of the three where unlimited amounts of relief were available. It was the safest and unquestionably the most sensible of alternative investments because there simply was no alternative which offered the investor the same benefits.

By the time of the 1988 budget, two benefits to the investor were on an ironic collision course. It did not take a genius to work out that with further income tax reductions to 40 per cent, forestry would not look very attractive at all.

But the Chancellor does not give away tax relief for nothing. The Exchequer needs private investment in woodlands. As a nation, we have fewer trees than almost anywhere else in Europe (9.6 per cent of our land is covered, as against an EC average of 25 per cent). We import 90 per cent of our timber, spending *every penny* of our North Sea oil revenue to do so, and we face at the start of the twenty-first century a more or less inevitable world timber shortage which will almost certainly force us to pay more. If we don't go on planting new trees – the government's target of 33,000 hectaresplantingayearhasneverbeenreached–wewillsoonbepaying*even*more.

New grants

The Chancellor's solution was to take forestry out of the tax system altogether, and to launch the Woodland Grant Scheme to sweet-talk investors back into the market. The scheme gives grants of around 50 per cent of the planting costs – less than the 60 per cent tax relief investors had been used to, but more than the 40 per cent that would subsequently have become their limit. Smaller woods get higher grants, as shown below in Figure 17.1. Broadleaved trees, which the government is trying to encourage as a sop to environmentalist dismay at relentless blocks of pine, get much higher grants but take much longer to grow.

Grants are paid in three instalments – 70 per cent at the start, and then two further instalments of 20 and 10 per cent at five year intervals. They come down heavily in favour of upland forestry, while lowland planting, demanding much heavier, longer-lasting maintenance costs, becomes virtual investor madness.

Fig. 17.1 Grants for woodlands

Area for planting (ha)	Rate of grant (conifer) (£ per ha)	Rate of grant (broadleaved) (£ per ha)
0.25–0.9	1,005	1,575
1.0 –2.9	880	1,375
3.0 –9.9	795	1,175
10 and over	615	975

THE RETURNS

Throwing forestry into the unsheltered market to compete for investment capital makes it a suddenly much hazier area to assess. For anyone considering *bareland planting*, the gritty truth is that you have to shoulder enormous costs at the start and then wait a very long time – until the trees are old enough to be sold as timber – to see any returns. The forestry cycle lasts around 50 years, and it is rare to see any income from *thinning* – removing some stems once the trees have reached a saleable size, thus benefiting the remaining trees – before year 20. If you do not want a two-generation investment, you can sell off your wood at a profit before it comes into production, or you can buy an *established wood* which is about to produce, or is already producing, income.

Costs of planting, setting up an infrastructure to support the plantation – fencing to keep out sheep and deer, roads to transport the timber – and of maintenance, used to be set against tax, making bareland planting the attractive side of forestry for anyone looking for a tax haven. In contrast, the new grants are restricted to the costs of planting, leaving the investor to meet the other expenses alone.

In response, forestry companies are looking at means of deferring the expenditure while trying to bring forward the income. Thinning is now suggested at 17 or 18 years rather than at 20 or 25, and road building is kept to a minimum, to be finished off just before the crop comes into production. There are also opportunities for sporting income.

Forestry companies are still juggling figures to try to produce yields as tempting as in the pre-budget days – when a conservative forecast suggested an annual return of 5 per cent – and their estimates vary from 3.8 per cent to 6 per cent above inflation.

The projected annual return of 4.9 per cent over inflation for Brerachan, an 189 hectare hill suitable for bareland planting, near Pitlochry, Perth-

Fig. 17.2: Projected timber volume — Brerachan (189 ha)

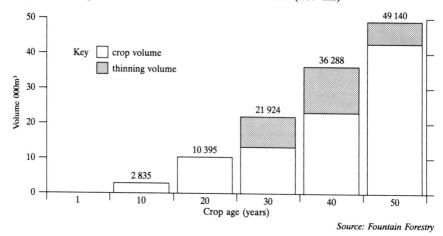

Source: Fountain Forestry

Fig. 17.3: Production forecast — Brerachan (189 ha)

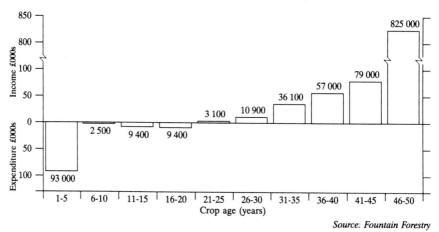

Source: Fountain Forestry

Fig. 17.4: Cumulative 5-yearly (expenditure)/income — Brerachan (189 ha)
(at current prices, assuming no inflation)

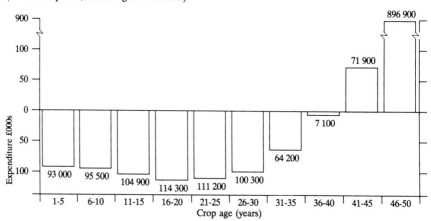

Source: Fountain Forestry

shire, on Fountain Forestry's books after the 1988 budget, is a good example. Figure 17.2 shows the projected timber volume for Brerachan and Figure 17.3 illustrates the production forecast. Figure 17.4 shows that although income starts coming in in year 21 (see Figure 17.3), investors have to wait a full 40 years of the cycle (unless they decide to sell their wood sooner) before they start to make a profit.

Timber prices have been running ahead of inflation since 1982; if, as is expected in view of an almost certain world timber shortage at the turn of the century, they move ahead of general prices by around 1 per cent, investors can look forward to better returns. Figures 17.5 and 17.6 show how dramatically this would affect income. Figure 17.7 shows the upward trend of timber prices against the RPI. There is undoubtedly a good case for timber as a valuable commodity in ever-decreasing supply, and with £600bn invested in timber processing plant in the UK since 1983, and the

Fig. 17.5: Projected timber volume — Brerachan (189 ha)
(Timber prices increasing at 0.6% per year, no inflation)

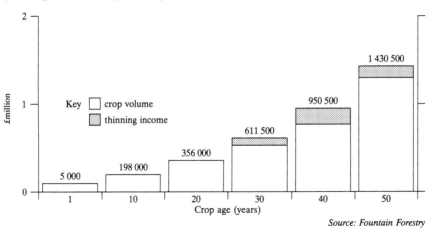

Source: Fountain Forestry

Fig. 17.6: Projected timber value — Brerachan (189 ha)
(Timber prices increasing at 1.6% per year, no inflation)

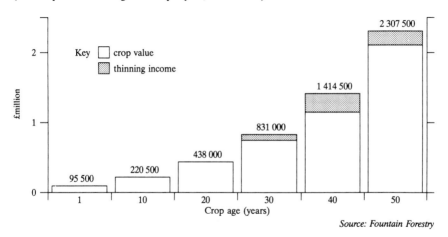

Source: Fountain Forestry

Fig. 17.7: Timber prices from 1968 to 1988

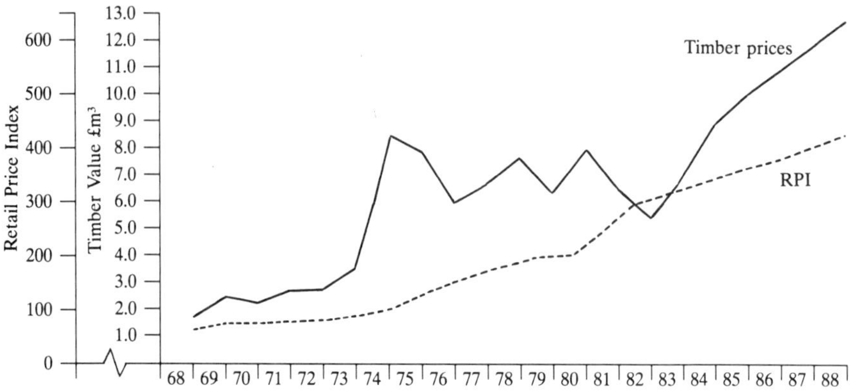

Source: Fountain Forestry

government still committed to the industry, it would be a pessimist indeed who would argue the case against a long term rise in the value of mature trees.

Nonetheless, investors are having to rethink their strategies, and many forestry companies believe there could be a temporary or even a permanent drop in the price of bare land and of those existing plantations far off the income-producing stage and still demanding maintenance costs. Prices for established and productive woodlands, on the other hand, are unlikely to go down; indeed, they may even go up if the market feels, as one forestry company suggests, that the great blocks of highly coniferous woodland formed over the past 25 years will not be repeated.

Capital growth

Buying a bareland site for planting or a youngish wood, however comfortably above inflation the return is guaranteed to be, is rather like buying in the futures market; established woodlands are the spot market equivalent. A good example is Pen Y Garn Goch, 160 acres of top quality woodland in Powys, where in 1988 the 26-year-old crop had just come into production from thinning. Fountain Forestry asked £210,000 for it, with a further total expenditure of £7,000 necessary before 1992. Then income starts to come in as shown in Fig. 17.8.

Like any wood, Pen Y Garn Goch is *a capital asset which appreciates in real terms to fund future long-term liabilities*. If that sounds like a pension fund, that is exactly what it can be – the ideal investment, say, for a man in his mid thirties looking for several large dollops of capital in his fifties. Each time you cut down some trees, you are, as it were, realising some of your capital, but the remainder continues to grow.

Tax benefits

With woodlands outside the tax system, *income* from timber sold is tax free. Woodlands also remain an attractive *capital gains tax* shelter. Plantations and standing timber are free of CGT; land is chargeable, but

---

SCOTTISH WOODLANDS LIMITED

FORESTRY INVESTMENT
CHANCELLOR CREATES NEW OPPORTUNITIES

Having taken forestry outside the scope of Income and Corporation Tax the Chancellor has created a unique investment medium.

Ownership of a professionally managed forest is an investment in a renewable resource with particular benefits—Substantial grants available for planting; Exemption of the crop from Capital Gains Tax; Roll-over advantages; Availability of Business Assets Relief and a delayed payment option for Inheritance Tax.

With timber requirements forecast to rise, an investment in forestry will secure an asset likely to remain in demand into the foreseeable future.

Scottish Woodlands has over 70 years experience of providing a wide range of professional forestry services, particularly in the field of investment.

For information on forestry as an investment and details of new grants, please telephone Ian Goodlet on 031-337 5350 or complete the coupon.

SCOTTISH WOODLANDS LTD
N.C.R. House,
2 Roseburn Gardens,
Edinburgh EH12 5NJ.
Tel: 031-337 5350

FTGAI

To: Ian Goodlet, Forestry Investment Manager,
Scottish Woodlands Ltd,
N.C.R. House, 2 Roseburn Gardens,
EDINBURGH EH12 5NJ.

Please send me information on forestry.
My interest lies in establishing a new forest/purchasing existing woodland.

Name _____

Address _____

Fig. 17.8: Pen Y Garn Goch production forecast

Period	(Expenditure)/income £
1988–1992	(7,000)
1993–1997	14,000
1998–2002	113,000
2003–2007	268,000
2008–2012	200,000
	588,000
2012 Sell Plantations	120,000
	708,000

long-standing woodland owners who saw the value of their land shoot up in the 1970s will benefit from the change in the base date to 1982.

For *inheritance tax* purposes, woodlands qualify for business property relief of 50 per cent after two years' ownership, an added attraction for a scheme that may well end up as a two-generation investment. Making a virtue out of necessity, the long-term nature of forestry makes it a neat, foolproof and lucrative way of keeping children or grandchildren away from the family fortune until they, along with the trees, have matured and know what to do with it.

An alternative pension fund

The great drawback of forestry investment remains the length of commitment and, linked to that, the inflexibility. Selling a wood is not like phoning a broker and arranging to have some shares sold; although there are always buyers, and many forestry companies have clients waiting for suitable woods to come up, it takes time and there is no guarantee of easy liquidity. Whether annual returns a few points ahead of inflation and gilts are enough to compensate depends very much on your individual position and even on your temperament. What seems possible, as is shown with Pen Y Garn Goch above, however, is that the lure of an imaginative pension fund will start to replace the lure of tax relief, and as such forestry stands up well.

Fringe benefits

But forestry is more than another cold-blooded investment, and many of its rewards do not show up on the accountant's balance sheet. One big plus is the control retained by the private investor. A management company will advise you, but the final decision on the site, the size and on what to plant where is yours, and you can inspect it at any time. Many investors, says Gittings, find this sort of tangible asset preferable to a few pieces of paper over which they have little say once they have paid for them.

There is no doubt that some very unimaginative planting took place over the last 30 years – not even the most committed investor can fail to shudder at the giant square blocks of unrelieved sitka spruce in the midst of some of Britain's loveliest countryside, to most destructive effect. These days, plantations are planned more sensitively; a proportion of broad-leaved trees like Japanese larch, birch, hazel or willow is always included to alleviate the pines, and some areas are left for recreation.

Among those to benefit is the investor. The most hard-bitten often end up falling in love with their woods, and there is certainly a lot to fall in love with. As well as beautiful scenery, many include shooting and fishing rights (inseparable from land in Scotland); some too have a shoreline and sailing facilities, a shooting hut or croft which can perhaps be turned into holiday accommodation.

As well as buying into a safe investment, you are buying an alternative way of life, even if you only indulge it for one week a year. You can do so for a minimum investment of around £40-50,000; mini-woods are sometimes available for less, and qualify for higher grants.

APPENDIX 1

ADDRESSES

These are limited by space to the major London salerooms and to some London dealers. There are many other good dealers both in London and in the rest of the country, and many reputable salerooms outside London.

SALEROOMS

Bonhams
Montpelier Galleries
Montpelier St
London SW7
01-584 9161

Chelsea Galleries
65 Lots Rd
London SW10
01-351 1380

Christie's
8 King St
London SW1
01-839 9060

Christie's South Kensington
85 Old Brompton Rd
London SW7
01-581 7611

Phillips
Blenstock House
Blenheim St
London W1
01-629 6602

Sotheby's
34 New Bond St
London W1
01-493 8080

DEALERS' ASSOCIATIONS, OTHER USEFUL ORGANISATIONS AND TRADE FAIRS

These include major associations, general fairs and the larger specialist fairs throughout the country

British Antique Dealers
   Association
Rutland Gate
London SW7
01-589 4128

The Burlington House
   Antiques Fair
Royal College of Art
Kensington Gore
London SW7

The Fine Art and Antiques Fair
National Hall
Olympia Exhibition Centre
London W14

The Chelsea Antiques Fair (twice
   yearly)
Chelsea Old Town Hall
King's Rd
London SW3

CINOA
27 rue Ernest Allard
B 1000 Bruxelles
513 48 31

Antique Collectors Club
5 Church St
Woodbridge
Suffolk
(0394) 385501

The Grosvenor House Antiques
   Fair
Grosvenor House
Park Lane
London W1

The West of England Antiques Fair
The Assembly Rooms
Bennett St
Bath

The World of Watercolours and
   Drawings
The Park Lane Hotel
Piccadilly
London W1

International Silver and Jewellery
   Fair
The Dorchester Hotel
Park Lane
London W1

The Park Lane Hotel Antiques Fair
Park Lane Hotel
Piccadilly
London W1

The British International Antiques
   Fair
National Exhibition Centre
Birmingham

The Northern Antiques Fair
Royal Bath Assembly Rooms
Harrogate
Yorks

International Ceramics Fair
The Dorchester Hotel
Park Lane
London W1

International Scientific and Medical
   Instrument Fair
The Cumberland Hotel
Marble Arch
London W1

PACKAGERS AND SHIPPERS

Gander and White
21 Lillie Rd
London SW6
01-381 0571

Featherston Shipping Ltd
24 Hampton House
15-17 Ingate Place
London SW8

Fentons Fine Art Packaging
Beachey Rd
Old Ford
London E3
01-533 2711

Cadogan Tate
Cadogan House
Hythe Rd
London NW10
01-969 6969

DEALERS

The fine arts

Arthur Ackermann
3 Old Bond St
London W1
01-493 3288

Thomas Agnew & Sons
43 Old Bond St
London W1
01-629 6176

Appleby Bros
8 Ryder St
London SW1
01-930 6507

Brod Gallery
24 St James's St
London SW1
01-839 3871

P & D Colnaghi
14 Old Bond St
London W1
01-491 7408

Crawley & Asquith Ltd
16 Savile Row
London W1
01-439 2755

Johnny van Haeften
13 Duke St
London SW1
01-930 3062

Christopher Wood
13 Motcomb St
London SW1
01-235 9141

Abbot & Holder
73 Castelnau
London SW13

Fischer Fine Art
30 King St
London SW1
01-839 3942

Richard Green
44 and 39 Dover St
London W1
01-493 3939

Stephanie Hoppen
17 Walton St
London SW3
01-589 3678

Alan Jacobs
8 Duke St
London SW1
01-930 3709

David James
291 Brompton Rd
London SW3
01-581 3399

The Leger Galleries
13 Old Bond St
London W1
01-629 3538

Spink & Son
5-7 King St
London SW1
01-930 7888

Wildenstein & Co
147 New Bond St
London W1
01-629 0602

Didier Aaron
21 Ryder St
London SW1
01-839 4716

The Fine Art Society
148 Bond St
London W1
01-629 5116

Waddington Galleries
11 Cork St
London W1
01-437 8611

Frost & Reed Ltd
41 New Bond St
London W1
01-493 7658

20th century pictures

The Redfern Gallery
20 Cork St
London W1
01-734 1732

Angela Flowers
11 Tottenham Mews
London W11
01-636 8824

Anthony D'Offay
9 & 23 Dering St
London W1
01-329 1578

Anderson O'Day
255 Portobello Road
London W11
01-221 7592

Nigel Greenwood
4 New Burlington St
London W1
01-434 3797

The Warwick Arts Trust
33 Warwick Square
London SW1
01-834 7856

Peter Nahum Art Gallery
5 Ryder Street
London SW1
01-930 6059

The Young Unknowns Gallery
82 The Cut
London SE1
01-928 3415

The Curwen Gallery
4 Windmill Street
London W1
01-636 1459

Furniture

Anno Domini Antiques
66 Pimlico Rd
London SW1
01-730 5496

H C Baxter
191 Fulham Rd
London SW3
01-352 9826

Apter Fredericks Ltd
265 Fulham Rd
London SW3
01-352 2188

Box House Antiques
105 Pimlico Rd
London SW1
01-730 9257

Church Street Galleries
77 Kensington Church St
London W8
01-937 2461

Geoffrey Rose Ltd
77 Pimlico Rd
London SW1
01-730 3004

Richard Courtney
112 Fulham Rd
London SW3
01-370 4020

C Fredericks & Son
92 Fulham Rd
London SW3
01-589 5847

Hotspur Ltd
14 Lowndes St
London SW1
01-235 1918

Ronald Phillips
26 Bruton St
London W1
01-493 2341

David Tron
275 King's Rd
London SW3
01-352 5918

Clifford Wright
104 Fulham Rd
London SW3
01-589 0986

Stair & Co Ltd
120 Mount St
London W1
01-499 1784

Ceramics

Adams Antiques
28 Old Bond St
London W1
01-629 0717
(Meissen)

Bernheimer Fine Arts
32 St George St
London W1
01-499 0293

Bluett & Sons
48 Davies St
London W1
(Chinese)

Cohen & Pearce
84 Portobello Rd
London W11
01-229 9458
(Chinese)

Eskenazi
166 Piccadilly
London W1
01-493 5464
(Chinese)

Jonathon Horne
66 Kensington Church St
London W8
01-221 5658
(English)

Klaber & Klaber
2A Bedford Gardens
Kensington Church St
London W8
01-727 4573
(Continental)

Spink & Son
5-7 King St
London SW1
01-930 7888
(Chinese)

Earle D Vandekar of Knightsbridge
138 Brompton Rd
London SW3
01-589 8481
(Continental)

Delomosne
4 Campden Hill Rd
London W8
01-937 1804

Contemporary ceramics

Craftsmen Potters Shop
7 Marshall St
London W1
01-437 7605

Crafts Council Shop
Victoria & Albert Museum
London SW7
01-589 5070

Contemporary Applied Arts
43 Earlham St
London WC2
01-836 6993

J K Hill
151 Fulham Rd
London SW3
01-584 7259

Silver

Armitage
4 Davies St
London W1
01-408 0675

Asprey
165 New Bond St
London W1
01-493 6767

J H Bourdon-Smith
24 Mason Yard
Duke St
London SW1
01-839 4714

Brand Inglis
9 Halkin Arcade
Motcomb St
London SW1
01-235 6604

E & C T Koopman & Son
The London Silver Vaults
53-63 Chancery Lane
London WC2
01-242 7624

B Silverman
The London Silver Vaults
53-63 Chancery Lane
London WC2
01-242 3269

S J Shrubsole
43 Museum St
London WC1
01-405 2712

S J Phillips
139 New Bond St
London W1
01-629 6261

Spink & Son
5-7 King St
London SW1
01-930 7888

Books

The Antiquarian Booksellers
    Association
45 East Hill
London SW18
01-870 8259

Bernard Quaritch Ltd
5-8 Lower John St
London W1
734 2983

Bloomsbury Book Auctions
3 Hardwick St
London EC1
01-636 1945/833 2636

Bertram Rota Ltd
9-11 Langley Court
London WC2
01-836 0723

E Joseph
Third Floor, 1 Vere St
London W1
01-493 8353

John Wilson (Autographs) Ltd
50 Acre End St
Eynsham
Oxford
(0865) 880883

Maggs Bros Ltd
50 Berkeley Square
London W1
01-493 7160

Scientific instruments

Harriet Wynter
50 Redcliffe Rd
London SW10
01-352 6494

Arther Davidson
78 Jermyn St
London SW1
01-930 6687

Wine merchants

John Armit Wine Investments
190 Kensington Park Rd
London W11
Tel 01-727 6846

John Harvey & Sons
27 Pall Mall
London SW1
01-839 4691

Berry Bros & Rudd
3 St James's St
London SW1
01-839 9033

Corney & Barrow
12 Helmet Row
London EC1
01-251 4051

Justerini & Brooks
61 St James's St
London SW1
01-493 8721

Cars

Coys of Kensington
2-4 Queensgate Mews
London SW7
01-584 7444
Coys also organises three major
auctions a year.

Straight Eight
152 Goldhawk Rd
Shepherds Bush
London W12
01-743 1599

Chris Drake Collectors Cars
21 Brook Mews North
London W2
01-262 6583

West One
142 Finchley Rd
London W1
01-794 7856
(Ferrari specialists)

Autovogue Classic Cars
Unit 1
Newington Industrial Estate
Crampton St
London SE17
01-708 5757

Michael Fisher Ltd
23 Charles Lane
London NW8
01-722 3449
(Ferrari specialist)

Hanwell Car Centre
86 Uxbridge Rd
London W7
01-567 9729
(Rolls and Bentley)

P J Fischer Classic Automobiles
Dyers Lane
London SW15
01-785 6633
(Rolls and Bentley)

Car storage

Storacar
65 Blandford St
London W1
023 065 206

Cabriolet Cars
Milton House
2 Fernshaw Rd
London SW10
01-352 8565

Angels

Society of West End Theatres
    (SWET)
Bedford Chambers
London WC2
01-836 0971

FORESTRY MANAGEMENT COMPANIES

Bidwells
Trumpington Rd
Cambridge
(0223) 841841

John Clegg & Co
The Bury
Church St
Chesham
Bucks
(0494) 784711

David Goss & Associates
Broomrigg House
Holywood
Dumfries
(0387) 720184

Scottish Woodlands
NCR House
2 Roseburn Gardens
Edinburgh
031-337 5350

Fountain Forestry
Mollington House
Mollington
Banbury
Oxon
(0295) 758471

Tilhill Forestry
Greenhills
Tilford
Farnham
Surrey
(0786) 811721

Information is also available from *Timber Growers United Kingdom*, an organisation representing the interests of private woodland owners:

Timber Growers United Kingdom
Agriculture House
Knightsbridge
London SW1
01-235 2925

APPENDIX 2

BIBLIOGRAPHY

General

The Economics of Taste, by Gerald Reitlinger, Barrie and Jenkins 1963 (3 volumes)

Christie's Guide to Collecting, ed Robert Cumming, Phaidon 1984

Christie's South Kensington Popular Antiques Yearbook, ed Huon Mallalieu, Phaidon 1987

The Phillips Guide to Tomorrow's Antiques, by Peter Johnson, Weidenfeld 1987

The Successful Investor, by Robin Duthy, Collins 1986

Is it Genuine?, by John Bly, Mitchell Beazley 1986

Dealing with Dealers, by Jeremy Cooper, Thames and Hudson 1985

Guide to the Antique Shops of Great Britain, by Rosemary Ferguson and Carol Adams, Antique Collectors Club (ACC) 1988

Fine arts

The Impressionists, by Michael Wilson, Phaidon 1983

Post-Impressionism, Royal Academy of Arts/Weidenfeld & Nicholson 1979

The Concise Encyclopaedia of Impressionism, by Maurice Serullaz, Omega 1984

Victorian Painters, by Jeremy Maas, Barrie & Jenkins 1988

British Landscape Painting, by Michael Rosenthal, Phaidon 1982

British Art, by Simon Wilson, Tate Gallery/Bodley Head 1979

British Watercolours 1750-1850, by Andrew Wilton, Phaidon 1977

19th Century Painters and Painting, by Geraldine Norman, Thames & Hudson 1977

The Dutch Painters, by Christopher Wright, Orbis 1978

From Van Eyck to Brueghel, by Max Friedlander, Phaidon 1981

Dutch Painting, by R Fuchs, Thames & Hudson 1978

The Golden Age, by Bob Haak, Thames & Hudson 1984

Modern English Painters, by John Rothenstein, Macdonald 1984

A Guide to European Painting, by Michael Jacobs, David & Charles 1980

The Art of Describing, by Svetlana Alpers, John Murray 1983

Understanding Watercolours, by Huon Mallalieu, ACC 1985

Modern British Paintings: Review of London Auction Prices, ACC 1988

Victorian Paintings: Review of London Auction Prices, ACC 1988

English Watercolours: Review of London Auction Prices, ACC 1988

The Dictionary of Victorian Painters, by Christopher Wood, ACC 1978

The Dictionary of British Artists, by Jane Johnson, ACC 1976

The Dictionary of British Watercolour Artists up to 1920, by Huon Mallalieu, ACC 1988

The Great Century of British Painting: Hogarth to Turner, by William Gaunt, Phaidon 1978

The Restless Century: Painting in Britain 1800-1900, by William Gaunt 1800-1900, Phaidon 1978

The Glory of Watercolour, by Michael Spender, David and Charles 1987

Practical Guide to Print Collecting, by Ann Buchsbaum, Van Nostrand Reinhold 1975

Building a Print Collection, by S Warner, Van Nostrand Reinhold 1981

Collecting Original Prints, by Rosemary Simmons, Studio Vista/Christie's Contemporary Art 1980

Discovering Antique Prints, by Ronald Russell, Shire 1982

Prints of the 20th Century, by Riva Castleman, Thames and Hudson 1976

Furniture

Collecting Antique Furniture, by Peter Johnson, Hamlyn 1983

A History of English Furniture, by Percy Macquoid, first published 1904-08, reissued by ACC

The Price Guide to British Antique Furniture, by John Andrews, ACC 1988

The Price Guide to Victorian, Edwardian and 1920s Furniture, by John Andrews, ACC 1987

Antique Furniture Prices 1968-88, ACC 1988

Oak Furniture – the British Tradition, by Victor Chinnery, ACC 1979

18th Century English Furniture – the Norman Adams Collection, by S Whittington and C Claxton Stevens, ACC 1983

Sheraton Furniture, by Ralph Fastnedge, ACC 1983

Regency Furniture, by Frances Collard, ACC 1985

The Macdonald Guide to Buying Antique Furniture, by Rachel Feild, Macdonald 1986

Insider's Guide to Antique Furniture, by Alan Robertson, Bell and Hyman 1985

Dictionary of English Furniture Makers 1660-1840, ed. Geoffrey Beard and Christopher Gilbert, Furniture History Society 1986

The Life and Work of Thomas Chippendale, by Christopher Gilbert, Studio Vista/Christie's 1978

English Furniture 1500-1840, by Geoffrey Beard, Phaidon/Christie's 1987

Ceramics

World Ceramics: an Illustrated History from Earliest Times, ed Robert Charleston, Hamlyn 1968

A Connoisseur's Guide to Chinese Ceramics, by Cecile Beurdeley, Leon Amiel, New York 1974

Studies in Chinese Ceramics, by Te K'un Cheng, Chinese University Press, Hong Kong 1984

English China, by Geoffrey Godden, Barrie and Jenkins 1985

English Pottery and Porcelain, ed Paul Atterbury, Owen 1980

European Porcelain of the 18th Century, by Peter Wilhelm Meister, Phaidon 1983

The History of Porcelain, by Paul Atterbury, Orbis 1982

An Illustrated Encyclopaedia of British Pottery and Porcelain, by Geoffrey Godden, Barrie and Jenkins 1980
The Chinese Potter, by Margaret Medley, Phaidon 1980
Chinese Blue and White Porcelain, by Duncan MacIntosh, David & Charles 1977
Chelsea Porcelain, by Elizabeth Adams, Barrie and Jenkins 1987
An Illustrated Dictionary of Ceramics, by George Savage, Thames & Hudson 1985
Meissen Portrait Figures, by Len Adams, Barrie and Jenkins 1987
The Price Guide to 19th and 20th Century British Pottery, by David Battie and Michael Turner, ACC 1979
The Price Guide to 19th and 20th Century British Porcelain, by David Battie and Michael Turner, ACC 1982
A Collector's History of English Pottery, by Griselda Lewis, ACC 1985

Silver

Discovering Hallmarks on English Silver, by John Bly, Shire 1986
Starting to Collect Silver, by John Luddington, ACC 1984
An Introduction to English Silver from 1660, by Eric Turner, HMSO 1985
The Price Guide to Antique Silver, by Peter Waldron, ACC 1982

Books

Discovering Book Collecting, by John Chidley, Shire 1982
Collectable Books, by Jean Peters, Bowker, New York 1979
A Directory of Dealers in Secondhand and Antiquarian Books in the British Isles, Shepperds Press 1977
The Bookbrowser's Guide to Secondhand and Antiquarian Bookshops, David & Charles 1982
Essays in Book Collecting, by John Gretton, Dereham Books 1985
Understanding Book Collecting, by Grant Uden, ACC 1982

Scientific instruments

Early Scientific Instruments, by Antony Turner, Sotheby's Publications 1987
Scientific Instruments, by Harriet Wynter, Studio Vista 1975
Encylopaedia of Antique Scientific Instruments, by John Fitzmaurice Mills, Aurum 1983
Antique Scientific Instruments, by Gerard L'Estrange Turner, Blandford Books 1980

Toys

The Price Guide to Antique Dolls, by Constance Eileen King, ACC 1977
Antique Dolls and Toys for Collectors, by Romy Roeder, Costello 1986
Understanding Dolls, by Caroline Goodfellow, ACC 1986
The Collector's Encylopaedia of Dolls, by Dorothy Coleman, Hale 1986
Collecting Teddy Bears, by Pam Hebbs, Collins 1988

Wine

How to Buy Fine Wines, by Stephen Spurrier and Joseph Ward, Phaidon 1986
The World Atlas of Wine, by Hugh Johnson, Mitchell Beazley 1977
The Wines of the World, ed Jeremy Roberts and Jose Northey, Orbis 1976
Christie's Wine Companion, ed Patrick Matthews, Webb and Bower 1987
The Wine Drinker's Handbook, ed Serena Sutcliffe, Pan 1985

Cars

Coys International Collectors' and Investors' Car Value Guide is published annually in October by Coys of Kensington. It includes market trends for all major marques and a price guide detailing prices at auction over the past 20 years and current values and a free six-monthly update.
The first *Dalton Watson Collectors and Investors Car Guide*, by Dalton Watson, 1988
The Great Classics, by Ingo Seiff, Orbis 1986
Great Classic Cars, by Alan Austin, Octopus 1986
The World Guide to Automobilia, by Nick Baldwin, Macdonald 1987
Vintage Motor Cars, by William Boddy, Shire 1985 (Shire publish a range of specialist motoring titles. All cost £1.25 and comprise a 5,000 word text and 40-50 illustrations.)
Collectible Cars, by Julian MacNamara, Hamlyn 1986

INDEX